Blair Justice, Ph.D., and J. Pittman McGehee, D.D.

RAISING LAZARUS

THE SCIENCE OF HEALING THE SOUL

For my wife, Rita, who does it all for me

Blair Justice

For Bobby, my wife and companion

J. Pittman McGehee

OTHER BOOKS BY BLAIR JUSTICE, Ph.D.

Visits with Violet: How to Be Happy for 100 Years

A Different Kind of Health: Finding Well-Being despite Illness

Who Gets Sick: How Beliefs, Moods, and Thoughts Affect Your Health

The Abusing Family

The Broken Taboo

Violence in the City

OTHER WORKS BY J. PITTMAN MCGEHEE, D.D.

The Invisible Church: Finding Spirituality Where You Are

Slender Thread: Reflections by Robert Johnson

TABLE OF CONTENTS

FOREWORD

A recurring theme in the annals of world mythology is the hero's journey, in which a restless, courageous individual ventures far from home, endures great trials, returns wiser than before, and shares his wisdom with those who stayed behind. Sometimes the hero finds help in the form of wise guides who suddenly appear, who ease his burdens and increase his odds of success. Yet the journey is never a happily-ever-after affair, but is always perilous and is sometimes fatal. Survival is not guaranteed, no matter how valiant the struggle.

Raising Lazarus is an archetypal hero's journey. The hero-journeyer is Dr. Blair Justice—psychobiologist, clinician, author, academic dean and professor—who has fallen periodically into the bottomless abyss of depression.

I first encountered Dr. Justice's work in the 1980s through his award-winning book *Who Gets Sick: How Beliefs, Moods and Thoughts Affect Your Health.* Over the years I came to revere this seminal work as a veritable encyclopedia of the emerging science in the rapidly expanding mind-body field.

The guide whom Justice encounters in *Raising Lazarus* is the Reverend Pittman McGehee, the renowned Episcopal priest, Jungian psychoanalyst, and self-confessed mystic. Justice, whose inner life is moribund from relentless, recurring depression, is returned to life with McGehee's help, like the biblical Lazarus whom Jesus raised from the dead.

McGehee's role in resuscitating Justice's psyche is profound. He is a modern Jedi Master Yoda—the wisest and most powerful of teachers and guides in the Star Wars saga. Yoda's name implies the power of guides; it may possibly derive from the Sanskrit noun *yoddha* ("warrior"), or from the Hebrew verb *yodea* ("knows"). McGehee is cut from this archetypal cloth. It is Justice's ability to set aside his pride and humble himself before Master McGehee that makes this interpersonal alchemy work and enables Lazarus to rise. In this process Justice enters another archetype—that of The Patient, a word derived from the Latin, meaning "a suffering or sick person." Justice is sick in the extreme—he is facing death—and he has encountered a healer who may be able to help him. It would be suicidal for him not to "be patient"— in modern parlance, to wait without annoyance or complaint before the person who possibly may save his life.

The theme of *Raising Lazarus* may be mythic and archetypal, but there is nothing archaic about the telling of this gripping account. By alternating "story" and "science," a contrapuntal rhythm is established that is original and enchanting. Personal accounts of depressive illness are now quite common, as it has become more acceptable to go public about one's "black dog," depression. But I know of no account that embodies the elegant structure, rich detail, penetrating honesty, polished prose, and sheer scope of *Raising Lazarus*.

As the Justice-McGehee journey unfolds, a worldview is revealed that embodies qualities of the universe often considered magical. Among these are synchronicities — those weird, acausal "coincidences" that are eerily meaningful to the individual experiencing them. These events were defined and elaborated by an earlier healer-patient pair, psychologist C. G. Jung and Nobel physicist Wolfgang Pauli. The concept of nonlocality—infinitude in space and time—surfaces also, with stunning implications for the unity of all minds and for some immortal, eternal quality of human consciousness. In these pages, consciousness in its many expressions—willing, wanting, intending, praying—comes to life as a mover of "the world out there." Matter transcends its status as inert stuff and becomes enlivened. The entire natural environment sings as rugged mountains, trees, and animals convey special meanings. The dead speak, sometimes through animal intermediaries. In other contexts these ideas might be dismissed as new-age, flakey nonsense; but Justice anchors them in emerging science and they assume uncommon stature.

So it is not only Justice's inner world that is transformed as his healing proceeds, but also his universe. This reveals how depression ravages the deeply depressed: they die not only within but also to the world without. It is true that effective therapy helps one feel better, but that is only part of its benefit. It can also catalyze a rebirth into another form of existence that involves not just a new mind but also a new world of unspeakable beauty and harmony, to which, one knows without doubt, one truly belongs. This is what it means to be born again. This is the cleansing of the doors of perception of mystic-poet William Blake, whom Justice quotes. Blake can speak of his ability to hold infinity in the palm of his hand and sense eternity in an hour because he knows he *is* infinite and eternal.

In the background of this spellbinding account, an amazing individual is always present: Dr. Rita Justice, Blair's wife, who is also a psychologist. Rita is a pillar of strength, unfailing compassion and unconditional love. This story would not have unfolded in the same way without her; indeed, it might not have unfolded at all, for it was her gentle nudging that helped Blair find his way to McGehee in the first place, when he was about to go under for good. Rita is literally Blair's lifesaver. She is the anchor that kept him from drifting away during the years it took him to beach finally on McGehee's shores.

This story needs desperately to be told. Depression is a major disabler of Americans, and it is on the increase for reasons that are not entirely clear. Its vengeance is underestimated because of the assumption that it can handily be dispatched by the various medications now available, such as Prozac and related pharmaceuticals. But this is not the case for many individuals, whose depression refuses to yield to the drugs that have proven salvific for others.

When medications don't work for depression, one then resorts to—well, what? For Justice, the alternative was something widely considered out of style, old-fashioned, retro, uneconomical, equivocally effective, and agonizingly tedious: sitting face to face with another person and slogging it out in "therapy." As Justice explains his choice, "Personally, I am one depressive not pursuing pills or surgery to make me more outgoing and lively. I am in search of overcoming my illness and doing it 'the hard way,' that is, to 'earn' my recovery, with the help of a teacher/therapist. The science that I trust to bring me to that end is not only providing empirical evidence in support of Jungian analysis, but also is demonstrating that 'mental effort,' along with resonance in relationships, can reshape neurons and balance brain chemistry."

But wait. *What* science? What is the empirical evidence that thoughts and mental effort can actually reshape the brain and balance its chemistry? Only recently we were assured that it's the other way around: The brain and its chemistry determine what we think and feel, not vice versa. If my neurotransmitters and synapses are out of whack, my mind goes haywire and I need a chemical, electrical or surgical tune-up. But the idea of correcting the brain's malfunction by mental effort is part of the new science—hard, rigorous *brain* science. This is one of the key contributions of this book. In chapter after chapter, Justice explains the neurobiological changes resulting from his mental activities and his interpersonal exchanges with his guide, as buttressed by the latest research findings.

The belief in the dance between mental activity and the brain has been a vision of key thinkers in psychology—most notably Sigmund Freud (1856-1939), as Justice makes clear, and also William James (1842-1910), who is regarded as the father of American psychology. Attributed to James is the oft-quoted remark, "The greatest discovery of my generation is that a human being can alter his life by altering his attitude." Justice puts scientific meat on the bones of James's assertion by showing that one's thoughts change one's brain. In our bottom-up era, in which higher functions such as emotion were believed to be solely determined by lower, deep-seated physical processes beyond our control the top-down possibility that James proposed seemed unthinkable. As a consequence, talk therapy almost disappeared in the twentieth century in favor of physical approaches such as pharmaceuticals. Yet talk therapy and cognitive approaches are poised to come roaring back, for reasons you will discover as you follow Justice on his journey.

When therapy works well, the healing vector always operates in both directions as healer and healee are mutually made more whole. In his epilogues, analyst McGehee acknowledges that he has indeed been transformed as well as his patient. But in *Raising Lazarus* an additional healing vector extends to the reader. I know this because I have been made more whole by reading this account. As I entered this story, healing flew off the pages and jiggled my mind-body nexus, strengthened my synapses, and boosted my neurotransmitters. After this book, I'll never look at my amygdala and prefrontal lobes in the same way, because now I understand more fully my brain's sensitivity to word and image.

There is nothing new here; we merely forgot what our ancestors knew. In *Raising Lazarus,* we encounter the power of shared story—the sort of communion that for eons took place around campfires, but which today is more likely to emerge through print and electronic media. As a consequence of the power of shared experience, Justice has written more than a book. He has written a healing.

I have had mini-epiphanies reading this book. I wish the same, dear reader, for you.

Larry Dossey, M.D.

Santa Fe, New Mexico

PREFACE

The raising of Lazarus in the title of this book refers to reviving a person who is virtually dead in all respects except the physical.[1] "Virtual death" describes the state of people who suffer from a major, clinical, unipolar depression. They feel mentally, emotionally and spiritually dead. The title also refers to any alienated or stigmatized human being—a leper or lazur in ancient times. These outcasts were allowed to look at life only from a distance—through a "leper's slit" in the wall surrounding the city within. Depression is a wall that keeps a person today from participating in the activities that make life worth living. It is a leading cause of disability in America; the World Health Organization (WHO) "now ranks major depression as one of the most burdensome diseases in the world."[2]

"The science of healing the soul," the book's subtitle, refers to what scientists now have to say about a subject whose existence has been either denied or viewed as so soft that no self-respecting scientist would consider discussing it. It was thus a groundbreaking event when the prestigious, 186-year-old New York Academy of Sciences sponsored a three-day conference on the soul, self and brain in September 2002.[3] This book is about how soul loss, if not death, occurs in depression and how the neurons physically responsible for such illness can be restored, not by drugs or shock therapy, but by experiences that reshape synapses and rewire the nervous system.

This is the story of two men—one committed to science, the other to religion. One is a psychobiologist and clinician who participated in the historic New York conference, the other a psychoanalyst and priest. Both are former deans—one academic, the other Episcopal. The first, who suffers from major depression, is treated by the second. Their experience together revives the scientist, who is the writer of this chronicle and thus the "I" in the story. Although neither of us has grandiose delusions of being a Jung or a Pauli, we cite their collaboration as an example of analyst and analysand working together to write a book about the analytical experience.[4]

What follows here is a collaboration combining the knowledge and experience of both patient and doctor—as well as the shared pain that bonded them. It is a story of soul, from death to rebirth, not only Blair Justice's soul, but Pittman McGehee's as well. It is also about what happens in the brain and body during such transformation. "Interpersonal neurobiology" is the subdiscipline that helps explain how relationships reshape synapses.[5]

Underneath our personas of academician and cleric are two mavericks. I (Blair) am classified by my wife, Rita, as a "nerd," in the kind sense of the word, meaning I become obsessed with what I am doing if I am not too depressed and can focus on what I am fascinated by. My fixations result in violations of all signs of order in my office, on my desk, in my car and in my dress.[6] On his part, Pittman led the open-collar, laid-back fashion of men at work long before Friday casual became fashionable. As always, he can articulate exactly why, as translated here from the Jungian, a language that he speaks fluently and I am learning: "Men cut themselves off from their feelings at work by tying knots around their throats. They stay strictly in their heads. They can't wait to rush home, enter the house, take off the tie, hug the wife and play with the dog, in that order. It is an archetypal imperative, which reconnects them to their hearts."[7]

Sharing a maverick quality in the faces we present to the outer world also goes deeper and has roots in feelings of being marginal men, living outside the mainstream.[8] As practitioners and followers of Jungian psychology can appreciate, Pittman's vocation takes him into a manner of talking and thinking that many people find arcane and impossible to grasp in social settings. "At a dinner party, when I am asked what I do," Pittman says, "I have no easy answer. Do I say I'm a Jungian analyst and then try to answer the question, 'What's that?' Do I say I am a preacher without a flock who sits and listens to people talking, and then try to answer my dinner partner's question, 'Why?'" However, Pittman has no identity crisis. He knows he is on this earth to expand consciousness, his own and others', and to contribute to the evolution of the cosmos. That may sound grandiose, but as Pittman explains to the uninitiated, "the cosmos is grand" and deserves nothing less.[9] In short, my analyst's calling is not an easy one. As for me, I have pursued a number of callings, the most pertinent to this book being science editor, academician, clinician and author.[10] My analyst says that my many occupational adventures, which have taken me worldwide, express a restless soul. The painful accompaniment has been a variety of both physical and emotional symptoms, which neither power nor prestige relieved. I have realized that the answer is to keep connected with something bigger than ego.[11] Until I make such a connection firm, I remain marginal. My multiple pursuits also express a bipolar aspect to my depression, which is largely unipolar.[12]

Whatever misinterpretations there are in this book on either side of the bridge between science and soul, they are my own and not my partner's. I have, though, depended on Pittman to keep me from falling off the spiritual side of the bridge and drowning in the deep, dark mystical waters underneath. How we came to an inner, if not outer, world different from the one introverts, who are less marginal than we are, may occupy will become plainer as our story unfolds. Because shame and guilt have a propensity to become locked in the very bowels of a depressed person, as in my case, chapter 1 of this story starts with a gut that ruptured. Some of the language we use is necessarily scatological and may not seem fitting for two professionals, regardless of how maverick or marginal they are—particularly since one is an agent of God. Yet just as it's been said that the sacred can be found in the profane and dross can camouflage gold, we have experienced that shit is good fertilizer for recovering the soul. We invite you to see for yourself, but first, an introduction, which includes the explanation of how a left-brainer and a right-brainer ever got together.

A final note: Because the heart of this book is a narrative, each chapter, as well as the introduction, starts with "The Story." Following this is a section on "The Science" that is pertinent to the narrative. We have tried to use our respective backgrounds and training to make understandable the many points pertaining to analytical, Jungian or depth psychology and to neurobiology as they relate to depression.

Blair Justice and Pittman McGehee

ACKNOWLEDGMENTS

We would like to thank Barbara Deal and Liz Williams, who helped us believe in this project. Further, we want to thank Feffie Bowers for her tenacious editing and tireless research, and Jasenka Deminovic, M.D., Ph.D., who filled in the blanks, researching the science notes and the references. These two are searchers and companions on the path. We acknowledge the Institute for the Advancement of Psychology and Spirituality for the advance of a grant which enabled the book to come into being. Pittman's administrative assistant, Cathy Trull Jenkins, held a steady hand in coordinating the many moving parts. Finally, we would like to thank our many students, who have helped us serve our purpose.

INTRODUCTION

...all of our provisional ideas in psychology will presumably

one day be based on an organic substructure....

– Sigmund Freud[1]

THE STORY

Every Thursday I sit with my psychoanalyst, reshaping my synapses to relieve a severe depressive illness. Neurobiologically speaking, we are engaged in a "cytoarchitectural" project to redesign brain structure and function enough to restore my biogenic amines.[2] My analyst sits opposite me, his feet on a coffee table in front of our chairs. He is a tall, balding man whose imposing figure I first saw in the purple vestments of an Episcopal dean. My wife and I would visit his cathedral to hear his Good Friday sermons, which, scriptless, seem to pour spontaneously out of his mouth as though he had a direct pipeline to God. Recently I asked him what it feels like when he speaks extemporaneously and his words start flowing without pause, producing, as he smilingly observes, an almost "hypnogogic effect" on his listeners. "Do you feel," I asked, "that the Almighty is actually speaking through you?"

Without hesitation, he answered, "Of course." My analyst has a self-certitude I have some hope of achieving.

Starting in 1999, I became better acquainted with the Very Reverend J. Pittman McGehee through sharing lecterns where we debated such subjects as the mystery of healing and whether the rift between science and religion is bridgeable. We felt a genuine kinship emerge, due in part to our mutual respect for both science and religion and, more personally, to our willingness to speak openly about our own wounds and near deaths.[3]

Pittman is an avowed mystic who gave up being a parish priest once he completed his training as a Jungian analyst. It was a step, he jokes, that took him off the church payroll and freed him to be "even more heretical," although he remains a priest in good standing. As a skeptic, I am always questioning what he mystically intuits as truth and feels in the marrow of his bones. His "proof" is what he experiences.

With humor on both sides, we have bonded as nonbiological brothers, joined as partners in what my analyst calls a "perichoretic dance." Perichoresis, he says, is "the play of psychic energy that translates eros and logos into agape"—eros being a connecting force; logos being rational understanding; and agape, "wise love."[4] I am still learning Jungian talk, so for me it is an experience that has made for new sprouts on my neurons. As depressives can attest, motivational energy—or, more accurately, the absence of it—is at the heart of our illness. As for how I can express humor while severely depressed, I don't know. I only know that on occasion something funny will pop out from some tiny islet in me even as the dark waters continue to rise. Other depressed people have experienced similar paradoxes in this little-understood and often misunderstood malady.[5] In the fleeting moments when I recapture the playfulness that Pittman and I have found in each other's humor, I like to imagine that a few green twigs have been added to my neuronal tree and synaptic connections.[6]

"Synapse" is the scientific term for the "clasp" or connecting cleft responsible for neuronal communication and sprouting. "Synchronicity," from the same stem as synapse, is a term coined by C. G. Jung, the godfather of analytical psychology, and Wolfgang Pauli, the Nobel Prize-winning physicist and longtime patient and friend of Jung.[7] Synchronicity is a different kind of connectivity, a joining together in *time* or *place* of meaningful inner and outer events without any apparent cause, a so-called "acausal" phenomenon. Chapter 1 tells of my experience with synchronicity, which led me to Dr. McGehee for an explanation. I came to a mystic and analyst for three reasons: I was deeply depressed; drugs weren't working; and I was now willing to explore, if not embrace, "mystery."[8] I also picked Pittman for his willingness to deal with shit, both mine and his own. On Pittman's part, he takes a secret pride in what has become known among local Anglicans as "Pittmanese," once lovingly characterized by one of his parishioners as "mythopoetic bullshit."

Although I have not had brain scans of my changed cerebral circuitry, the progress I have made could not have occurred without some remarkable rewiring. Where antidepressants failed to stop my descent into deep waters, therapy with Pittman has reversed my trajectory. I have had much talk therapy before, some helpful, some not, but what I am engaged in now is a new and advanced form of what has been termed "relational analysis." It differs from interpersonal psychotherapy, whose roots date back some seventy-five years to Harry Stack Sullivan, in its emphasis on the relationship between patient and therapist and the importance of self-disclosure by each.[9]

It is new in the sense that traditional psychoanalysis never allowed for self-disclosure on the part of the therapist, who served as a blank screen on which the patient was to project fantasies, fears and conflicts. Freud, who himself could be quite chatty in the waiting room, insisted that "the doctor should be opaque to his patients, and, like a mirror, should show them nothing but what is shown to him."[10] My analyst shows me his personality as much as I show him mine. "We made a lot of mistakes by being too much in our heads," according to Dr. Elio Frattaroli, a psychoanalyst affiliated with the University of Pennsylvania, and author of *Healing the Soul in the Age of the Brain: Why Medication Isn't Enough.*[11]

Jung, who believed in the neurological or "organic" basis of mental illness as much as Freud did, never advocated that the analyst should be anonymous to the analysand. Such a stance would have precluded the twenty-six-year relationship he had with the physicist Pauli. In fact, Jung described his therapy as "demanding" a true partnership between analyst and analysand.[12] So treatment now is being recast as an endeavor that requires doctor and patient to work together in a *two-way* relationship. No longer functional is the old medical model of *vis curativa,* in which healing presumably flows down from doctor to patient, without the doctor ever being known as a person to the patient.[13] Partners are on the same level, not one above the other, with one being responsible for "fixing" the other. Jung, my partner tells me, insisted that an analytic alliance must transform the analyst as well as the patient. So Pittman changes as I change.

It has been pointed out that "therapists reveal things about themselves, not just by what they say, but also by what they don't say, their facial expressions… and the way they dress and decorate their office."[14] During the five years I have been sitting across from this former jock—I am referring to my analyst—he has never taken a note. Pittman has an aversion to writing anything except poetry. He confesses he once feared graduate school because he was not accustomed to thinking and writing. He still relies on intuiting and sensing to lead him to answers, which he then expresses effortlessly in a stream of poetic and/or pontificating pronouncements.

As we noted in the Preface, Pittman also never wears a tie at work. I have stopped wearing ties except on days when I am at the bedside of cancer patients or at church. Ties, I argue, may symbolize respect and not just blockage of the heart chakra.[15] I still wear my university ID badge when I see him, although he thinks I shouldn't have to be reminded of who I am. Another habit of mine is to stick pens or pencils in my shirt pocket for easy access. Engineers are identified for Pittman by this display of left-brain dependence. One asked him after a lecture, "Isn't all this just theory?"

"Why, of course," the teacher answered patiently. "Isn't all truth mystery?"

Studies since Freud and Jung have confirmed that appropriate self-disclosure by the doctor, as well as the patient, promotes trust, bonding and understanding.[16] In the case of my therapist, I have listened to hours and hours of taped lectures and talks he has presented to professional and public audiences. In many of these he draws on his own experiences to illustrate the "involuntary" archetypal energies that he is convinced shape our lives. He talks of the people who have brought meaning and healing into his life. Pittman was nearly burned to death as a child, and an Oklahoma Indian named Dr. Orange Star, "half medicine man and half M.D.," saved his life and gave him his first lesson in becoming a "wounded healer." Pittman also had, as I did, a mother with undiagnosed depression. Pittman's mother used to place his head in her lap and repeat to him, "When you grow up, I hope you will help people with their sadness."[17] His father, like my father, was kind and gentle, but a reserved person who never expressed feelings, as was the custom of men then.

I don't just sit and expect Pittman to show me his wounds or discuss how we have bonded around mutual pain. I have not escaped the responsibility as a patient to be the first to open up, no matter how tongue-tied or dead in the head I am feeling. I hate to abandon that safe lobe of my brain, used for reason and logic, and dive into a deeper and darker emotional pool. Pittman is good at seeing when I am holding back, not letting what is unconscious have a voice. Freud, I read, said many years ago that "the therapist catches the drift of the patient's unconscious with his own unconscious."[18] So Pittman, who as a poet practices catching feelings and words with "a butterfly net," is good at catching my drift. And that, I am learning from both therapy and interpersonal neurobiology, is how deep connections are made—out of consciousness.[19] "Feeling felt"—meaning one person in a relationship feels that the other person is feeling what he or she does—is the kind of experience that reshapes synapses.[20]

Dancing, then, with Pittman—hearing the same music, moving in synchrony to the same internal rhythm and "feeling felt"—is slowly becoming less awkward for me. Our "perichoretic dance" seems to express some implicit knowing we share.[21] Our similar mothers, though long dead, brought us to this dance, or so my mystic friend reminds me in explaining how synchronicity operates. As for our fathers, both dispirited by the Depression, they lived "lives of quiet desperation" that we have tried to make up for.[22] A favorite premise of my analyst is that children are destined to live the unlived lives of their parents, or, in the words of Jung, "What usually has the strongest psychic effect on the child is the life which the parents... have not lived.... that part of life that they have always shirked from, probably by means of a pious lie."[23]

Science is only lately coming to explain that what moves us—whether it is poetry, myth, music, mothers, art, religion, God, mystery, love or science itself—has profound effects on body and brain. Neuroscience is now identifying brain structures, both conscious and unconscious, that respond to universal symbols and images. This means that identified correlates in brain scans, based on cerebral blood flow, are associated with emotionally moving experiences, including archetypal and spiritual ones.[24] The implicit part of the self, the nonverbal region of the limbic system, is full of emotion and movement. It is the unconscious, deeper-than-words area where soul stirrings "tingle our amygdala," in the words of Nobelist Eric Kandel, the neuroscientist who proved how experiences reshape synapses. Kandel delights in the abstract art of Mark Rothko[25] because he feels that reductionism as a methodology, in art as well as science, reveals basic truth.[26] I am learning that myths and stories that cut to the bone and move us accomplish the same thing. As another eminent scientist, biologist E. O. Wilson, puts it: "People need a sacred narrative."[27]

My analyst is a master storyteller who defines a "comfortable crowd" as one that has pew space enough to lie down when he puts his listeners into a state of altered consciousness or the J. Pittman McGehee "hypnogogic" state. One reason I am sticking with Jungian analysis is that Jungians do have a sense of humor and, though they take their reifications seriously, they seem to be able to laugh about them. I also am attracted to analytical psychology because it seeks to integrate what seems universal to human experience, including the soul, into a theory of human nature—human nature now having been "rediscovered" once again by science.[28] The emerging field of cultural biology, which explores both the nature we come endowed with and the culture that shapes it, seems to parallel Jung's theory of archetypal imperatives.[29] Another "rediscovery" that I sense the healing sciences—if not brain sciences as well—are making is the importance of taking imagination and imagery seriously. "Jung's analytic method is based upon the healing function of the imagination."[30] The seminal work of Achterberg and Lawlis and that of Simonton and Simonton[31] has been replicated so that imagery is now a powerful modality for behavioral medicine, particularly in treating cancer.

For my part, I must rediscover what I once experienced—that imagery and imagination can have measurable effects on the brain and body. I must relearn what I once knew so that I can again feel my amygdala tingle from the effects of imagery. In imagination and symbolically, I am dancing with my analyst so I can reconnect with my soul and bring life to my withering neuronal tree.

Our metaphorical dance is meant to reawaken the energies that have gone dead in me. My role in this partnership, at the invitation of my teacher, is to take the abstractions and analogies of Jungian therapy and try to anchor them in the hard stuff of science—specifically neuroscience and what it takes to change the synapses and circuits responsible for new ways of thinking and being. The neurobiological evidence tells me that for loving bonds, in or out of therapy, to heal depressed people like me, such relationships must do three important things: [1] Provide felt experiences in which we sense a distinct, recurring shift and resurgence of energy; [2] Learn more about who we are at the core levels of soul and shadow; and [3] Discover meaning, benefit and purpose in our very illness, suffering and depression.

Writing a book with Pittman was the idea of my wife, Dr. Rita Justice, another therapist (non-Jungian) and avowed mystic whose intuition I have learned to trust. Normally analysts and analysands work very privately together and don't disclose what they do. After deliberating the pros and cons of breaking this convention, Pittman and I decided that what is most personal in therapy is often the most universal in human experience. If what we do together in therapy can help others among the growing number of depressed people, then sharing our work seems a moral obligation. Pittman tells me that Jung described analysis as a personal relationship in a professional context.[32] We keep our relationship confined to that context, whether it is in his office or at public forums.

Pittman had a personal motive for wanting to collaborate on a book that examines the neurobiology of love as well as soul. The thesis he wrote more than a decade ago for his Jungian diploma was titled, "Love in the Analytic Container: The Place of Eros, Logos and Agape in Psychoanalysis." Pittman wrote, "speaking of an analyst 'loving' his patient might send chills up the ethical backbone of some analysts, yet as Jung asked, how can this 'immemorial psychic driving force of humanity' be denied? Our inability to speak of love returns us to the impoverished comprehension of this concept by the English word."[33] My analyst believes American culture has so equated love with sex that the word has lost its rich primordial meaning and almost become a taboo subject in the relationship between doctor and patient. Eros has become eroticized, although according to Pittman's etymology, its principal meaning is one of "union" and "connection" at the level of heart and soul. Not many years ago, psychotherapists could speak freely of "loving the patient" and being committed to a loving relationship without fear of misunderstanding.[34]

Neurobiologically, the loving relationship in the analytic container is limbically distinct from being "in love." In therapy, "loving is synchronous attunement and modulation... [and] depends critically on *knowing* the other."[35] Finding oneself "in love" may be based on brief acquaintance and little knowing in terms of the limbic brain. I know much about the person opposite me in the analytic container and he knows even more about me. The eros we experience is a connecting energy.

The attention we pay to neuroscientific anchors is meant to emphasize the new evidence confirming the healing power of talk, relationships and attachments to something larger than ego. The two of us offer whatever wisdom we have gained from our experience to all Lazaruses yet to be raised. Our story starts with a resection, my own, and a dissection, my daughter's, in New York City.

THE SCIENCE

We live immersed in unseen forces and

silent messages that shape our destinies.[1]

At a point where the curving lines of an aquatic creature known as a seahorse touches "almond joy," the brain gives us much of what makes for a soul—memory that goes deeper than awareness, motivation that reaches to the stars, and love that is stronger than death.

If this sounds mythical or poetic, it is some of both. However, it is also real and physical—and thus intersects with science. The seahorse is our hippocampus, so named because its cluster of neurons forms the graceful lines of this tiny oceanic denizen. The almond is the shape of each of our amygdalas, a small neural aggregate in both temporal lobes that is proximate to its aquatic mate. The amygdala not only defends us against dark shadows, but also gives us vitality for joy and affection, friendship and play. Without our limbic system, in which the hippocampus, amygdala and hypothalamus are prime players, we would be much older in evolutionary time and far less human.[2]

"Soul" is being reclaimed by scientists, who, in many past centuries, when they were known as philosophers, couldn't get enough of it. Wisely, they are not now trying to define it. The neuroscientists who presented at the 2002 conference of the New York Academy of Sciences seemed to assume that everyone agrees that soul has to do with our essence, our core self.[3] No one said it was a mechanistic "thing" or a "part" in the head or torso. Yet neither did anyone claim that it is totally disembodied, completely out of reach of mind and brain. When Eric Kandel, the Nobel Prize winner and godfather of much cutting-edge brain research, spoke movingly of Rothko's art and the chapel that houses it in Houston, he let it be known that his amygdala "tingles"—which listeners understood as meaning his soul is stirred. If there had been any Jungian practitioners present, they would have rightly heard Kandel also saying that art, as well as soul, is archetypal in its symbolic power to bring spirit and soma together and move mortals physically. In fact, the Nobelist told his audience that "in every culture art meets a spiritual need."[4]

So when Pittman McGehee, the priest and analyst, sits with Blair Justice, the psycho-biologist and patient, we have no trouble finding common ground. "Whatever the soul is," Pittman says, "it is complex, deep and substantial."[5] Knowing too well what clinical depression is, I venture to say I am working with my analyst to regain my soul. It is what animates me and gives color to my life. I know because I can remember what it is like to be un-depressed, to live life fully—"abundantly," my therapist calls it. In those times, Rothko bands of light and color seem as sacred to me as the chapel they are in. When my amygdala is really in high gear, I can go outside and feel the Milky Way sparkle in my soul— particularly at "Chateau les Justices," the house we built in 1983 high in the Colorado Rockies and so named by my Francophile mate, Rita.

My therapist reminds me that Jung regarded the Self as an archetype that stands paradoxically for both the essence of who we are and the totality of our psyche. Analytical psychology thus seems to agree with neuroscience about what the soul is. Just as our unique personalities are an expression in analytical psychology of the soul, neuroscientists have concluded that "synapses are simply the brain's way of receiving, storing and retrieving our personalities, as determined by all the psychological, cultural and other factors" that shape them.[6]

The amygdala permits us to experience the nuances of emotional tone and color not only in a painting on the wall, but also in transactions with other people. This tiny clump of nuclei has such sensitive radar that it can tell us almost immediately whether another person we encounter communicates in the silent language of the limbic system and whether our amygdala is attuned to this communication.

When Pittman the priest tells me he feels God speaking through him, I may show a sign of incredulity, but I am aware that the brain does provide a structure for such transmission. Neuroimaging demonstrates that experiencing God through dreams or the way Pittman does activates components of the limbic system as well as the right temporal lobe. Transcendent experiences increase blood flow to specific areas of the brain, as demonstrated by PET (positron emission tomography) scans. This does not mean that science is trying to "neurologize" things spiritual or religious. Neither God nor religion needs to be justified or "made real" by scientific findings of their brain scan correlates.[7] It doesn't mean that there is a specific "God spot" in our head, although Rhawn Joseph, director of the Brain Research Laboratory at the Palo Alto Veterans Center, has written a book on the brain entitled *The Transmitter to God.*[8] What it does mean is that feelings of being one with God and other moving experiences are expressed, after all, in the brain and have neurobiological substrates. The limbic system, which is inextricably connected to other parts of the brain, is involved.

The limbic system is receiving increasing attention by psychotherapists as well as neuroscientists for several reasons. One has to do with the potential it offers for changing neurochemistry without drugs. In my case, which is not atypical, antidepressants have failed to keep me from sliding into another depressive episode, my fourth over the years. This may be due to a "Prozac backlash," in which receptors no longer will respond to SSRIs or tricylics.[9] Even at best, directly manipulating the neurochemistry of emotions by drugs is a tricky business. In severe depressions, which I experience, limbic circuits shut down and seem immune to "the healing force of others."[10] Only a strong commitment to trusting the process of sitting in the presence of another will give the limbic loops time to repair and reconnect one with one's soul.[11]

Limbic circuits are inextricably linked with a more cognitive part of the cortex, so the evidence isn't telling my analyst or me that insight and interpretation don't count anymore, that talk therapy just has to be "relational." I need to learn something new about myself, but learning—or perceiving things differently—is not just neocortical. It is also interpersonal. To the extent that I experience "emotional attunement" with my analyst and learn from his words, the scientific evidence suggests that neural change and new connections will occur in my brain, resulting in a positive alteration of my neurotransmitters.[12]

Another compelling reason for the scientific attention being given to the limbic part of the brain is a renewed focus on perception without awareness.[13] When Joseph Ledoux, who chaired the 2002 soul and brain conference, says that "we are more than what we are aware of," he is referring to the "silent" self in us that has its own memory and learning systems.[14] This is the implicit self that communicates at a level deeper than words. This is the arena where emotional nuances, facial expressions, tones of voice and postures send and receive messages. It is where our deepest connections with others are made and where we feel moved by art, poetry, music, nature, religion and dreams. It is the arena of the amygdala— and the soul. In saying this, we are not contending that the soul or unconscious has a physical existence inside our heads.[15] Nonetheless, they do have neuronal correlates that express them. These synapses, dendrites and axons, interconnected in a marvelous neuronal forest, are shaped and resculptured by culture and our interaction with others.[16]

The amygdala is a doorway into the limbic system, which is full of movement and sensory awareness. The system both receives and transmits human emotions.[17] It constitutes a liminal border across which the physical and psychological, the seen and unseen, the emotional and spiritual interplay. Its doorkey is the synapse, which connects cell to cell for intercommunication within and among parts of the brain.

Relationships that promote cell connections and "arborize" our neuronal trees— making them bushier—are the kind of experiences that heal, according to neurobiological research.[18] However, only certain connections qualify. These are the ones that give us felt experiences of attunement, resonance and synchrony. When humans or other mammals are attuned to each other's inner states, there is limbic resonance.[19] When there is mutually responsive interaction, there is synchrony. In plain talk, we are bonding with another and speaking the same language of knowing. The more mutual limbic literacy between us, the deeper the knowing.

Such connections affect our electrochemical circuits and fertilize our neuronal soil and root systems. However, this connection does not simply consist of feeling close to someone. It is not touchy-feely stuff; it is understanding and meaning, involving the neocortex as well as the limbic system. In other words, we must learn something to heal. What starts as implicit, unconscious "emotional learning"[20] can serve as the "motivational core" for sending the experience on as explicit memory in the hippocampus and from there to the neocortex.

We must learn something so well, both implicitly and explicitly, that it encodes a new story about who we are and why we are here into the very grooves of our brain.[21] This process involves not just encoding in our right brain, but also left brain rewriting and rewiring. Thanks to a neuronal root system, linking countless axons and dendrites in the brain, what starts in the amygdala spreads across the neocortex and into our moods and behaviors.

In the language of depth psychology, arborizing depends on tapping into archetypes that we have denied or neglected.[22] When we pay too much attention to the need for power and prestige and not enough to affiliation and attachment, an imbalance occurs in body and spirit. We have overemphasized what we do and how we look in our roles at the expense of who we are and what we are meant to be in our souls. When we "perform" as extraverts even though we are introverts, we also are not being who we are and are meant to be. The effects reverberate throughout the brain and body. Our autonomic nervous system becomes incoherent, with too much sympathetic stimulation and too little parasympathetic activation.

Sooner or later, we get sick from the imbalance, and our soul disconnects. Our emotional brain, which is limbic, and our thinking brain, which is neocortical, recede into darkness. Perhaps worst of all, our social brain, which is embedded in both our emotional brain and our thinking brain, suffers. It flees not only from face-to-face contact and interpersonal communication, but also from any communion we had with God. At this point we are in deep depression and have lost our soul. What follows is the hard work of recovering it.

CHAPTER 1

SHADOW OF DEATH

THE STORY

It's 1:00 A.M. Sunday, March 15, 1999, and I am lying on a stretcher next to the operating table where I am to have emergency surgery. I am on the sixth floor of Tisch Hospital at 560 First Avenue in Manhattan, a neighborhood I recognized as vaguely familiar as Rita rushed me by cab from the Gramercy Park Hotel, where we are staying. It has been a wild night of unrelenting pain in the gut, a fever that has now climbed to 105° F, and a cacophony of banging steel doors hit open by the hospital stretcher that speeds me from the emergency room to radiology, where X-rays show that my lower bowel has ruptured. Sepsis, blood stream poisoning, will kill me if my perforated sigmoid colon isn't promptly resected.

I am strangely calm as a surgery resident makes small talk while we wait for the summoned chief surgeon, Dr. Elliott Newman, and his anesthesiologist to enter the operating suite. I hear the young doctor's voice, but I am not listening. I have the same eerie quietude I felt in facing death twice before—once from a reckless misstep hiking high in the Rockies and once from having the steering wheel of a car wrenched from my hands by a psychotic young man, my son, in the front seat beside me, causing us to veer off the narrow road and head down a steep embankment.

A question from the resident brings me back to the here and now. He is asking if my wife and I have any children. I say we do. Then the image of the neighborhood comes back to me. The image of the large, imposing building next door from a few hours ago, when the cab pulled under the neon Emergency Center sign and delivered me to the hospital, flashes before my eyes. I ask the resident, "Are we anywhere near the medical examiner's office, where the morgue is?"

He nods. "Yes, it's the building adjoining this one. The hospital and morgue are connected. Why do you ask?"

"That's where we went on a Sunday morning four years ago to claim the body of our younger daughter. It's her birthday tomorrow, and she's been on my mind." The young doctor doesn't know what to say, and there isn't time for a reply anyway because I am being rolled on to the operating table for anesthesia and my disembowelment.

The morphine gives me crazy dreams. I wake up telling Rita we need to pull out of a real estate transaction involving a piece of property right where the hospital is standing, the corner of First Avenue at Thirty-third Street. By now I am back from ICU and in a small fourteenth-floor room with no windows, the only one available. Rita is insisting that a fold-up bed be brought in for her to spend the night on. Suddenly I remember, with a start, having handed the resident in the operating room my wedding ring before the anethesiologist placed the mask over my face. It has hieroglyphic engravings that carry deep memories, and I am afraid it's been lost. Rita assures me the ring has been returned. I smile in relief and think of what she has said from the very beginning of our June-and-January marriage of almost three decades: that we have been soulmates forever. She's the first self-avowed mystic I ever met and loved. Rita leans down to kiss me and whispers something about my being her knight on a white horse. Always the skeptic, even in my post-surgery daze, I want to ask how many more belly wounds and lifetimes I have to experience before I get my karma right, but the morphine takes over again as Rita puts her cheek against mine.

At Rita's insistence, I am moved to a larger room, a corner room that, luckily, becomes available. My address becomes Room 1452, Kahn Pavilion, for the cards and flowers that follow. I can see the Fifty-ninth Street Bridge over the East River through the construction scaffolding outside my window. My first visitor is a Hasidic Jew with a long dark beard and black hat. He blessed me, I will never forget, as I lay the night before in an emergency room cubicle next to one his wife occupied, with only a thin white curtain separating us. She is now on the same floor as I am, and I will become accustomed to her husband's visits and prayers.

As the daze from my anesthesia gradually wears off, I remember the welcoming by Hasidic Jews in Brooklyn in the two marathons Rita and I ran in New York. They gathered at the curbside and, though they were silent, we felt their support for the streams of runners. This time we came to New York for Rita to attend a board meeting of body psychotherapists, and again we receive Hasidic spiritual support.

As I gradually regain consciousness I suddenly remember something else more immediate and physical: I now have a bag attached to my belly. I recall asking the surgeon before I went to sleep what I could expect as an outcome from the operation. A colostomy pouch for sure, he said, and a rupture that, with luck, is not related to cancer. As my fingers feel around the plastic wafer that seals the bag to my left abdomen, I get the good news from Rita that no cancer was found. "They think you had a diverticulum, but no tumor, that led to the rupture."

Even in my twilight consciousness I experience my brain waking up enough to question the diagnosis. "I just had a physical and colonoscopy before leaving Houston, and there was no diverticulitis."

"I know," Rita says. "It's strange, isn't it?" Then, reading my thoughts, she wonders aloud, "How can a single diverticulum, if there was one, suddenly occur and cause your colon to rupture?"

I put the mystery aside for the time being and fall back asleep. There is a liminal state between sleep and wakefulness where I am to dwell for a number of days. In it, I wrestle with anxiety over the impending deadline for the unread page proofs of my new book; over meetings in Houston I had scheduled in my job as academic dean and that now need to be postponed; and—underneath all of these worries—the nagging, vaguely depressing question of what to do with my life once I become professor emeritus. In my twilight zone, I also dread waking up and having to adapt to my new appendage, the colostomy bag on my belly.

By now, our elder daughter, the doctor, has flown in to join Rita at my bedside. Cindy, a board-certified internist with Baylor Hospital in Dallas, has detailed, technical questions for Dr. Newman, my attending surgeon, and his retinue of New York University Medical School surgery residents. One or more of them show up at my bedside night and day, probing, pricking and inspecting my anatomy tirelessly. She's satisfied that they are doing a good job and does me the favor of not bringing up the subject of a second operation that I will have to undergo in three and a half months to take the colostomy bag off and reconnect the two ends of my remaining bowel. Meanwhile, a nurse arrives to give me my first lesson in removing the colostomy bag, where my feces will start to collect once my shocked bowels resume working. She is laboriously—from my perspective—cleaning the surgical hole where a properly sealed fresh pouch is attached and rests on my sore abdomen. The lingering morphine and post-op painkillers keep me drowsy enough not to worry about learning to sleep on my back for the next four months so I won't roll over on my shit. A pretty nurse from the Bronx named Theresa McGrath rescues me from some of the frequent rounds of taping and retaping that the young residents do to look at my wound, ostensibly treating it, but invariably yanking out pubic hairs with the peeling off of surgical tape.

Mystery keeps intruding into my consciousness as more of my neurons penetrate the pain medication and start to turn on. Before the anesthesiologist put me to sleep for my resection, I wondered how I had ended up in such proximity to where we had claimed our daughter Liz's body. Rita and I had sat in tears viewing her lifeless form on a gurney separated from us by a sheet of glass, stained by other grieving viewers identifying a lifeless loved one. Now, I am in a bed in the same Mount Sinai-NYU Medical Center as the one where Liz's body had been dismembered in autopsy. I remember with gratitude the young pathologist who performed the autopsy. Interrupting her analysis of a mounting number of necrotic tissues from a Saturday night of killing, she consented to visit with Rita and me. I still remember her name, Dr. Yvonne Milewski. She just happened to be still on duty that Sunday morning when we arrived at the morgue. Leaving her basement laboratory and autopsy tables, she came upstairs to answer our questions about the drugs and injuries from a drug-induced fall down a flight of stairs that killed our daughter. Liz had died at 1:00 A.M. on a Sunday, at the same time of day and on the same day of the week that I had walked through my valley of the shadow of death in the adjoining Mount Sinai-NYU complex.

As the Sunday sunrise shafts through the construction boards outside my window and with questions still circling like scavengers in my psyche, the Very Reverend Pittman McGehee, in Houston, three hours away by plane, is finishing a second cup of coffee. He is mentally rehearsing two talks he is to give this Sunday—one in Houston and then, after a two-hour flight, another in Louisville, Kentucky. The first is at the largest Anglican church in the US, Saint Martin's, an affluent parish in a neighborhood of tall pines and wide lots. Pittman reflects passingly on Jung's statement that we are destined to live the unlived lives (and dreams) of our parents and wonders what his maternal grandfather, the fiddle-playing preacher, would do in front of such a crowd. As is his custom, Pittman will talk without notes, convinced that what needs to be said will pour out of him if he gets his ego out of the way and lets his soul speak.

The second presentation is the one to which he has to give more thought. After a flight to Louisville, Kentucky, he will speak that evening at Saint Francis in the Fields, where he had previously served. What makes it even more important is that the occasion honor Robert Johnson of San Diego, author of three best sellers—*She, He* and *We*—and Pittman's Jungian godfather. It was a talk on male psychology by Dr. Johnson that Pittman heard as a young priest that convinced him to enter the long training required to become a Jungian analyst. Dr. Johnson became the Reverend Dr. McGehee's mentor as Pittman took six years of weekend coursework and hundreds of hours of therapy training. Now, as an experienced analyst himself, he wants to impress not only his former parishioners, but, even more, his most influential supervisor. Such an assignment, Dr. McGehee decides, requires letting his ego get into the act and relieving God of the sole responsibility for what comes out of his mouth.

That evening in Louisville, Pittman reads from the thesis that earned him his Jungian diploma, "Love in the Analytic Container: The Role of Eros, Logos and Agape." To warm his audience up, Dr. McGehee confesses that he has a "seductive monotone" of a voice, which risks putting his listeners into an altered state of consciousness. It is the voice that he also describes as "hypnogogic," meaning it puts some people to sleep. It's a voice with which I had some acquaintance.

Two weeks before these events, he and I were keynote speakers at a three-day conference at the University of Texas M. D. Anderson Cancer Center in Houston. The conference theme was "Open Questions on the Mystery of Healing." I acknowledged to the audience that, as a scientist, I had trouble both understanding and accepting mystery. I confessed to being more comfortable with what is known by science about pain and healing and how to relieve the one and promote the other. Pittman argued that science considers mystery to be a puzzle yet to be solved while religion defines it as unsolvable, unknowable. He spoke of living with the mystery of pain, of having his own brush with death as a child. I spoke of my own pain, of having had cancer four years earlier when our daughter was slowly killing herself with cocaine and heroin despite all our attempts to change the inevitable. I told of David, my schizophrenic son by an early marriage. David had a schizophrenic break as an adolescent. He has spent the rest of his life in institutions and continues to live in a halfway house, too ill to be employed or attend school. Listening to me from the audience, even the intuitive Dr. McGehee had no hint of the gods that would soon bring us together again under less sanguine circumstances.

After my New York doctors become convinced that my bowels and kidneys are functioning again and my long surgical wound—dividing the two sides of my belly like a Berlin Wall—is starting to heal, I am discharged in the care of my loving wife. Now on the plane taking Rita and me back to Houston, she has her arm around my shoulders, knowing that the pain around Liz's death has once again been reawakened. In my own state of altered consciousness, I once again replay the sad story.

Liz was a brown-eyed, golden-haired little girl sought after by photographers. Early on, she announced her intention of becoming an artist. At her boarding school near Princeton, she was taken with her class to Europe, to the museums of Paris, Madrid and Rome. On summer breaks, she went with us to our beloved Indian Peaks Wilderness in the Rockies and to Blue Lake, whose sparkling waters became a subject of Liz's watercolors. Whitewater rafting in Idaho, she was excited to see bighorn sheep gazing down on us from their steep mountain perches. They, too, became part of her art. In Hawaii, on Kauai, as we hiked after a rain, she saw a double rainbow. Thereafter, rainbow colors took over her paintings as she struggled to be an artist in New York City.

Liz left her last painting with the Reverend Ashton Brooks, Canon of the towering Cathedral of Saint John the Divine, where she volunteered in the soup kitchen for the homeless. On a late Saturday night, three blocks down Amsterdam Avenue, Liz went to the room of a drug buddy on the fifth floor of a seedy single-room-occupancy hotel. After getting high, she staggered from the room and plunged down sixteen hard marble steps in the stairwell of the old building, rupturing her spleen. Within minutes she was taken to the nearby Emergency Room of St. Luke's-Roosevelt Hospital, just blocks south of Columbia University, where I had attended graduate school. There Dr. Daniel Roe, the attending resident physician, tried to save her life. When he couldn't, he was kind enough to call me later and say, "We did everything we could, but we just couldn't stop the massive internal bleeding."

Now, back in Houston in the weeks after our return from Manhattan, mystery becomes a much more personal subject than when Pittman McGehee and I debated on it at M. D. Anderson. The pain from the surgical hole in my gut compounds the depression I feel coming on. I toss in bed at night and get up each morning asking what the point of it all is. I return to the caring psychiatrist and friend who had seen me through an earlier episode of depression. I go back over what she heard from me only a few years ago: the sense of shame and failure I feel from having a daughter who ended up selling sex for drugs on the streets of New York. Some crazy god rubbed it in by giving me such a pain in the gut that it exploded and caused me to be cut open next to where Rita and I had seen our daughter dead. Now I have something more to be ashamed of: a bag of shit hanging from my belly. Antidepressants do nothing to help me understand what has happened or any meaning it has. Calling it a "coincidence" doesn't satisfy me. I feel I deserve the stigma of shit and shame. I grow gloomier and gloomier and keep asking both my doctor and my wife, "Where do I go from here?"

Rita answers, "You need to see a mystic, and his name is Pittman McGehee."

THE SCIENCE

C. G. Jung, chastised by Freud as too mystical,[1] joined with Wolfgang Pauli, winner of a Nobel Prize in physics, to research strange "coincidences" that he found occurring in the lives of many people. In their book *The Interpretation of Nature and the Psyche*, Jung and Pauli wrote: "In most cases they were things which people do not talk about for fear of exposing themselves to thoughtless ridicule. I [Jung] was amazed to see how many people have had experiences of this kind and how carefully the secret was guarded. So my interest in this problem has a human as well as a scientific foundation."[2]

Jung and Pauli introduced the idea of "synchronicity" as a natural phenomenon worthy of scientific attention and not just a fancy word standing for a fantasy or superstition.

They proposed the term to indicate another kind of synchronous—meaning, occurring together—phenomenon found in nature. Albert Einstein, also considered a "mystic" by some, had earlier conducted an experiment with two of his contemporaries on a "togetherness-in-separation" phenomenon. The scientists demonstrated that "quantum entities that have once interacted with each other retain a power of instantaneous mutual influence, however far apart they separate."[3] On the non-quantum level of reality, a father has been thinking of the birthday the next day of his daughter, now dead. He ends up having a colostomy next door to where he and his wife had claimed her body. Is this a "togetherness-in-separation" experience? I wonder.

Science calls the kind of interconnectedness that transcends time and place the "EPR experiment," named after Einstein, Podolsky and Rosen. The counterpart in the inner world of psyche and soul is synchronicity. In the billiard-ball, cause-and-effect world of Newtonian physics, one ball affects another when it hits it. In the less visible mental and spiritual world, events can be brought together by "meaning." Pauli regarded "meaning" as a force or feature operating in both the external world of physics and the inner arena of the psyche. Synchronicity is a meaningful "coincidence"—the coinciding in time and/or space of two meaningful events (such as my sigmoid bowel removal in proximity to our daughter's dissection, with the operation occurring on the very eve of her birthday). According to Jung, what makes a coincidence something more than random chance is its "peculiar interdependence of objective events… with the subjective (psychic) state of the observer."[4]

Jung contrasted mere coincidence with synchronicity by this illustration, as cited by Wilmer:[5] "A wife gives a man a new pipe for his birthday. He takes a walk and sits under a tree in a park. Sitting next to him is a man smoking the same kind of pipe. He tells the man that his wife gave him his pipe for his birthday. The man says, 'Mine did too.' It turns out that they both have the same birthday. They introduce themselves. They have identical Christian names. This is not a synchronistic event because there is no simultaneous, inner-meaningful, subjective event."

If a dog suddenly barks and whimpers in the night and wanders bereft and aimless through the house and, as later discovered, the dog's master has been killed in another city at the very same time that the whimpering began, this is an example of synchronicity. So is this: Norman Mailer wrote in his novel *Barbary Shore* about a Russian spy. After the book was finished, the U.S. Immigration Service arrested a man who lived one flight below Mailer in the same building, whom the author had never met. The man was Colonel Rudolph Abel, accused of being the top Russian spy in the United States at that time.[6]

In synchronicities, a person may act as a "nexus into which events from the external world, past and future," flow and out of which synchronous phenomena emerge.[7] For instance, a young woman is visiting friends when all present suddenly smell the odor of a burnt-out candle. After a careful search, all agree no candle is to be found in the house. Later in the evening, the woman receives a transatlantic phone call saying her father has unexpectedly become ill and is about to undergo surgery. A few weeks later, he dies, and the woman flies home to her parents' house. On the morning of her father's funeral, as she is standing in the living room, she sees a large painting, a wedding present given to her parents, fall to the floor from its place on the wall.[8]

Happenstance? Not to the young woman. She is convinced that the burnt-out candle odor, which came before the telephone call about her father's illness, meant he was failing. The painting crashed to the floor on the day his body was lowered into its grave. Synchronicity, "non-locality" and "action at a distance" describe "an essentially mysterious connection between the personal psyche and the material world, based on the fact that at bottom they are only different forms of energy."[9] The forms this energy takes is still fascinating scientists, including those pursuing the bridge between matter and mind, body and soul. At the most fundamental level of both mind and matter, according to one theory, there is only form and flux, order and energy. These phenomena constitute a unity called "intelligence," which pervades all being, all existence.[10] This nonlocal intelligence, or universal information, is seen as a basic feature of all there is and is not thought to be derived from something more elemental. It is a "given," a nonlocal consciousness or mind, that is infinite in time and space. It "works through the body but is not limited to it."[11] In this sense, it is like the soul, which uses the limbic system and amygdala to manifest itself, but the source of which is not to be equated with any part of the brain.

Jung, who recognized the soul as such, personally experienced the powerful connection between strong internal feelings and sudden external events. When the close connection between Freud and his "adopted son," Jung, was showing signs of increasing tension, an incident occurred as the two sat talking. Freud was chastising Jung for being too spiritual and interested in the "occult." Jung suddenly experienced "a red-hot sensation in his diaphragm, and at the same time, the two men heard a loud crack from the direction of the bookcase. Jung suggested that this was an example of 'catalytic exteriorization,' to which Freud replied, 'sheer bosh.' The younger man then predicted that a second event would occur, and sure enough, another report was heard, the sound of which shook Freud considerably."[12] After the break between the two became final, Jung began to focus more on the forces of intuition, sensation, thinking and feeling, as well as the inner structure of the unconscious. Freud continued to see the unconscious as the dwelling place of repressions and drives. In analytic circles, Jung's reputation grew as a mystic whose theories were antithetical to the teachings of Freud.

Dr. McGehee's personal experience with synchronicity was confirmed one Sunday at the Holy Trinity Episcopal Church in Midland, Texas, where he was the featured speaker at a weekend conference. His subject was "The Wounded Healer," and he told the story of his discovery, early in life, that this is his archetypal calling. He was reading one of his poems, titled "Incarnation," which tells the story of his being nearly burned to death at age six. When he got to the lines that read:

> The physician, tall with a plow
> Horse's girth and hair, a shock of
> White wheat. Black bag, with O. Star
> M.D. carried salvation in a syringe...[13]

A woman in the back of the audience let out a high-pitched scream. Pittman didn't know her, and she didn't know him. Nonetheless, both had been deeply affected by the Cherokee Indian physician/medicine man in a little town in northern Oklahoma called Drumright. The woman was Dr. Star's granddaughter. The meaning of the coincidence? It seemed to be that Pittman was there that night to help, with his words and manner, a woman he had never seen who needed to hear them. It was a debt repaid to the stately gentleman, long dead, who had saved Pittman's life when he was six years old.

It has been said that humans make meaning as spiders construct webs. It is an evolutionary means of survival. Viktor Frankl's experience in Nazi concentration camps proved that the will to live depends on making meaning out of the most horrendous of circumstances. If suffering or dying is the task before us, we can choose between doing it well or poorly.[14] We can choose to say there is no meaning to my New York coincidental experience or to Pittman's experience in Midland, but in both instances, brain and body recognize that choice and respond accordingly. It's a biopsychosocial consequence.[15]

Synchronicity sometimes literally flies in through a window. Jung told of a patient of his who was not making any progress in therapy because, he felt, she was so highly rational. She could not accept the existence of unconscious, deeply emotional aspects of herself. One day she was relating to Jung a dream in which a golden scarab appeared. Jung knew that to the ancient Egyptians such a beautiful beetle was a symbol of rebirth. As the woman was talking, there was a tapping on the window behind Jung. He drew the curtain, opened the window, and a gold-green scarab flew into Jung's hands. He presented it to his patient as hers. It was the turning point in her therapy.[16]

David Rosen, a contemporary Jungian analyst who describes his own depression in a fine book entitled *Transforming Depression,* reports in the epilogue a similar experience: A university student, Beth, had been hospitalized for severe depression and became Rosen's patient after discharge.[17] "Her depression was relentless and seemed to be unending," Rosen wrote. She "plummeted into a psychic black hole associated with difficulty in functioning and the feeling that she was dead."

She walked into his office for a session one day and reported that "she had just seen a yellow butterfly outside her window." Rosen said, "I was struck by this observation because it was winter, when there usually weren't any butterflies around. Much to our mutual amazement, at the precise moment when she was telling me about the butterfly (which she interpreted as a hopeful sign), a yellow butterfly appeared outside my office window, and then another butterfly joined the first, and then they danced together, almost as if in a mating ritual. After a long silent period spent staring in awe at the two butterflies, Beth asked: 'How do I pull myself out of this well of depression?' In response to her question I asked, 'How does the butterfly get out of the cocoon?'" Rosen said that this incident "turned out to be transformative for Beth. Following this session, she was no longer psychologically paralyzed by depression…. She had somehow found her lost soul…."[18]

Such dramatic changes don't usually occur from synchronicities, which themselves may be more subtle and appear to many to be coincidental. F. David Peat, a quantum physicist, says that while synchronicities can be dismissed as mere "coincidences," such an "explanation" makes little sense to the person who has experienced one. "Indeed the whole point of such happenings is that they are *meaningful* and play a significant role in a person's life."[19]

Just as we can perceive the 2002 New York Academy of Sciences conference as underscoring a connection between the nonmaterial soul and the material brain, "synchronicities challenge us to build a bridge with one foundation driven into the objectivity of hard science and the other into the subjectivity of personal values."[20] In other words, synchronicities form a bridge between matter and mind.

Science long insisted upon the separateness of the physical and psychological realms.[21] The growth of mind/body medicine and health psychology has put to rest such misconceptions. I have written extensively on this subject.[22] Thoughts, feelings, moods and meanings affect bodies and health. Loss of health brings up questions of meaning.[23] As the father who experiences a synchronicity linking my mind and body with that of my dead daughter, I feel that there has to be meaning involved, some purpose served. This felt experience comes from my insula, a part of the emotional brain that monitors disquiet in brain and body. What I don't know is what its meaning or purpose is and how I can pull myself out of my own deep well of depression.

CHAPTER 2

THE NIGHT BEFORE

…wrestling with a vine of despair that wraps

around you, sucking out your energy[1]

THE STORY

It is 6:30 P.M., the evening before my appointment with the Reverend J. Pittman McGehee, Jungian diplomate and savior of psyches and souls. It has been a month now since I walked through the valley of the shadow of death at Mount Sinai-NYU Medical Center. My emergency colostomy has left me severely depressed, and I've run out of therapeutic options. Although it is still daylight outside, I am getting ready for bed.

I feel dead in the head, meaning that nothing excites, stimulates or even interests me. To hide my true state from others, I use the word "down" to describe how I am feeling, but it is too weak a word. I am "dead" in spirit as well as thought. My only feeling is dread. I look forward to nothing except sleep. Before I can go to bed, my wife makes sure I keep up a routine of getting down on the floor and playing with our dog, Tashi, but she and he can tell my heart isn't in it. My mind is preoccupied with two things: the bed in the next room and the hole in my belly, the anatomical site requiring me to take a course in the care and cleaning of my colostomy. An experienced "bag lady," a vocational nurse, comes to our house to teach me the fine art of colostomy pouch attachment, removal and replacement. While I undress and check my shit bag for any sign of leakage around the seal, I find dark humor in wondering if I should list this training on my resume—my academic vita— under postgraduate courses.

My body shames me by requiring that my shit come out from a hole just below the waist instead of from my anus. I know I should be thankful that I am alive instead of bitching about how to pass inspection in shit handling. However, depression, as depressives well know, darkens everything and allows for no appreciation or gratitude—even for life itself, which becomes more than just a pain in the anatomy. I feel guilty for feeling this way.

I also feel guilty for being a drag on my wife, although Rita is such a cheerleader she would never acknowledge I am sapping her emotional, if not physical, strength. Books have been written by wives, children and parents of depressives on how contagious unrelenting darkness becomes.[2]

"Look at the bright side," some minority part of me whispers to the dark, brooding part. Other than the appendage that my body has acquired, my soma seems to be accommodating itself to the sixteen-inch gash down my middle, where the sigmoid section of my colon was cut out. The incision and the pouch have taught me new sleeping positions—back, left side, right side, anything but the stomach, which had been my favorite. The position I mostly find myself in is fetal, with my wife's arm around me to defend against the frightening light of a new day. I am amazed that my body manages to heal despite my psyche's feelings of doom.

My head tells me I should know by now what goes on in the battles it has waged against depression. As a psychobiologist I am aware that my brain serotonin, dopamine, norepinephrine and oxytocin are in fast retreat. From three previous episodes of clinical depression, I have become well acquainted with antidepressants, psychotherapy, supportive therapy, bibliotherapy, writing therapy, jogging therapy, cognitive-behavioral therapy and prayer. The treatment I am receiving now, pro bono from my loving psychiatrist friend, is strictly pharmaceutical. Nothing is working, including prayer. I keep saying pious words, but, if I were God, I, too, would be deaf to them, because—let's face it—I have a beautiful wife who still loves me, a dog that gives me kisses, friends who sent me flowers and get-well cards when I was in the hospital, a well paying job and money in the bank. So what do I have to be depressed about? *No wonder,* I say to myself, *that depression is regarded by so many as a weakness, not an illness.*

My lack of progress mockingly proves that I can't practice what I preach, teach and have written books on—namely, coping with stress and adversity and finding well-being despite illness. My failure to walk my talk compounds my shame and pain. There are only two alternatives left for me—Dr. McGehee or electroshock therapy. I admit to being skeptical of things otherworldly and unexplainable, but if I have to choose between a mystic and running electricity through my amygdala and memory banks, I will choose Pittman any day.

So if I'm stuck in such inner darkness, why am I here on a warm spring evening closing the blinds and pulling the curtains shut as though I can't wait for outer darkness to descend? From my bed, I can see tall pecan trees sprouting green and the blue sky fading to orange outside my window. They are lovely sights I used to delight in. Now I see myself as invalid, in-valid, unworthy of such sensory pleasure, and hide my eyes from it. As quickly as I can, I am making it dark in the room to match how I feel in psyche and soma. I know that if I don't close out every crack of light, I will lie in bed too immobilized by dysphoria to move my body even three feet to adjust the blind. A paralysis of not only will but also movement goes with the illness. I remember a line from one of Jane Kenyon's poems describing her depressive paralysis, which fits mine:

> *I had to ask two times*
> *Before my hand would scratch my ear*[3]

I have given up on being "saved" by God or Zoloft or Wellbutrin or Prozac or any of the tricyclics that once pulled me out of previous depressive episodes. I know my depressed self painfully well, a knowing that first began when I was a young man, full of energy, enthusiasm and promise. Depression knocked me to my knees then, and did so, with more or less severity, many times in the following decades. This time I feel my last hope is a self-described "heretical" agent of the God I have given up on. I manage a small smile thinking of my having bandied and dueled with him on public forums. We share some sense of quirky humor. Tomorrow he will see me as a patient without humor, quirky or otherwise. I don't allow myself to expect anything, although I am seeking magic. I know what therapists do, because in a better life I am one. I know the scientific literature because I am also a professor. I know what darkness is because I not only live in it, but also know that darkness is the word most frequently used to describe depression.

This is the earliest I dare to go to bed. Even an understanding spouse like mine will ask how many more hours can I sleep each night. The only pill I take that really works is zolpidem tartrate, better known as Ambien. It sends me into a dreamless sleep, a state of nothingness that I both embrace and fear. I embrace it because my anxiety, despondency and futility do not haunt me for a few hours. I fear it because of what my depression is doing to me. I wake up repeating as a dopey mantra what Ernie Pyle said in *The Battle of Iwo Jima*: "There's no point to the struggle but to struggle." I'm terrified of running out of struggle. I'm certain I can't keep up much longer the charade I practice upright day after day. The mask I wear over the depression is wearing thin. Yet what's the alternative to being a mechanical man who has lost his soul? Suicide? It depends on how much longer Ernie Pyle's line can sustain me with its existential angst.

I think of what Jungian analyst James Hollis has said about fear of shame being a driving force behind the experience of "wounded" males, which includes depressed ones.[4] We fear the shame of weakness, of sickness, of failure, and each generation carries the fear and shame of its fathers, he said. Most men would never acknowledge fear or shame. I don't admit to it. I hate myself for being weak and "not acting like a man"—an "unwounded" one.

While I wait for the Ambien to take effect, I tell myself not to be so ashamed that I have failed to help myself. I am in good company. On the shelves in my study are books by other scientists and psychologists who have struggled mightily with the depression of malfunctioning synapses and dead spirits.[5] The consensus is that depression is not only "a wrestling with a vine of despair that wraps around you, sucking out your energy," but is also "a trip to the country of nothingness."[6]

Some, maybe many, of my fellow depressives finally found relief in the psychopharmacology of Prozac and other SSRI's—selective serotonin reuptake inhibitors. I haven't. One clinical psychologist, Dr. Martha Manning, found that electroconvulsive therapy was "the tractor" that pulled her "out of the mud."[7]

I have been dodging the ECT bullet—electroshock therapy is now called electroconvulsive therapy—since my first major depression came out of the blue decades ago. I was flying high as a prize-winning science writer when a pain in my belly could find no relief from internal medicine. Without knowing its reputation, I ended up traveling for psychiatric treatment to what was then the "shock capital of the world," at the University of Texas Medical Branch in Galveston. My doctor, the chairman of the department, was a gentle, fatherly type. After seeing me every day for a week of evaluation/psychotherapy, he advised me to consider EST. I considered it for one day and decided against it. I returned home and went back to bed.

I have also made myself read the accounts of gifted writers who are professionals at depicting the vicissitudes and darkness of the human experience. Even they struggle for the right words to describe their depression. It has been described not only as a "vine of despair that wraps around you" on "a trip to the country of nothingness," but also as "soul loss"[8]— or soul death, as I experience my depression.

"To most of those who have experienced it," author William Styron observes, "the horror of depression is so overwhelming as to be quite beyond expression, hence the frustrated sense of inadequacy found in the work of even the greatest artists."[9] The "horror" may be so great that it kills because it cannot be borne. To Styron, it is "Darkness Visible," the title of his best-selling "memoir of madness."[10] To many, depression is experienced as "the black struggle," derived perhaps from "the black dog" that Churchill, and Samuel Johnson before him, called their depressions. To Andrew Solomon, a widely-published writer who has written a 569-page "atlas" of depression, it is "The Noonday Demon."[11] Speaking of his own depressive paralysis, he mentally rehearsed the steps required to get to the shower, which became "twelve steps... as onerous as a tour through the stations of the cross."[12] But I identify most with the scientists and physicians who have come out of the closet to admit their illness—and their shame and guilt. The British applied biologist Lewis Wolpert of University College, London, confesses,

> It was the worst experience of my life. More terrible even than watching my wife die of cancer. I am ashamed to admit that my depression felt worse than her death but it is true.[13]

Such shaming self-involvement is not uncommon and describes what I feel. For Dr. John Horder, past president of the Royal College of General Practitioners in London, depression is "total... it is oneself and not part of one's machinery, a total form of paralysis of desire, hope, capacity to decide what to do, to think or to feel except pain and misery."[14] I am struck by the paucity of psychiatrists who are willing to disclose their own depressions. I know of only Jung himself[15] and David Rosen, who wrote about his in *Transforming Depression.*[16] I am also aware that psychiatrists have the highest rate of suicide among physicians and that this is often preceded by undisclosed major depression.[17]

Anthony Stevens, a physician and Jungian psychiatrist, notes that "in every doctor there is a patient, and in every patient a healer. What draws most of us into the profession of healing, I suspect, is the sick patient in ourselves questing for its other half for completion.... As therapists, consciousness of our wound and our personal therapeutic quest is a primary duty."[18] In turning to a "wounded" priest for my redemption and a way out of my paralysis, I think about where "soul" is in all this. Then I recall the words of Dr. Wolpert: "If we had a soul—and as a hardline materialist I do not believe we do—a useful metaphor for depression could be 'soul loss' due to extreme sadness. The body and mind emptied of the soul lose interest in almost everything except themselves."[19] In my soul loss or death, I can no more escape being self-absorbed than a locked-in-syndrome patient can move his body. I am thinking of the once high-living Jungian analyst Dr. James Hall, whose brainstem stroke left him able to move only his eyelids, and, after much rehabilitation, a finger, which enabled him to write using a word processor.[20]

To escape my prison, I am now turning the sheets back and unplugging the phone to disconnect for a few hours from conscious morbidity. The Ambien will soon take over, freeing me from the pit in which mind and body hold me, and surrendering me to the deeper darkness I seek. If I had any ego left, I might feel proud that I have an affliction that great poets—Milton, Dante and Keats, as examples—have experienced. The history of depression is a catalogue of noteworthy figures since Socrates and Plato, who had "black bile," or the melancholic disease.[21]

As for Lazarus, Martin Luther confessed to being "a true Lazarus, and well tried in sickness," and he said, "When our heart is grieved and sad, the weakness of the body follows."[22] As mentioned previously, in Luther's time and even in the fourteenth century, a Lazarus or lazar was someone afflicted with a stigmatizing disease, such as leprosy. To Luther, sadness and sickness of the heart, which is what depression delivers, is included in this definition.

If my left brain were clear of fog, I might also try to understand the mystery that my kind of depression presents in these more enlightened times: why the sickness comes and goes when it wills, why it gets worse each time, why it won't respond to the best and latest that medicine has to offer. Jung said a person often has to suffer to find out who he is and what he is here for.[23] Even if my depression ultimately gives me an answer, I am at the point of asking: *Is it worth it?*

I am turning to a man who embraces mystery as a calling. As I face him tomorrow for the first time in therapy, I will probably practice, out of habit, a favorite technique of depressed souls: faking and masking. We fake facial expressions, tone of voice, body movements and all the rest so as not to attract attention and to keep others from looking at us and seeing us for what we are: a Lazarus who walks and talks, but is otherwise dead.

Why would I play such charades in front of a priest and therapist to whom I go for help? First, he is someone who knows me from sharing speaker platforms on such weighty subjects as the science and mystery of healing—about which, in my better days, I knew something, and now feel I know nothing. Second, I fear acknowledging to anyone how sick I feel, believing that my worst doubts about myself will be confirmed. Third, I fear being pitied. My disdain for pity is so deep that I not only don't want it from others but have resolved never to manifest self-pity, regardless of how close I come to drowning in dark waters. I will do my best not to convey that feeling even to an understanding agent of God.

What I *will do* is be honest with Pittman about the episodes of depression I have had recurringly over the least three decades: what triggered them, including a sick first wife whom I climbed through a window to save from an overdose of pills, a schizophrenic son by that marriage, a painful divorce and career change, a golden-haired daughter who killed herself slowly with heroin and cocaine, and, most recently, the explosion of my gut in proximity to the New York City morgue where my wife, Rita, and I had claimed my daughter's body. This is not an inclusive list of triggering events, but it should be enough material for Dr. McGehee's therapeutic mill to start grinding.

So I lie in bed thinking about my appointment with Pittman, the therapist-priest who has heard confessions far worse than mine, knowing that I will nonetheless play it safe and mask some of mine. The last glimmer of daylight is now sneaking through the bedroom shutters as I close my eyes. Although I have given up on being saved, I still pray. "Fake it 'til you make it," I used to hear in twelve-step programs I attended for parents of children derailed by drugs. What do I have to lose?

I am determined to keep going, a walking Lazarus or not, if for no other reason than to find out the meaning of being resected next door to where Liz was dissected. I manage a faint smile as I drift off to sleep. Despite my paralysis of desire, I have something to desire after all: to learn the meaning of the mystery connecting me, on the very brink of death and on the day before what would have been her birthday, to Liz, whose body we had claimed next door.

THE SCIENCE

The epidemiology of depression tells us that the illness is on the increase.[1] Some form of it affects one out of every four persons in the United States.[2] Rates are even higher among adolescents.[3] Regardless of age, most depressed people do not seek treatment.[4] Eighty percent of those depressed complain primarily about physical symptoms such as aches and pain, fatigue and sleeplessness, according to the American Psychiatric Foundation. Unlike depression, these symptoms carry no stigma and are openly acknowledged.

In this country "the treatment, morbidity and mortality associated with depression are estimated to cost $44 billion annually"[5] and are second only to heart disease in healthcare costs. As a debilitating disease, depression also ranks second among causes of disability in the U.S. and first worldwide. In the United States, depression is the main cause of disability in women.[6] The amount spent annually on antidepressants alone now stands at $14 billion. The estimate for the year 2006 is $22 billion.

But antidepressants are not the number one treatment of choice. Alcohol is. Many, if not most, depressed people prefer self-treatment, and alcohol raises serotonin, just as antidepressants do. The side effects, of course, are more dangerous. The estimated number of people treated in emergency rooms for attempted suicide is 500,000 per year. Many are depressed but have never been diagnosed or treated by a physician or psychologist. According to research on the subject, "fewer than half of those with depression are treated."[7] Depression can kill not only through suicide, but also through higher heart disease rates, lowered immune function, and serious injury—the "comorbidity" problem.[8] Alcohol, like other addictive drugs, provides an ill-advised "shortcut" that attempts to get the brain's reward system to provide a sense of relief without individual effort.[9]

Another problem with alcohol, as well as many antidepressants, is that the drug stops working. Limbic system receptors become resistant and keep less and less serotonin from entering brain cells. The initial episodes of depression often follow distressing external events in a person's life, some failure or loss that seems devastating. If there is no treatment or if drugs have stopped working, the episodes start recurring without any well-defined external "cause." Despite the danger that depression poses in the lives of persons who experience it, a stigma persists, branding the illness as a weakness. Wolpert's wife was embarrassed that he was depressed. She told others that he was "exhausted from a minor heart condition."[10]

Depressed doctors are particularly vulnerable because they fear disclosure of their illness will jeopardize their careers. "The message is: Don't talk about it, don't mention it. It's perceived as weakness," said Wendy Hansbrough, wife of a prominent surgeon who killed himself during a severe depression.[11]

I have been acutely aware that disclosure of my depression could stigmatize me. Suffering a ruptured colon is accepted as an illness. Depression is not. Even in academia, men are supposed to be strong physically as well as mentally. While I was academic dean, a promising young biostatistician failed to write up and publish papers because of major depression. In committee meetings on the problem, little recognition was given to his depression as an illness. The prevailing opinion was that "everybody gets down in the dumps and has tough times, so let him get himself together and move on or get out." He got out.

Andrew Solomon, the writer, was once told by an editor, "I don't buy into this whole depression business," meaning that it has become an easy excuse for weak people to escape the stresses of daily life.[12] Seventy percent of the public believes mental illness is due to "emotional weakness."[13] Solomon believes "depression is so scary and unpleasant that many persons would just as soon deny the disease and repudiate its sufferers."[14] Besides, "real" sickness puts people in bed, and most depressives will do anything to keep from giving up and going to bed. So we sit and stand and move and pretend. Nonetheless, there is no hiding depression. All of us live around people and have families, relatives, bosses and others to whom we are accountable or who pry into our lives.

Although depression is always biological in the sense of causing upheaval in brain and body chemistry, at the same time it occurs in a social context. It has roots in relationships, starting with one's family of origin. Both Freud and Jung recognized the psychological power that relationships have on our mental states, both unconscious and conscious, and on external behavior. Both of these famous physicians sought to account for causes and effects scientifically. However, as medicine became increasingly dependent on the advances of chemistry, physics and biology, neither the psychoanalytic theories of Freud nor the analytical psychology of Jung earned the respectable mantle of science. Freud died before his "Project for a Scientific Psychology" was ever completed, and Jung's collaboration with the physicist Wolfgang Pauli seemed too esoteric for medical science to countenance.

"Real" science, meaning the "hard" sciences that make for Nobel Prizes, has great difficulty dealing with something called "the unconscious," whether it is Freud's repressions of the personal unconscious or Jung's archetypal imperatives and the collective unconscious. Nonetheless, the unconscious is inextricably embedded in relationships, which are at the root of depression. On the other hand, strictly biological psychiatry can now argue that since depression is "caused" by too little serotonin in the neurons and too much cortisol coursing through the bloodstream, then logically the treatment should be biological, meaning drugs like Prozac. Whatever part, if any, the unconscious is seen to play becomes irrelevant if medication does the trick.

Although dysregulation of serotonin (or 5HT, 5-hydroxtryptamine) is involved in depression, the "cause" is more complex. Behind neurotransmitter malfunctions are genetic factors and gene-environment interaction to be considered. All of this leaves neuroscientists to sort out "epigenetic factors." These are ways in which experience influences how genes are expressed, and how "a 'genotype' (genetic template or information) becomes expressed as a 'phenotype' (genetic transcription function leading to protein synthesis and external manifestation as physical or behavioral features)."[15]

Patients—and I am one of them—are only too willing to buy into the idea that the dysfunction in our lives is due strictly to faulty brain chemistry. And physicians are only too willing to prescribe drugs to change the chemistry. Even if relationships are part of the problem, what medical doctor has the time or training to sit with a patient and listen long to what's happening in the patient's life, both inner and outer? Anyway, the patient is much more comfortable believing that what's making him sick is his body and brain—in this case, his neurotransmitters and circulating cortisol—than what's happened in his relationships, past or present, conscious or unconscious. So we'll fix it with a prescription, we tell ourselves, and let our busy doctor call the next patient into his busy consulting room.

"Before the advent of SSRIs, psychiatrists prescribed most antidepressants. Now, nonpsychiatrists prescribe most antidepressants, writing almost 90 million prescriptions in 1998, up from 32 million in 1988," according to a 2002 National Health Policy Forum white paper issued by George Washington University.[16] The point here is that physicians who are not psychiatrists are not trained to sit and probe into the lives of patients. Many are too rushed to sit at all, and the probing they do is of the body, not relationships. The evidence shows that for psychotherapy to relieve depression, a relationship with the doctor must occur, meaning a connection or bonding deeper than that which fifteen-minute visits allow.[17]

For a depression to end, a patient must learn enough in therapy to connect and bond outside the doctor's office, including with a refurbished self. However, the number of treated depressed Americans who receive psychotherapy is declining as use of antidepressants only is rising.[18] The rise of "biological" psychiatry has put psychopharmacology into the forefront in the minds of some practitioners who previously favored talk and analysis. T. M. Luhrmann, an ethnographer who now specializes in psychological anthropology, sees this issue as part of "the growing disorder in American psychiatry."[19]

Whether drugs preclude relationships in treatment priorities may depend not so much on efficacy as on time. Relationships, in and out of therapy, take time. Drugs don't. Talk therapy, particularly the analytic variety, also requires money, a lot of it. Health providers as well as patients, therefore, have to consider cost/benefit ratios and make tough decisions.

The point is that relationships are not antithetical to "science." They are integral to biology, psychology and sociology—to life itself. Whether the relationship is with another person, a group or a cause, if it takes us out of our self-preoccupation, it engages us both physically and emotionally. Relationships have something to do with harmony, union, belonging and loving. Solomon says flatly that "the climbing rates of depression are without question the consequence of modernity."[20] What does that mean in terms of my brain chemistry or the malfunctioning neurons in any other depressed person? Solomon continues,

> The pace of life, the technological chaos of it, the alienation of people from one another, the breakdown of traditional family structures, the loneliness that is endemic, the failure of systems of belief (religious, moral, political, social—anything that seemed once to give meaning and direction to life) have been catastrophic.[21]

Martin Seligman, a research psychologist who has done seminal work on depression for some forty years, gives a one-word answer to the question of why the illness is increasing to epidemic proportions in prosperous countries of the West: "Shortcuts." He is convinced that "every wealthy nation creates more and more shortcuts to pleasure: television, drugs, shopping, loveless sex, spectator sports, and chocolate to name just a few."[22] While "the pleasures come easily... gratifications (which results from the exercise of personal strengths and virtues) are hard won." His remedy for reversing the rising tide of depression is establishing a national ethos that encourages people, particularly the young, to identify and develop their personal strengths and virtues. This often means doing something that helps others so that a person gets in touch with the gratifications that altruism bestows.

Solomon believes that while medications are needed, other therapies are necessary to deal with the emotional turmoil of chronic disease,[23] of which depression is one. Whether ECT should be included among the other therapies is a point of contention. Solomon says it can be a "miracle" for some long-suffering depressed people. Shocking the brain certainly produces physical effects. Less obvious and harder for many people to accept is that words do, too. They change neurons and electrical circuitry, often more permanently.[24] If words and relationships did not create physical effects, then alienation and loneliness couldn't be blamed for emotional upheavals that cause autonomic imbalance and limbic dysregulation, each of which is involved in depression. The problem is simultaneously psychological and biological.

The therapy, then, that works for depression is not *either* a drug *or* a talking therapy. It is both, plus an ethos that values developing personal strengths and virtues instead of shortcuts to pleasure. The self, the site of the battle, is not *either* a body *or* a mind. It is both, plus a soul.[25] Feelings, which relationships depend on, are not just the "soft" stuff of emotions, but also the "hard" stuff of biology. Serotonin and cortisol are not affected only by a biological predisposition causing dysfunction or by a diet deficient in tryptophan (a precursor of serotonin). At its roots, the chemical imbalance represents failure to connect not only with one's true self, but also with other people, with nature and/or with God. In other words, our biology reacts to a lack of belonging, of feeling part of something outside of and bigger than the ego self. The reward circuit of the brain, which dispenses dopamine and other feel-good endogenous chemicals, responds to relationships, cooperation and trust.[26]

But is this "science"? It is if science depends on measurement and empirical proof. Neuroimaging demonstrates that synapses of brain cells can be changed in a relationship where one person feels close to another and connects not only by words, but also by the emotional nuances of bonding and limbic resonance. For instance, when nuclear brain images are made by single photon emission computerized tomography before and after talk therapy, significant positive changes are visibly apparent in the deep limbic system where depression and anxiety are rooted.[27] PET scanning shows that mood improvement lights up the left prefrontal cortex while the negative affect of depression is registered in the right hemisphere.[28]

Imaging studies also reveal that depressed individuals, who often show reduced facial expression, have a blockage "in the activation of right-hemisphere facial perception centers. The implication here is that the expression and perception of facial affect may be a neurologically linked process." Because of shame and/or masking of one's depression, chronic blocking of affective expression may lead to a shutting down of circuits controlling display of emotion. The right hemisphere, particularly the orbitofrontal cortex and the amygdala, is involved.[29] The orbitofrontal region is important in reading others' feelings and being aware of one's own. According to psychiatrist Daniel Siegel of UCLA, when we repeatedly block consciousness of our emotions, or refuse to let them into awareness, the results may be a feeling of not knowing who we really are and a sense that "life is meaningless."[30]

Self-perception—meaning the story we have encoded in our neocortex about who and what we are—can change when we learn something about ourselves in a healing relationship. When we have a change of mind, we have a change in the brain. When we gain meaning, we mold matter.[31] All of this I know—theoretically—on the night before going to Pittman McGehee for the first time. All I now have to do is prove it.

CHAPTER 3

UNEXPECTED MEANING

Depression can force one to look inward

and ask very difficult questions about oneself:

what is it all about, what is the purpose, and who and what am I?[1]

THE STORY

I am sitting nervously in the darkly paneled reception room of the Broadacres Center for Psychological and Spiritual Renewal, located in a stately two-story brick home overlooking well tended gardens. A bronze bust of an unidentified Roman looks blindly in the direction of a fancy aquarium several feet away. The aquarium and its occupants are similar to others now populating reception rooms of doctors seeking to calm waiting customers. My anxiety causes me to look with envy at the colored specimens swimming serenely in the tank.

What was once an expanse of green lawn on the property's east side is now a paved parking lot for patients, with a galvanized shed at the far end for the SUVs of therapists and counselors who work there. The founding psychiatrist and his wife occupy the upstairs of the home, while the first floor of the building has become the site for those seeking renewal of psyche, soma or soul—or all three, as in my case. It is a place I remember only in shadows from the days that Rita and I were doing long, predawn training runs in preparation for marathons. I was "up" then and am "down" now. Even at my best I have never been very comfortable in the kind of old-wealth, tree-lined, private-park neighborhood of large lots that the Broadacres Center borders.

My colostomy bag is new enough to me that I am still self-conscious about carrying my feces on the outside of my belly, producing a bulge that I worry people will notice at my belt line. Psychotherapists are used to people bringing their shit to them, but not in the literal, as well as metaphorical, sense that I am doing. In these genteel surroundings, talking about shit seems gauche. Nonetheless, shit or no shit, I am here to consult the charismatic therapist, teacher and preacher I have long known by reputation and, more recently, by sharing podiums with him.

In the waiting room I get up from one of the large imposing chairs, under the watchful eyes of an ornamented big bird perched above my head, and go to the hallway where there are certificates of achievement and testimonies of recognition displayed on a black wall. As I stand reading the framed credentials of J. Pittman McGehee, Jungian Diplomate, Doctor of Divinity and Carolyn Fay Professor of Analytical Psychology, he approaches and remarks, "I also walk on water."

I reply, "Good. That's why I came." Buttoning my jacket across my protruding left belly, I try to respond to his hyperbolic humor. "Weren't you also once an all-state basket-ball player?" I ask. "You should have your trophies on display."

He shakes his head. "There's not enough room."

Pittman is a tall, balding, middle-aged man dressed in khakis and a soft, long-sleeved shirt open at the neck. He strikes me as someone who would like to fish, which I learn he normally would be doing with one of his colleagues on this Wednesday afternoon. For whatever reason, his weekly pastime has been canceled, and he's available to see me. We walk to his office where he promptly puts his feet up on the coffee table in front of his large stuffed chair. A soft settee is opposite him, but I pick instead a hardbacked straight chair, which is more compatible with my tense back and belly.

During the many months to come Dr. McGehee will be my teacher as well as therapist in analytical psychology. In return for the professional courtesy rate he charges me, I will tell him what I know to be the neurobiological evidence that talk therapy changes synapses and chemistry. Since in this case it is my own neurons at stake, I have more than an academic interest in the experience—or experiment—I am embarking on with him.

Although Pittman is a mystic and I am a skeptic committed to empirical evidence, we make the propitious discovery that our personalities seem to balance each other in ways that bond us. He's intuitive, I'm cognitive; he's analogical, I'm logical; he's spontaneous, I'm reserved; he's orderly, I'm disorderly; he perceives the world mythologically, I see it scientifically; he's certain about God, the soul, where we come from and are going; I'm not, doubly so in my depression. The self-deprecating humor we share has a connecting chemistry that guides our first steps in the "perichoretic dance," which Pittman describes as the energy, the resonance and rhythm, he thinks are essential in any caring relationship, analytic or otherwise. We will do this metaphorical dance, I learn, in what is called the analytic container, the crucible in which therapy takes place.

"I'm here," I tell him, "because I am deeply depressed and antidepressants aren't help-ing me. Nothing matters to me anymore but sleep. I drag myself out of bed each morning repeating a mantra, 'There's no point to the struggle but to struggle.' I don't know how much longer I can go on this way. I'm also here because I can't understand why my lower bowel burst in New York—why it ruptured at the time and place it did—when tests a few weeks earlier showed it to be normal."

Pittman takes no notes. He just listens and looks at me, then responds, "You mean you can't understand the meaning of what happened."

"Yes, the meaning." I tell him the story of our daughter, Liz, her death in New York and our claiming her body at the morgue on a Sunday four years ago. I tell him of my emer-gency colostomy last month, early on a Sunday morning, on the eve of Liz's birthday and in a hospital adjoining the morgue. I describe my efforts since then to stave off a depression that keeps deepening and of going to a loving friend and psychiatrist who treated me in the past when Liz's irreversible drug addiction first began to threaten her life. I tell him that my friend has been prescribing antidepressants for me. I'm fearful that the medicine's potenetial benefit will come too late to arrest a spiral into despair that will be insurmountable. I also know from research and from my previous encounters with the "black dog" that medication alone does not have the best effect.

"I have been haunted," I say, "by the coincidence of having been partially disemboweled next door to where Liz was dismembered on an autopsy table. I keep asking myself, is there any meaning to it beyond the physical, beyond the medical explanation which was sent to me in the pathology report." The physical facts, I tell him, are that my sigmoid colon ruptured from a single diverticulum. "Before leaving Houston," I add, "I underwent a colonoscopy and was told that my bowel was okay. Then suddenly, two weeks later, I'm laid low in New York by emergency surgery caused by a diverticulum in my bowel. Why then, why there?" I keep asking. "Maybe my 'gut brain' caused my bowel to explode from all the powerful emotions it was feeling," I suggest.

Then I hear Pittman use the word "synchronicity," which, as I already knew, refers to a coincidence that seems to have significance beyond being just a chance occurrence. He immediately gives me a meaning that I find unbelievable but strangely moving. "It means you went to purgatory," he announces, "to release Liz."

I don't know whether I am hearing this from Pittman the mystic, Pittman the priest or Pittman the analyst. "There's an ancient belief," he says, "that those who commit suicide—as your daughter did by slowly killing herself with drugs—go to the realm between hell and heaven. There's also the belief, steeped in mythic traditions, that they can be unstuck in their struggle to get to heaven by sacrifice. You made the sacrifice in her behalf."

"And my sacrifice," I ask, "was what?"

He answers: "Having sixteen inches of your colon surgically removed. And almost dying on her behalf." I am stunned by his words. I feel tears welling up. As a father who felt he never did enough to save his daughter, I am now being told I did save her—after death, to be sure; nevertheless, making a sacrifice that helped her escape purgatory. I've never even believed in purgatory. I want to know how Pittman knows what he says is true. "There are at least two kinds of truth," he replies. "Science identifies objective facts that are empirically true. Myths are about subjective truth, about the mystery and truth of human experience that can't be measured."

As a psychobiologist I have written extensively on how the subjective in us—our thoughts, beliefs and attitudes—have profound effects on the objective parts of us—our bodily tissue and organ systems. However, Dr. McGehee is in some higher or deeper realm of discourse, one that scientists would consider illusory. My questioning nature leads me to ask for some supporting evidence. He goes to a bookcase on the wall behind his chair and shows me pages from his literature on dismemberment. It's an important mythic theme, he points out, not only in Egyptian and Greek traditions, but also in Oriental, Celtic and Germanic legends.

This is not what I consider "proof," but I cannot question what I have experienced in my body, if not my soul, by the meaning he attributes to my "dismemberment." I feel, for the first time, that some higher purpose could have been served by my surgical "sacrifice," but the understanding of it is beyond me. There were two purposes served, Pittman tells me: first, a rebirth for Liz in terms of her moving on in an afterlife; and, second, a chance for an emotional and spiritual rebirth in my own life, which, since New York, has been a living death.

I acknowledge that I desperately need new spirit, in the sense of some vitality, meaning and color to restore my life. "If you mean," I say, "a spiritual rebirth in terms of a connection with God, I need that, too." I tell him I no longer feel any experience of God, that God has been dead for me since I sunk into my depression. "I go back and read what I have written about finding well-being despite illness or transcending the self through God. Now it sounds like so much shit." I am aware that four-letter words don't offend this agent of God, so I continue.

"God as an idea, a concept," I say, "still dimly exists for me, but a cognitive deity does me no good." I then confess to Dr. McGehee that, in my desperation for some relief from a living death, I have sought God's rescue, despite what I said just a few minutes ago about it being "so much shit." When I realized that the antidepressants weren't going to help me, I tell Pittman, I resumed a writing therapy ritual I used to practice daily and have taught in my graduate course on coping processes and health outcomes. It consists of spending fifteen minutes a day writing one's deepest thoughts and feelings on what is most painful and troublesome in one's life.

"But what I found myself doing," I say, "was writing entreaties to God to come help me, to save me." I open a folder I brought on my Mount Sinai experience and its aftermath. It includes the pathologist's report on my resected sigmoid, the list of antidepressants I have been given and examples of my daily writings. I read him a sample:

> Help me heal, please God, from my ruptured colon and broken spirit. Help me understand what part, if any, my pain over Liz's life and death contributed to what happened to me in New York and my depression now. Let me experience an easing of my belly pain now that I have written the sordid details of Liz's life of addiction and death in *Visits with Violet* [my recently published book]. I acknowledge the mistakes I made in not always being there for her. I need to know what else I must do to redeem myself and regain some meaning in my life and some relief from my pain. I am living in my own excrement, facing it, handling it and sleeping in it when the seal on my bag leaks during the night. Help me to live without shame or fear and with some human dignity....

There is more, but I stop. "It sounds so self-pitying. No wonder God is silent and does nothing."

Pittman asks, "Isn't that what a major clinical depression is like, being so self-absorbed you can't get outside of yourself? It's what makes the illness so insidious."

I nod. "That and feeling sick of my own helplessness to do anything about it." Pittman notes that cancer is also an illness that people can't do anything about by themselves.

"I know that," I reply, "but cancer is something people can understand is a disease. Depression isn't, despite all the publicity on Prozac and the celebrities who suffer from it. Prozac does nothing for me but make me feel more agitated." I am surprised to hear myself say, "Maybe I need shock therapy."

Pittman tells me he has had patients who have responded well to EST, administered by a psychiatrist he respects. "I have refused shock therapy before," I reply, "and my wife has made me promise not to have anything to do with it yet because of the effects it can have on memory. It was her idea that I need spiritual guidance because I'm so obsessed with trying to understand the meaning of what has happened to me."

Jung was convinced, Pittman tells me, that the causes of any illness include its meaning. It has occurred for some purpose. In addition to the medical causes, there is a teleological cause—"teleos" referring to some end the illness is pointing one toward. "And the end in my case being my mythical sacrifice on behalf of Liz?" I ask.

"More than that," Pittman answers. "It can mean an end in the sense of seeking a completion, of making the self, your own self, whole. The unconscious may use illness to stir us up so that we embrace a part of ourselves we have kept out of consciousness. It can force us to discover who we are and what we were created to be."

I tell him that prior to my emergency surgery in New York, I would have rejected his "explanation," at least the part that related to saving Liz from purgatory, as unbelievable and therefore untrue. However, I am beginning to acknowledge that what I experience is more important than what I believe. I am also aware that experience is what changes synapses. Experience is deeper than belief. What I experienced when I was stunned by Pittman's words was something visceral that felt like truth. I don't know if that single experience was encoded in my corticolimbic brain and changed my synapses. Nonetheless, it's a start, and I feel better. I know I have a long way to go yet. I know that for talk therapy to work, the new learning I must experience for my brain to change its mind—its chemistry and circuitry—must occur in a close relationship between my therapist and me over time. I feel ready to start the perichoretic dance.

"Would you have space in your busy practice to take me on as a patient?" I ask.

"I would be honored to be your therapist," Pittman replies, "and your priest, if that's what you would like."

"I need all the help I can get," I answer, "spiritual, psychological, physical, the whole works."

There is a long pause at this point. Pittman looks at me; I look at him. He is hesitating because he's not sure that even "the whole works" will be enough to raise the Lazarus I am at this point. He sees me as depleted, flat, without anima, meaning without soul, or at least any contact with it. He wonders why I seem determined not to cry over my own pain, apart from the pain of having lost Liz. After all, I almost died, and my body was deeply invaded. He thinks ECT may be the only piece of machinery strong enough to pull me out of my mud. Yet since I haven't hinted at suicide, he will see if sitting and listening and letting our bonds deepen will jumpstart our perichoretic dance. However, he is also pausing because he fears I might reject, in my commitment to empirical gods, the blessing he wishes to give me. It's a healing ritual he reserves for the sickest patients he has seen across twenty years of practice.

Finally, he says, "I take that to mean you wouldn't mind if I bless you with some holy oil that I got from a bishop a number of years ago." He goes to a lamp table by his bookcase and picks up a small vial. Pittman, the therapist, mystic and priest, then turns the vial up on his thumb and rubs the oil of unction on my forehead in the form of a cross as he asks God to hear my story and heal me.

I thank him and, as we head for the door, I remark, "I hope you have a pipeline to God that I don't." He smiles but doesn't deny it. Whether it is true that his prayers will have more influence than mine I don't know. *Then again,* I tell myself, *it's the experience that counts, more than what I believe.*

THE SCIENCE

Limbic resonance is best defined as two people being "in tune" with each other. It is an attunement to one another's inner states. "Because limbic states can leap between minds, feelings are contagious, while notions are not," according to *A General Theory of Love.*[1] As neuroscience advances its knowledge of the physical correlates of mind and emotions, the nonverbal self is increasingly recognized as central to the formation and maintenance of human connections. Words, generated and processed in the verbal parts of the self and brain, are still important, but they cannot convey on the feeling level what the unconscious and nuances of facial expressions, tones of voice, touch, gestures and eye contact contribute to the "symphony of mutual exchange." It has been said that good listening can even connect souls. Dr. Kandel's molecular brain biology suggests to me that just as a synchrony of feelings can be wordless, so can the learning I need for remorphing my synapses by way of the amygdala.[2]

For attunement and attachment to take place, whether in therapy or in any other close relationship, "feeling felt" is essential. As indicated in the Introduction, "feeling felt" is a "form of resonance" between two individuals in which each is able to feel what the other is feeling. According to Siegel, "whereas empathy is 'a state of understanding another's experience,' feeling felt is 'feeling another's feelings.' We can feel sad when other persons feel sad, and we can rejoice in their excitement and joy."[3]

The silent language that bonds people involves an energy that science is just beginning to describe. Historically, the heart has been regarded by science as a muscular pump and mechanical device that operates outside the influence of love, appreciation, devotion or any of the metaphors that poets, philosophers and painters have ascribed to it. Nevertheless, the major languages of the world and their many cultures have spoken of the heart as if it really is a source of love, caring, tenderness, strength and even personality. Some people speak of hearts talking to each other or having a language of their own, yet such musings remain outside the realm of science. Even more, some spiritual traditions posit that a "life force" issues from the heart and that spiritual suffering is a disruption of this force, which pervades a person's entire being.[4]

Researchers who study the heart as a generator of electromagnetic waves and neuronal power are measuring its effects outside the body as well as within it.[5] Such effects may be involved in the longstanding assumption that a person's energy or "aura" can affect another person. We can feel a change in our internal environment by just coming into the presence of certain people or settings. Healing techniques continue to evolve based on the belief that touch, prayer or the mere presence of a person can transmit positive effects to organs and tissue.[6] But science demands to know the nature of such affective or energy transfers. Over the last decade, a growing number of studies have explored this question.[7]

What good evidence is now telling us is that the expectations, beliefs and intentions of one person toward others can have healing effects. Understanding how these effects occur requires some appreciation for the nature of consciousness, described by science as the capacity not only to be awake and aware, but also to experience and respond.[8] Physicists as well as neuroscientists and research psychiatrists suggest that consciousness is a fundamental feature of all there is, both animate and inanimate, and an "intelligence" or "information" that can be tapped into by prayer, healing intentions, intuitions and other "action at a distance."[9] Under this rubric, I don't have to believe that Pittman's good heart will help heal me. It is his healing presence and our relationship that will prevail. Nonetheless, I wish I understood the mechanisms by which such welcomed effects occur.

One of the greatest living physicists, John A. Wheeler, claimed by both Princeton and the University of Texas, has come to the following conclusion: All existence can be likened to "an idea, to the manifestation of information."[10] We are told that all of us carry this information and, even though we die or our brains falter or grow old, the information is still all around us. Even though a radio or television goes on the blink, the electromagnetic radiation it was using and manifesting is still present in the universe.[11] Some scientists even use the word "wisdom" synonomously with "information." It is encoded in every particle of matter, including the stuff that makes up humans. Yet, as with radio waves, if we don't tune in to the indwelling information or wisdom, or fail to have a perceptive receiver to make full use of it, then we slog along with a lot of static in our lives.

If we do connect, then our mind, body and spirit are "informed"—infused with character and essence. This view of consciousness, Pittman notes, is consistent with what Jung foresaw as a fundamental feature of existence. How much of it we have in our lives depends on how attentive we are to raising our consciousness and understanding its meaning and value.[12]

So, in my case, when I experience any attenuation in my clinical depression in the presence of my therapist priest, such a response may come from our having accessed some of the wisdom that makes for healing. Outside of our awareness, the subliminal communication of our limbic systems contributes to such healing. If I experience something deep in me being touched by Pittman's blessing and unction, a real change in my brain chemistry may very well start to occur.

The late, great Richard Feynman, who won a Nobel Prize in physics, played bongo drums and stood on seashores wondering about the cosmos. He was fascinated with how the atoms of his being could have evolved to wonder about the being of all that is.[13] He believed, as I do, that science is as much about wonder, awe and curiosity as it is about evidence. Confirming evidence is now accumulating about this invisible intelligence that infuses our atoms as well as all the particles of the cosmos. It is the fundamental wisdom that Feynman wondered about on the seashore. So, as metaphysics folds into quantum physics, there will be those—and I hope I am one of them—who will tap into the wisdom and knowledge that are so close to us we fail to recognize them for what they are.

And what has all this to do with my depression? The most telling feature of clinical depression is the depletion of energy. Depression deadens the mind, the body, and the spirit. As indicated in the previous chapter, depression is a closing down, which I can feel in my very blood and bones. In the temporal lobe of my brain is an area called the cingulate gyrus. Like the amygdala, it is part of the limbic system. Normally, it joins with the amygdala in transmitting good as well as bad feelings. In depression, the cingulate gyrus simply "burns out" and "goes to sleep."[14] Hence the "nullity" of major depressive disorder.

To know now that I am enveloped in a wisdom that pervades my being at fundamental levels—deeper even than limbic tissue, blood and bones—is an expansion of my consciousness, which I have experienced as shutting down. To know that there is present in me a countervailing force to the darkness of depression gives me hope and a resolve to tune in to it with Pittman's help and heart.

As indicated above, the heart, it turns out, is a more powerful oscillating organ than the brain. Both generate waves of electromagnetic energy. The heart, in fact, generates the strongest electromagnetic field produced by the body.[15] Its influence can be measured acting on another individual at a distance of several feet. Most important is that its electromagnetic field becomes more coherent—harmonious, "connected"—when its source, the person whose heart it is, shifts to sincere feelings of love or care. The evidence suggests that such a shift benefits both the sender, the person whose love it is, and the receiver, the one who is in its presence.

Interestingly, the heart has its own brain, as does the gut.[16] The 40,000 neurons of the cardiac brain emit a hormone that is an atrial peptide known as ANF (atrial natriuretic factor). It regulates blood pressure, body fluid retention and electrolyte homeostasis. Its "nickname" is the "balance hormone," meaning it brings systems of the body into harmony. When there is cardiac coherence, the cerebral brain is "entrained"—gets into orderly steps —with the heart and good things happen. The fast beta waves of our "main" brain slow to alpha. The sympathetic and parasympathetic branches of the nervous system come into alignment and balance, which makes for the possibility of healing of mind and body, if not soul. And a major player in all this is our little friend, the amygdala.

So when Pittman McGehee, the analyst and priest, sits with his skeptical patient, we don't need insights of great meaning to be delivered for healing to seep in. As therapist Edgar Levenson has observed, "The significant insights in therapy… are not solutions but connections…"[17] Connections and chemicals go hand in hand in both psychotherapy and neuroscience. Connections are experiences, and as LeDoux reminds us:

> ... life's experiences leave lasting effects on us only by being stored as memories in synaptic circuits. Because therapy is itself a learning experience, it, too, involves changes in synaptic connections. Brain circuits and psychological experiences are not different things, but rather, different ways of describing the same thing.[18]

I like to think that the connections my therapist and I are making in the arenas of my amygdala and cingulate gyrus, in my emotional brain, will lead to insights at the higher, cortical level. If I only experience the feeling of a healing presence, this may matter more now than what I believe or disbelieve in my head. I do not discount the possibility of learning something new from the experience, but I am willing to accept that the experience comes first. This may mean, in "Feynman physics" as well as "Pascal poetry," an endorsement of "heart over head." However, as LeDoux suggests, what is important is the felt experience, not whether it comes to our malleable synapses by way of rhyme or reason, eros or logos.

As much as I am convinced that the unspoken language of the amygdala is the doorway to the soul, I am aware that the science of trauma insists that, for my hurting to be relieved, the emotions lodged deep in my limbic brain must be moved to upper levels, to the hippocampus and neocortex.[19] This can occur only through giving them words that express the truth—words that may be too painful to be spoken, but must be. The brain is a beautiful complex of neuronal connectivity; it is impossible to hide what is in the lower levels from the upper and vice versa. So words must move within me from the unconscious to the conscious to free myself from my demons.

Meanwhile, I remind myself that I can also rely on my heart. If the heart can transmit love as energy, as the evidence seems to suggest, then this might explain the mechanism by which most of the religions of the world help people through prayer and other rituals. Religion is another slippery slope that science has to negotiate. Feynman was an agnostic, if not a card-carrying atheist, who reveled in the beauty and awe he felt from quarks to quasars. He felt the experience in every fiber of his being and acknowledged to his fellow scientists that if these feelings constituted a "religious experience," then so be it. For me, Feynman's closest counterpart in religion is the priest who sits besides me. To those outside the priesthood, mavericks like Pittman are seen as "heretics," he tells me. To those inside the institutional structure, they are called "prophets." Paradoxically, according to Dr. McGehee, prophets inside the walls of religion are considered heretical, which takes us back to square one. Such circularity, I am learning from my teacher, is common to the antinomies or paradoxes of Jungian insights.

Although McGehee and Feynman would agree about using felt experience as a measure of what is true, science requires objective evidence for proof of truth. Medical science uses randomized, controlled, clinical trials as its gold standard. What science is now testing is the power of prayer, the centerpiece of religion. It doesn't matter that the best controlled scientific studies have been done on non-human subjects, such as yeast and plants, to show that prayer at a distance affects growth, which it does at a level of significance beyond chance.[20] What medical clinicians want to see is "hard" evidence of effects of prayer on human subjects. Such evidence is increasingly available, but not widely recognized in medical circles.[21] Medicine also wants to know how prayer works, if it does—how the loving entreaties and intentions of others can make a difference. Larry Dossey, a physician who has written widely on the subject, is convinced that the mechanism involved in such action at a distance is "nonlocality," which was discussed in chapter 1 in connection with synchronicities. In short, we live in a nonlocal universe, which means that all of us are connected by a fundamental feature of consciousness. Alexis Carrel, a Nobel Prize winning researcher in perfusion and organ transplantation, called prayer the strongest healing force known in this shared consciousness.[22]

I don't doubt that prayer is good for the sick and suffering. I don't doubt that well designed scientific studies will continue to demonstrate its effectiveness. However, petitionary prayer—meaning praying for myself—has not helped me out of the shit I am in. I am not willing to ask others for intercessory prayer on my behalf, because I still feel I should be able to help myself. In the privacy of Dr. McGehee's chambers, I gladly accept his weekly unction. Nonetheless, the stigma of weakness haunts me enough so that I seek no prayers from others.

I am also too ashamed to cry for myself, much less have others cry over me. Even if other people were convinced that depression is an illness, most would prefer praying for someone with an obvious life-threatening disease, like cancer. Terrence Real, who has written on "the secret legacy of male depression," has it right: "He who has been brought down by it [depression] will most likely see himself as shameful."[23] So I doggedly hold to my no-tears position despite knowing that research shows that release of tears has positive physical effects. I myself have written about how tears contain ACTH, which is a stress hormone, and leucine-enkephalin, an endorphin that modulates pain. Unfortunately, hubris, shame and my shadow still keep me from crying.[24]

As to petitionary prayer, my therapist prays for himself and good effects seem to occur. Maybe I have made my self-prayers too long or involved. Pittman's prayer for himself is simple. He uses the Jesus prayer, which goes like this: "Lord Jesus, Son of God, have mercy on me, a sinner." He repeats it to himself every time he gets up to address a congregation or lay audience. It's his way of "staying humble," he tells me, and not getting carried away by his own impressive intonations. To Pittman the priest, "sin" stands for estrangement from God or "missing the mark" rather than a moral transgression. When he preaches or lectures, he feels he has to stay on the mark for God to feed him the words that flow out of his mouth. I have started including the Jesus prayer in my own morning meditation, but I must still need more humbling.

Until I can reconnect, then, with God and my soul, I will have to rely on my heart to save me. I am counting on Pittman's loving energy to sustain me if my heart stays in tune with his. It's a heavy load to put on him, but I remind myself that he is an ex-jock who captained football and basketball teams that won state championships. So between his big heart and the holy oil, even my shit should start turning to fertilizer and help fuel our analytic container.

CHAPTER 4

PSYCHIC STORM AND RIDING THE WAVES

How weary, stale, flat, and unprofitable

seem to me all the uses of this world!

— *Shakespeare, Hamlet, Prince of Denmark.*

THE STORY

The analytic container is the crucible in which a patient sits with a healer and is tested.[1] The test in my case is whether I can trust what my analyst calls "the process."[2] Because neurobiological evidence indicates that internal processes may occur without my awareness and contribute to changing my neurons for the better, I trust that "the process" of my analyst will qualify as a subliminal healing change agent.[3] In other words, something may be going on—both cognitively and affectively—when I don't think anything is happening.

I learn that "the process" consists of not just the "perichoretic dance" that Dr. McGehee and I are doing in an attempt to awaken the life energies in me. If I am to undergo transformation, the point of analytic alchemy, I must also sit in the belly of the whale and trust that through my partner's ways with marine mammals, we eventually will be deposited safely on the shore. Until that time comes, he and I are committed to a long, dark sea journey of the soul. There are risks for both of us. I may become more depressed and refuse to go on, and he may lose faith in his navigational skills and influence with denizens of the deep. A psychic storm is inevitable, but it is in crisis, my guide reminds me, that soul-making occurs and we discover who we are and what we are meant to be.[4]

Fish, Pittman also reminds me, are a symbol of the unconscious, of the deep waters under consciousness. So, since I am committed to going deeper this time in therapy than ever before, it helps to have as a guide one whose vocation is in that realm. Fish are also a sacred symbol of the faith that Pittman preaches, Christianity, so he should be doubly qualified. I am diving into the unconscious by recording my dreams, which I bring to my therapist. There have been no whales so far or any other aquatic creatures in my dreams. Shit and toilets, yes. I am relieved to hear my analyst say that shit is the most "popular" dream subject of his patients. That surprises me. Are they a skewed sample, I wonder.

Ernest Becker, award-winning author of *The Denial of Death,* figuratively rubbed his readers' noses in shit when he posited that a great beast of a god may gobble us up at death, metabolize our proteins, and then excrete what's left.[5] Becker graphically compares this egregious endpoint to our own feeding off of creatures lower in the food chain and excreting the remains. My analyst disagrees with Becker, now dead, but, we hope, not excreted, taking him to task for suggesting such an unseemly end while ignoring the soul in the process. I ask Pittman if lecturing on this subject so much could have somehow brought to his practice a fecal-prone group of dreamers. I suggest that by synchronicity or morphic resonance such an attraction might occur. He humors me with a so-be-it shrug.

Pittman is much more familiar with the fish in our metaphorical sea journey of the soul than he is with outerworld trout, bass and the like. I got to the top of his waiting list of people wanting to see him only because I happened to call on the very day his weekly fishing outing washed out. A psychiatrist buddy at Broadacres Center is teaching Pittman each Wednesday afternoon the secrets of large catches. My analyst has assigned himself this half-day off to prove that he is not a closet Type A workaholic. His calm demeanor hides the multiphasic personality that got him chosen captain of the football team, president of the Key Club, vice president of the student body and all-state basketball forward, all in his senior year of high school. From there he won a scholarship to the mecca of basketball glory, Oklahoma State University, where he played for the legendary coach Henry Iba and majored in business. In college, he was a BMOC (big man on campus), a fraternity jock who loved the limelight.

Everyone, including Pittman at the time, thought he was destined to become a power broker, either a big-time CEO or moneymaking lawyer for the rich and famous. So, in an effort to live as others now see him, composed and priestly, Pittman has taken up fishing. When Henry Iba came to Houston to give a talk, Pittman was asked to pick him up and escort him to the banquet. On the way, the coach turned to Pittman, shook his head and remarked, "You are the only one of my kids who turned out to be a goddamned preacher boy." Pittman doesn't blush often, but he did then.

Existential issues—a.k.a. religious questions—are very much a part of this journey we're on. Religion has been both praised and dismissed as a psychological defense against the terror of "the grave we cannot escape," as Pittman calls it. Mortality is one of two irrevocable conditions for having been, in the words again of my analyst, "invited into the human experience." The other is "a birth we did not request." More than forty years after *The Denial of Death,* the scientific literature in psychology is still accumulating studies on "terror management," known in the vernacular as what to do in the face of annihilation.[6] The basic premise for both Becker, an anthropologist, and Otto Rank, a psychoanalyst, was that humans are driven by a self-preservation instinct, on one hand, and an inescapable awareness of finitude, on the other.[7] "Death is the great unmentionable," which makes denying it imperative for many mortals.[8]

So, just as I cannot escape the mantra in my head when I get out of bed each morning insisting that there is no point to the struggle but to struggle, I am equally vulnerable to the metaphysical fears and questions haunting most human beings—depressed and otherwise—across the lifespan.[9] At the top of the list are: (A) Why are we here only to die? (B) What happens to us when we die? and (C) Why is there suffering? "B" is a variation of what has been called the "Great Question," which includes "do we float away from our bodies... do we go to heaven or Valhalla, or does our brain simply short out and our consciousness end?"[10]

Fortunately, my helmsman is experienced in talking about such issues, so talk we do on this boat trip across troubled waters. Pittman is a preacher who gets to the point even though it might take a few hundred words: (A) We're here because our souls were plucked out of eternity and invited into the human experience; we're here to live that experience abundantly and, in the process, to contribute to the evolution of the cosmos by raising our own consciousness; (B) When we die, we leave the spatial-temporal box we've been invited to experience and remain in the eternity from which we came; and (C) Suffering, which is different from pain, offers us an opportunity to transform and transcend. My analyst insists that the human vocation is a complex, difficult calling, and included in it is suffering. "It's all part of the process" is a refrain I often hear from Pittman. Through suffering, he says, we make soul and have a chance to experience the sublime and transcend ego.[11]

When I first heard my therapist on these subjects, I thought I was listening to more "Pittmanese," indelicately characterized by one of his longtime parishioners "as mythopoetic bullshit." The Greeks were great mythmakers and spawned the Platonic idea of souls being plucked out of eternity and into the human experience. Wordsworth was a great poet and wrote the memorable lines about our coming trailing clouds of glory from God, our home. Pittman is a great admirer of both the Greeks and Wordsworth. Oddly enough, I am, too. Long before I knew there was anything lovingly called Pittmanese—or, indeed, of the existence of Pittman himself—the romantic in me loved reading Plato and Wordsworth and referring to them in some of my writings. However, as my immersion in science grew, I became more rational and wanted empirical proof for the meanderings of myth and poetry. Then I became depressed again and stopped reading, and my soul, along with my neuronal tree, began to wither. I am now on a trip with my mystic partner to revive both of them.

My friend is big on exercise, both spiritual and physical. He works out to keep his large frame straight and his weight proportional. I run and swim even though depressed. We exchange blood pressure readings and worry about rising diastolic numbers. Nonetheless, it's the embodied spirit and soul upon which we focus in our container and crucible. In my energy-deficient condition, I ask the basic question: What enlivens the spirit and feeds the soul? We start with definitions: Soul is a symbol for something deep, complex and substantive, Pittman tells me. Spirit is a psychic energy, a motive force, which drives us upward and onward, acting as an arrow rising out of the circle that is the soul in us. Pittman seldom speaks of soul without mentioning William Blake, another great English poet, and (by coincidence or synchronicity, again) a favorite of mine. Blake says our five senses are the inlets of the soul.[12]

I am convinced that what makes clinical depression so deadening is that it cuts off or ties into knots the transmission lines extending from our sensorium to the soul. As a consequence, I can no longer feel my soul stir—or my amygdala tingle—when listening to a Mozart adagio; standing on Gray's Peak, atop the Continental Divide, and viewing the verdant forests and meadows far below; bathing in the golden hue of aspen trees each Indian summer; tasting a fine vintage wine; smelling azaleas in the springtime; or feeling my wife's loving embrace. So whatever my analyst has in his bag of spirit and soul reconnectors, I am ready for it. He starts with spiritual exercises.

Humor is a spiritual exercise to Pittman and is to be welcomed especially in sacred places, he believes. The homily he gave at a requiem for a parishioner at Pittman's cathedral expressed the humor he had shared across the years with the man who had died. Pittman spoke of the many memos he had received from the deceased. He thanked the man for the dozens of articles, opinions and book reviews he had sent, "much of it to counter 'Pittmanese' or 'mythopoetic bullshit,'" in the words of the deceased.[13]

In his tribute, Pittman assured his late parishioner that life "on the other side" would be less stressful, even though "heaven is full of people who didn't go to Princeton and are Democrats." In heaven, he told his friend, "[1] You won't have to argue; [2] You won't have to make lists or send memos; [3] You won't have to raise, make or lose money; [4] You will be able to hear; [5] You will now know the subtle notes of all the music you love; [6] You can wear your plaid coat and white bucks (in eternity they'll never be out of date); [7] Your roaring lion is now a lamb; [8] Your sleeping prince is now a king."

When I borrowed from Pittman a portable lock box of his sermons, I found this homily neatly filed along with ten years of other messages from the pulpit. At my next sitting in the container, I said, "I liked the homily you gave for the man who wrote you all the memos to counter mythopoetic bullshit. Will you give the homily at my funeral?" He agreed, assuming I leave this spatial-temporal box we're in first, which is likely considering that I am sixteen years older.

Humor, of course, can be used to defend ourselves against the terror of annihilation. Depressed people live with heavy awareness that "death is a canker in the bowels" of humanity, quoting the Reverend Carlyle Marney, Baptist preacher, on the subject and referring to an anatomical site I know well. But humor can lift me out of some of my heaviness, so I engage in it when I can with my analyst. While belief in immortality may be an antidote for terror of death, I am indebted to Dr. Larry Dossey for reminding me that there are many "immortality haters."[14] Included, he says, are hard-core, incorrigible introverts like himself. Dossey is put off by the popular image of heaven. "You've got to admit," he says, "that heaven sounds a lot like a permanent social event designed by and for extraverts, with all that strolling, chatting and singing...." Dossey asks, "What if one doesn't like this sort of thing?" He goes on:

> It concerns me that no one ever emphasizes privacy in heaven. Is heaven the
> end of solitude? Can you still go to your room up there? In all the religious
> and spiritual literature dealing with the afterlife I've read, I can't recall a
> single instance in which privacy issues are discussed. It's as if you've got to
> take the Meyers-Briggs personality test and be branded an extravert before
> being admitted.[15]

My therapist has talked long and hard on the afterlife, but I have never heard him address privacy issues. Dossey is right. Maybe heaven is for extraverts, and God is the cheerleader. I have heard Pittman define himself in Jungian typology as an intuitive, feeling type. He classifies me as a thinking sensate (meaning I have to analyze, use my senses and study something before I know whether I like it). On Jung's attitude scale, we're both introverts. McGehee shudders at Dossey's popular portrayal of the American afterlife. "If heaven is one big cocktail party," my companion tells me, "I consider that a living hell and want no part of it."

When groups—churches, Jungian societies, women's clubs—advertise a lecture by J. Pittman McGehee, he is invariably described as a "widely known" speaker. It's true that he does speak all over the country on a wide range subjects. He cracks jokes, turns ponderous questions from the audience into light humor and displays all the signs and symptoms of being as outgoing an extravert as one would expect on the celebrity circuit—one who, like a genial "Dr. Phil," is only too glad to converse with audience members who come up after the talk for more talk. Pittman is also the epitome of phenotypic pantomining, meaning that, by appearance and behavior, he adapts to extraverted occasions as if they were his archetypal calling. However, it's all show business. My friend and heretical prophet is an introvert who, by his own admission, hates crowds and people. "Being dean and head of a cathedral with a large congregation and argumentive vestry was exhausting me. I had to leave so I could retire to my room and write poetry," he confesses. "I was an adaptive extravert the whole first half of my life. I'm sixty now and want to be my introverted self. I never liked going to church."

All of which is to say that Pittman is the perfect partner for a long, dark journey in the belly of a whale. In between stretches of golden silence, he is only too glad to ponder metaphorically where we go when we die. Suffice it to say, he doesn't see heaven or hell as physical places where a person has to worry about fitting in or sharing a room. His idea of heaven is continued "transformation and transcendence." Hell is remaining stuck.

I take death seriously, and so does Pittman. As a hospice volunteer I have been at the bedside of many patients as they were dying. I have seen cancer patients die. And, most unforgettably, my wife and I sat for many hours in ICU with our daughter Liz, knowing, as she did, that she would soon die. Because my analyst-priest has conducted funeral services standing above, next to or near the corpse of the newly departed, who lies in an open casket, and because he hates AstroTurf even on baseball diamonds, Pittman is determined to keep the mortuary business from making his own death look artificial. He wants to be buried in a pine box, looking like himself and not a plastic, prettied-up mannequin.

Dr. McGehee has left written instructions prohibiting the placement of AstroTurf around his gravesite, as was done without his permission at his own father's burial. Pittman disrupted those proceedings by scooping the false carpets up and throwing them as far as he could. "I want to be buried in dirt," he has instructed, "in the dirt from which Adam and I came." (I learn from Pittman that the word "Adam" means "red dirt"—red because of the first man's embarrassment of letting the first woman talk him into eating the forbidden fruit.) Anyway, Pittman tells me he has the name and number of someone who still makes pine boxes for coffins. I remember well buying one in which to bury an old gentleman I knew many years ago in Fort Worth. It doesn't take too long in one to return to dust.

Pittman and I have both been at death's door ourselves, and we are astounded at times that we are still here, living the human experience into which we have been invited. My goal is to live it abundantly again, and I am very much in favor of humor as a spiritual exercise if it will help me. Among Pittman's "death instructions" is a strong demand to die at home. "I want with me my two sons and my wife," he has announced. "Not at my bedside, but in bed with me. I want a bouquet of peonies in the room, country-western music on the stereo and a baseball game on the television."

My own written wishes require a small amendment. I wrote that "I would like to have for my dying times images of mountaintops, music of the masters and the voices of those I love. If our Tibetan dog, Tashi, is still alive, I also want him there so I can feel his rich fur, receive his kisses and relive the joyous times of reaching peaks atop the Continental Divide, which for me is as close as a mortal can get to heaven."[16] My beautiful, still-young wife of more than three decades has agreed to my amendment. We have a second Tibetan now, and I want her with me as well. Her name is Bodhi, and her boundless energy promises to keep my wife young and run me ragged. I would like to die with images of Tashi and Bodhi making Rita and me laugh every evening with their own pantomime—wrestling and boxing each other like two clowns feigning a fierce fight. All this qualifies as a spiritual exercise for me, as Pittman's deathbed scene does for him.

For humor to be a spiritual exercise and to meet my analyst's guidelines, it has to be authentic, meaning true to one's self, and it has to stir the spirit and nurture the soul. When I feel myself backsliding—sinking again into despair—I try to recall some pithy piece of Pittmanese I have in my collection. This means that when I feel bogged down sitting with my spiritual guide in the vessel that is our analytic container, I find myself defaulting to the scatological to wake my spirit up.

I quote my guide's own words to him: "Because we are born between piss and shit, but come trailing clouds of glory, humans are infamous in their inability to be human. Angels seem to have no trouble being angels; dogs seem to have no problems being dogs. However, human beings are infamous in their inability to be human. The word 'human' comes from 'humos,' meaning dirt. We are an odd combination of mysterious grandeur and pompous dust."[17]

The dust part appeals to my scientific soul. Even when I feel dead in mind, body and soul, I continue practicing some of the religious rituals. I have no trouble accepting dust applied to my forehead in the form of a cross on Ash Wednesday. The stuff that makes up DNA is in dirt just as much as it is in me. In me the base pairs are organized in a human genome. When I think of being cremated and reduced to ashes at death, I imagine a baseball team disbanding at the end of summer. The players are just as real as ever; only the team is broken up. The "code" for what it takes to be a team is not gone. Nor is my code destroyed in my dust. For this recognition, I am indebted to Max Delbruck, winner of two Nobel Prizes; one in physics and one in biology. He said that Aristotle should be awarded a posthumous Nobel Prize for having discovered that the soul is the form of the body—meaning it is the body's code, its DNA blueprint, and not subject to death.[18]

When I ask Pittman to elaborate on what happens after death, he talks of heaven as returning home and hell as staying separated. Like other mythologists, Pittman sees life itself as a journey in which we leave home, we struggle with temptations and demons along the way, and through sacrifice and with luck, we return to home. "It's the same story whether we are talking about Ulysses or Dorothy or the great American pastime, baseball."

Baseball? I played it; he played it. I never perceived anything mythological about it. He didn't either as a boy. But as a priest and Jungian, he's convinced that baseball has such appeal because it is archetypal in the story it tells in every game. "You go to home plate to bat, you take your cuts, you finally connect and run like hell to get on base. And thereafter, you struggle to get home. A sacrifice is often necessary to bring you home. Then you go back to the dugout, underground." But where and what is our home? Dossey raises the question in his book *Healing Beyond the Body: Medicine and the Infinite Reach of the Mind*.

> On this planet we behave as if we were strangers in a strange land, fish out of water. Although we call ourselves the most highly evolved species, when we look at our situation from the widest possible perspective, we humans are a greater mess than any other form of life. We are chronically unhappy, anxious, and malcontent, unable to rest in the moment, always looking to the past or into the future. It's as if we were trying to reclaim the memory of whence we've come and where we're headed. We are only dimly aware that we don't belong here.... What remains is a vast uneasiness and the gnawing sense that we are better suited for some other form of existence than this one. But the old whisperings of our blood have not totally disappeared. From time to time humans arise who know how to listen to them— the great saints and mystics, poets and artists who periodically catch fire and bring back messages about another realm.[19]

So the Greeks, Wordsworth, Blake and McGehee are not alone in suggesting that "home" is a powerful symbol for the strong trophic pull that we feel drawing us to where we truly belong. An unknown poet, writing about Mexico's Day of the Dead, echoed Wordsworth in his opening stanzas:

> We only come to dream, we only come to sleep,
> It's not true, it is not true
> That we come to live on Earth.
>
> Where are we to go from here?
> We came here only to be born.
> As our home is beyond. Where the fleshless abide.[20]

But since we can connect here and now with the power behind wherever "our home" is, we should be able to experience transcendence without becoming "fleshless." My teacher talks about the immanent and transcendent side by side, about the presence of God in life's shit as well as its beauty. So while we're on this planet, in these bodies and with these minds, we should honor the earth and stop misusing the powerful technology science has given us. As physicist Peter Russell advises, "We have misused our newfound powers, plundering and poisoning the planet."[21] Russell is convinced that we have "reached what Buckminster Fuller called our 'final evolutionary exam.' The questions before us are simple: Can we move beyond this limited mode of consciousness? Can we let go of our illusions, discover who we really are, and find the wisdom we so desperately need?"[22] In the process we will discover our connectedness to all things and the immanence of the nonlocal mind that envelops us. With a little effort and much luck, we might even see the world "as it really is, infinite," to quote Pittman's favorite "wild-eyed" eighteenth-century poet, William Blake. Neuroscientists as well as preachers find truth in what Blake said about cleansing the doors of our perception so that we can see the infinite and transcendent in "everything." Walter Freeman, brain scientist for forty years at the Graduate School, University of California, Berkeley, is a case in point.[23]

Because I use science as a way to ground myself, Russell, if not Freeman, helps me understand both the physical and metaphysical. When I start feeling that my right brain is taking me too far into the clouds, I decide to talk a little more science to Pittman, even though our talk is on the same metaphysical subjects. I am struck by the advances in quantum physics and biology that take both fields to the very threshold between the physical and metaphysical. In the opinion of some experts, the border has been crossed and the threshold has turned out to be "the thin places" where two worlds meet.[24] As physicist Gerald Schroeder puts it: "...science has discovered a reality it had previously relegated to the mystical. It has discovered the presence of the spiritual."[25] The spiritual he is talking about is the recognition that every atom of every human is informed with an essence that, when tapped, joins that person to something transcendent.

When I choose to use up my time in the analytic container with such intellectual musings instead of embracing some nemesis in my unconscious, Pittman doesn't stop me. Either he is humoring me or I am educating him. Whichever, he offers me a little more Pittmanese, which seems appropriate to speculations about lofty homes. It's not original, but that doesn't stop him from claiming it: "Angels are able to fly so high because they take themselves lightly."

My soul is struggling to be lighter, so let my depression have wings. Pittman thinks the mist on our voyage is thinning, and the fog lifting. It's about time. Soon I should be able to confront my shadow.

THE SCIENCE

What a piece of work is a man!...

And yet to me, what is this quintessence of dust?

— Shakespeare, Hamlet, Prince of Denmark.

The "science" of immortality would be considered by most scientists and some mystics to be an oxymoron. Science is about establishing what is true by objective measurement.

How do you measure the hereafter? You don't. You can't prove its existence or nonexistence, much less measure its quantity and quality. Nonetheless, science *is* about medicine, health, psychology and sociology. So, since most people believe in an afterlife,[1] and beliefs activate neurotransmitters and hormones, affecting body, spirit and soul, should science be interested? Of course.

I am old enough to remember when the "science" of stress was considered an oxymoron. In the 1980s a colleague of mine at the Texas Medical Center, who had recently been diagnosed with breast cancer, asked if I would join her in a study investigating stress and malignancy. She was an epidemiologist; I was a psychobiologist and mind-body clinician. We went across the street from our school to the world-renowned M. D. Anderson Cancer Center to get permission to recruit subjects. The head of the department of surgery, to whom we were referred, looked at us incredulously and said, "I have been doing cancer surgery for more than thirty years. I have never operated on anyone and found 'stress.' What does it look like?" He made it plain that if you can't cut it out, weigh it or biopsy it, there's no such thing. It doesn't exist. So much for stress affecting people who get cancer. Now, twenty-five years later, after reams of evidence in the scientific literature has demonstrated the effect of stress on the immune system, cardiovascular system and health in general, no one argues that stress is outside the realm of science or is irrelevant to cancer.

Does it follow that there must also be a "science" of immortality that will demonstrate proof of an afterlife? Of course not. It does mean, however, that because science includes health as a focus, it cannot ignore stress or religion, spirituality or the soul. More than 70 of the 125 US schools of medicine now recognize this and include courses that teach how belief in a God or supreme being affects health.[2] As to the soul, if it is so chimerical, why does the New York Academy of Sciences offer a three-day conference on the self, the soul and the brain? Maybe the academy foresees growing evidence causing the fine line to fade between the metaphysical and physical—or at least between the scientific disciplines that recognize the spiritual and those that don't.

Even in the disciplines that have no immediate application to health, there is a growing conviction among some physicists and biologists that every atom of every human carries an essence that, when tapped, bestows in us a sense of union with a greater reality. In the Big Bang 15 billion years ago, "all of us and all we see were part of a compact homogeneous ball of energy.... Once we were all neighbors."[3] The stuff that made stars also made us. The "eternity" created out of the Big Bang pervades and envelops all of its "offspring," big and little. My 75 trillion cells have their counterparts in almost all living creatures, big and little. There's a kinship among us. As for things much larger, "spirituality can't be weighed, but our emotions tell us there is an aspect to life that transcends the physical."[4] Years ago, in the early 1950s, as a young reporter and science writer, I interviewed a salesman who had suffered a massive heart attack while calling on a customer. He reported to me what later became known in the press as a "near-death experience," complete with viewing himself from above and seeing a light ahead of him, as if in a tunnel, representing the afterlife. There is still skepticism among scientists about near-death experiences proving anything. However, there are now more than anecdotes and mounting NDEs to go on.

What I said above about there being no "science" of immortality requires amending. Dr. Gary Schwartz, a much published, well respected professor of psychology, psychiatry, medicine, neurology, psychiatry and surgery at the University of Arizona, is conducting what he calls "The Afterlife Experiments."[5] He is testing whether communication can be established with "the other side." Schwartz is convinced that science itself offers the foundation for conducting research on the living soul hypothesis. Using an experimental design, Schwartz tests the ability of reputable intuitives to "read" the thoughts and mental messages connecting someone alive with a close relative or friend who has died. His co-investigator, Dr. Linda Russek, gave him the idea for such a project after her beloved father died. Russek, a psychologist, had done research with her father, a physician. Now, as part of the afterlife experiments, Schwartz is investigating the continuation of the father-daughter collaboration as well as communication established by intuitives with "the other side."

Dr. Schwartz, in researching "the living soul hypothesis," considers his experiment as a test of faith in the scientific method itself as well as in the belief that there is an afterlife. He believes that his work will lead "to the hypothesis that the universe is more wondrous than imagined in our wildest flights of fancy."[6] On a personal level, he foresees all of us becoming more aware of our interconnections with others, both in this life and after—both here and there. Many academics would consider Schwartz's hypothesis preposterous. They would argue that for an "establishment" scientist to take the hereafter seriously enough even to frame a hypothesis, much less test it using standard methodology, is unheard of. Outside the academy, many who believe in heaven consider it sacrilegious for any scientist to put God to a test, to seek "objective" evidence to prove God's existence. Dr. McGehee, my religious authority and teacher on such subjects, has no comments. He only smiles like one who knows what it is like to be outside the mainstream.

Nevertheless, words such as "soul" and "afterlife" not only have been restored to the vocabulary of reputable scientists but are a focus of other serious research. For Dr. Rachel Naomi Remen, another respected clinician and academic, where there is soul, there is mystery.[7] She has been drawn to mystery by having lived with a severe chronic illness—Crohn's disease—for nearly half a century. When diagnosed at age fifteen, she was told that the disease would kill her by age forty. Thanks to "the power of the will to live," she is now in her sixties. On the faculty of the University of California, San Francisco, Dr. Remen gives talks to medical students and physicians around the country on "the power of mystery." She also treats terminally ill cancer patients and is the medical director of Commonweal, an educational cancer center for doctors and patients in Bolinas, California.

"Everyone," Dr. Remen says, "has had things happen to them that they cannot explain." Nor can science explain them, she contends. "Life is larger than science. These things are not replicable or measurable. But they are touching, moving, inspiring and powerful." Such occurrences are opportunities to explore mystery, which she defines as "the unknowable." In telling our stories about the strange or "funny" happenings in our lives, we often connect with what is genuine and true in us—in other words, our essence and soul. Even the most skeptical scientists admit to experiencing awe and wonder in nature and the universe. Dr. Remen would say they are touching their soul in such experiences. "Mystery is not only moving, it is strengthening and healing."[8]

For science itself, mystery is a motivating force. The biologist Erwin Chargaff, who contributed mightily to our knowledge of DNA, said "it is the sense of mystery that, in my opinion, drives the true scientist"; the confrontation with it may produce "a cold shudder down his spine" and "move him to tears."[9] So "the shoreline between knowledge and mystery" is often the place where even scientists feel "the tingle," an experience that is deeply moving. According to physicist Chet Raymo, "We live in a universe that is infinite, or effectively so. Our brains are finite, a mere 100 billion nerve cells. Our mental maps of the world are therefore necessarily finite."[10]

Whether God is mystery or metaphor, what counts is our *experience* of either as unconditionally real. Problems arise when science assumes that what cannot be measured and verified is not real, or when religion assumes that the only truth lies in its sacraments and symbols, which point to the Absolute and contain the numinosity of God. Science, just as religion does, depends on symbols, more mathematical than verbal. The numbers represent a lawful reality that technology powerfully uses to give us the gadgets and machines which help make our lives easier and longer. Nonetheless, science, as well as religion, still is not inside "Einstein's watch" or clock. We see the hands move and hear the ticking, but we are not inside the wonder of the workings and the Mind behind them.

The "religion" of many scientists is their experience of the universe and nature, together with the awe and wonderment, even humility, they feel in their materialistic souls. Some are poetic about their experience, describing the universe as elegant and intrinsically beautiful. "Art and science flourish at the boundary of the known and unknown."[11] So scientists are not strangers to mystery and the unknown, and the best use both to understand more about life, nature and the cosmos.

Dr. Remen has watched many people "confront the unknown in the face of death. I have watched them recover from a sense of numbness or cynicism. I have watched them become truly alive. It's almost as if they have remembered that life is holy and to live is a blessing." She sees life itself as a mystery and an invitation to wonder. "We are all process, and process has mystery woven into it."[12]

My own interest in the subject of mystery is more than academic. Like Dr. Remen's patients, I have confronted the unknown. I encountered "mystery" in my Mount Sinai Hospital experience in New York and was led to Dr. McGehee to explain something I couldn't understand. He gave me a story that touched the same place in me that awe and wonder do. So on this ride in the belly of the whale I am thrown back to the mystery of Jonah and his attempt to escape from God's calling. I have no mystical experience to report as yet, but I carry a mystery inside me that connects me to someone beyond the grave. Jonah had to experience a great psychic storm to wake up and honor who he was and what he was called to be—a prophet. Pittman preaches that illness, a form of suffering, is a requirement for health, for becoming whole and your true self. I have to keep reminding myself that Jungians speak a language that often sounds like the talk of quantum physicists, who say that truth often requires looking at things backwards.

Just as many cosmic truths remain shrouded in mystery, so do the secrets of psyche and soma. Although the word "mystery" is being readmitted—along with "soul"—to the vocabulary of mainstream scientists, "anomalous experience" is still the preferred, neutral term. Whereas the noted Harvard psychologist William James, described *The Varieties of Religious Experience*, its counterpart today is *Varieties of Anomalous Experience: Examining the Scientific Evidence*, a weighty tome with contributions from a score of academic authors.[13]

My boatmate on this trip is comfortable with both mystery and immortality, so he has little need to talk about "anomalies." As it turns out. Pittman's spatial-temporal box inside eternity is not so farfetched after all, and parallels some of the theories of quantum physicists. To review, Dr. McGehee posits, along with Wordsworth, that we come trailing clouds of glory from God, which is our home. My therapist holds that we are invited into the human experience and our assignment is to live it abundantly and to raise our consciousness in the process and, if possible, to "become whole." He believes, as almost everyone else does, that this life is limited in time and space; thus the "spatial-temporal box." To stick with the poets for a minute, Blake said that if we cleansed our lenses, we would be able to see the world in a grain of sand.[14] If we had clear perception we might also see the truth of Wordsworth's words. We might become aware that our tiny sandbox is just a temporary playground, which opens in every direction to the eternity we were born in and will never leave, according to my therapist the priest.

Science has its own counterparts to what poets, philosophers and theologians have told us. The British mathematician, astronomer and physicist Sir James Jeans invites us to think of it this way: Life as we know it involves the phenomenon of "individuals carrying on separate existences in space and time, while in the deeper reality beyond space and time, we may all be members of one body."[15] Pittman, being Christian, preaches that all of us are one with the body of Christ. Other faiths hold we are one with their gods. Erwin Schrödinger, whose wave theories won him a Nobel Prize in physics, proposed that "mind by its very nature is a *singulare tantum*," which he obligingly translated as meaning "the overall number of minds is just one."[16] So we are one, not only with an eternal body, but with a reigning non-local Mind, which is God for most religions.

What various scientific theorists are proposing, then, is that "mind" or "consciousness" really is, as suggested earlier, a fundamental feature of the universe on a par with matter and energy.[17] And, to repeat, it's so much around us and close to us, we don't see it for what it is: a given. As my teacher says, whether we are Ulysses, Dorothy or Babe Ruth, we always will have a Home, because we are already there. Only we may not realize it or recognize "home" until after we leave our little box. Meanwhile, we have a spatial-temporal sandtray to play in.

Do I believe all this? Maybe on a clear, blue-sky day, I do. But, remember, I'm the depressed one. I look down, not up. I do believe what my therapist says about "the process." The process is pain from the beginning. Fetuses have to be pulled out of their womb, infants separated from mothers, children have to be held by the hand the first day of school, and adult kids these days keep coming back home after they have already left. My analyst is convinced that every place where we get comfortable we have to leave. It's part of the process. Why? Only God knows, and maybe my analyst. I haven't been told why by the Almighty One, but my companion on this trip with me says, "It is the only way we grow, the only way to transform ourselves, to get beyond ego, to make soul, to transcend and to find God, our Home." A more immanent translation that Pittman gives to all this is that the home we seek we already have. It's the God within—including the ineffable power and mystery of which scientists such as Feynman, E. O. Wilson and Raymo stand in awe.

However, if home is the place we always have to leave, will we get kicked out of heaven? Pittman's idea of heaven is that it is a place where we are continuously in the process of transformation and transcendence. I get a little dizzy from such lofty projections, pessimistic mortal that I am. I can sympathize with the woman who wanted assurance from Dossey, who writes widely and wisely on spiritual issues, that her fear of heights won't bother her when she is floating around on clouds.

My helmsman has long had the conviction that the world of science is "strictly" materialistic. He tries to make his point by emphasizing that to science, the opposite of "material" is "immaterial"—meaning (quite literally) of little matter.[18] Science, he contends, equates the non-material with being trivial and worthless. In truth, as physicists have proved, a little matter can be so explosive with energy that a tiny, invisible dot of it creates a universe. More relevant to everyday life is the fact that it is through science, not theology and not religion, that we are learning and proving the physical power of experiences and relationships. Such invisible, nonmaterial phenomena affect the hard matter of the brain and can lead to a change of mind by changing neurons. The Bible teaches love, which comes through relationships and experiences, but science is making the case for it.

The technology of brain SPECT imaging, fMRIs (functional magnetic resonance imaging) and PET scans provides the before-and-after evidence. The brain looks one way before love, before meaningful experience, before talk therapy, and another way afterwards.[19] The synapses of our corticolimbic loop, including our soulful amygdala, reconfigure. Neurotransmission changes. The electrical pulses within our neurons cause a change in released chemicals. And our story, how we look at ourselves and our lives, undergoes revision. A different message is encoded in the story synthesizer of our neocortex .[20] Our autonomic nervous system stabilizes; our very heart rate expresses coherence. These are all materialistic, measurable processes, belying my teacher's belief that science considers the nonmaterial to be immaterial.

I quote to Dr. McGehee the words of the physicist David Bohm: "Everything material is also mental and everything mental is also material. The separation of the two—matter and spirit—is an abstraction."[21] Has my friend seen the light yet? Probably not. But I have hopes he will if I start using words, as Jungians often do, that express contradictory, paradoxical meanings, antinomies. For example, at the most fundamental level of reality—of matter—there is "nothing," literally no material, less than "of little matter." In this invisible world of super-high-energy physics, scientists posit the existence of "sparticles"—invisible partners of known particles such as quarks and electrons. The *New York Times* headline of this discovery read: "Years of Research Yield Nothing, and That's Good News for Physicists."[22]

If nothing particles boggle your mind, try spelling "enantiodromia," which Pittman had to do to become a Jungian diplomate. This jawbreaker, which my friend still has trouble pronouncing, is a Jungian psychological law that says that sooner or later, everything turns into its opposite, a principle first proposed by Heraclitus. The Bible recognizes the equation of opposites, such as black turning into white and "the darkness and the light are both alike to thee" (King James Version, Psalm 139). The link between religion, Jungian mythology and the discovery of nothing takes us to this basic reality: Beneath and beyond even the sparticles is only an eternal dance of form and flux, order and energy—pure "Intelligence" with a capital "I"—which even some materialistic scientists believe is God.

In reply to all this Pittman says nothing, which seems appropriate to the subject. So I stop talking, and we lapse into a long stretch of golden silence, each with his own metaphors and musings about the hereafter and thereafter. I start thinking about where my temporal, this-world home is. Every time my wife and I—and our two Tibetans—leave the place we have high in the Colorado Rockies to return to our urban home, I cry. The pull of the earth, the mountains, the forests and meadows is so strong they even penetrate momentarily the deadness that depression brings to soul and spirit. Someday, I will let myself recognize that on this earth, at least, I can have two homes, one in the city, near citadels of learning and medicine, and one in the mountains, even closer to God. In both, I will feel at Home.

So with God coming into my meditation, I start thinking of Mother Teresa, a Nobel Prize winner herself, who spent her life serving the poor and hungry in the slums of Calcutta, knee-deep in shit—a substance of unforgettable materiality that I have some acquaintance with. Since Mother Teresa was very religious, she was asked by a visitor what is it that she prays to God for. "Oh, I don't pray," she replied. "I just listen." So, her questioner wanted to know, what does she hear from God? "Oh, he doesn't talk, he just listens," she answered.[23] That just about covers it. Another koan. Or Jungian antinomy. Or theological promise that "though this body be destroyed, yet shall I see God."[24]

Somewhere during and in between the stretches of silence that a depressed skeptic like me and a re-visionist like Pittman share with one another, something healing is happening. It is so immaterial it can't be seen, and we can't measure it. The effect can only be felt and experienced by both of us. I am convinced, and I believe I have convinced my teacher, that this felt experience has the power to affect the very material neurons and synapses of my brain and heart, arborizing them with love—and reaching even deeper to stir the soul. Time will tell.

CHAPTER 5

FATHERS, MOTHERS AND SONS

Depression is the flaw in love. To be creatures who love,

we must be creatures who can despair at what we lose,

and depression is the mechanism of that despair.[1]

THE STORY

It's the Fourth of July in the little town of Drumright, Oklahoma, known then as the friendliest town in the state. It's the first and last time Pittman McGehee, then a boy in the sixth grade, sees his father drunk. With young Pittman and his father at the sandy rodeo grounds are Mr. Nash the town lawyer, who is wearing wire-rimmed glasses, and Dr. Orange W. Star, whose white hair stands like a shock of wheat atop his imposing head. Dr. Star, a full-blooded Cherokee Indian, is the town doctor who saved Pittman from dying of third-degree burns at age six. The three men are joking about how Mr. Nash keeps dropping his glasses in the sand, and Mr. McGehee, by then a little tipsy, has tried to light them three times, thinking they are firecrackers. Young Pittman is embarrassed to see his usually reserved and serious father so uninhibited and full of spirit. It's his first recognition of the use of spirits to inspirit people, a subject he will speak on decades later after concluding that what we seek in alcohol is a feeling of being lifted out of ourselves and truly experiencing what life is meant to be.

The scene and time shift, and now it is a Sunday afternoon at Reverchon Park in Dallas, Texas. I am sitting by my father's side watching sandlot hardball from bleachers with a high tin roof slanting overhead. The baseball game is sponsored by Magnolia Oil, whose "Flying Pegasus" sign spirals at the top of the highest building downtown, two miles away. It's the first and last time I see my father so excited—so spirited—that he stands on his feet and claps his hands at the sight of a home run hit by a batter. On every other day of the week, the home run hero circling the base wears the uniform of a filling station operator. Today he is dressed in a pinstriped baseball uniform advertising his employer's gasoline and looking to me as grand as what the New York Yankees wear when they win another World Series.

I am taken by surprise by my father's show of spirit as the batter rounds third base and heads home. Sam Justice, like J. B. McGehee, is normally reserved and serious. However, now the deep furrow of frown between his eyes, where his wire-rimmed glasses pinch his nose red, softens as he claps home the runner. I recognize the runner as Mr. Bianchi, who, on any other weekend, fills up the tank of my daddy's 1936 Chevrolet and wipes spattered bugs off the windshield.

It is the last time I am to see the frown soften. The Great Depression catches up with the Justice family, and my father loses both his bookkeeping job and his spirit. Daddy can't find any other office job. So he doesn't know what to do with himself, and with a friend he builds a green ping-pong table, which folds in the middle. We put it up in the narrow side yard under the glare of one outdoor bulb and play the game monotonously, trying to blot out the tough time as lightning bugs float by in the summer night. My father struggles to fill his days. Finally, he sells the mustering-out war bonds he has kept all these years from World War I service in Europe and buys a six-seat hamburger stand downtown across from the post office. It's time for me to grow up and to join my brother in selling magazines and newspapers. My mother, shamed by my father's new line of work, nevertheless cooks big pots of soup at home to take every day to "Sam's Good Eats," where she stands for long hours behind the counter serving customers alongside my father.

The attendance at Sunday baseball games with my father stops. Sam Justice becomes too worn out even to toss the ball with his two boys in a game of catch in our side yard. He has no heart for it. Even the stories he would occasionally tell after a highball on New Year's Eve cease. My daddy also stops smoking cigars, not only to save money, but as a sign that he doesn't feel man enough any more. My uncle, my mother's cocky younger brother, also stops when the Depression takes the wind out of his sails. Sam Justice's best friend, Frank Gilbert, always the practical joker and pool partner, is the third to give up acting important with a cigar in the side of his mouth.

My father's frown deepens, and the smiling face of my cheery mother becomes a mask. Behind it I see sorrow for what she feels has been lost. Her hopes for a fur stole, invitations to occasional country club dances, courtesy of a well-off cousin, and dreams of moving to a two-story house in Highland Park, all evaporate. Her father moves in with us because he is too frail and poor to take care of himself. He brings with him his carving pocket knife and his battered baritone horn. We call him "Dadoo" and marvel at what he can make out of pieces of wood—doorstops that look like cats, slingshots and whole teams of little wooden football players, painted in colorful uniforms. His stories of playing the baritone horn in circus bands and doubling on the coronet thrill me and entertain the neighborhood kids. My brother, three-and-a-half years older, and I try to learn to play the baritone with our grandfather's help.

However, Dadoo, already disabled by a hernia, held in place by a leather truss, brown with wear, gets sick. He is seventy-two, an age I can't even imagine. Now that he is sick, his false teeth remain in a glass of water on top of the toilet bowl in our bathroom. His tattered houseslippers stay under the rented hospital bed placed in the crowded living room for him. The veins in his arms seem as big as his thin wrists. His hands grow cold and turn as blue as his veins. I feel scared when I go up to the big bed, raised under his knees to support circulation and tilted behind his back to prop him up so he can breathe better. I hesitantly touch his hand, knowing that Mama wants me to. It's cold, like I imagined, and I feel sad.

Dadoo dies in the living room holding a glass of milk while my mother is reading to him. I come home from my magazine route and am led by my mother to see him, still and ashen in the hospital bed, too big for our living room, which is the largest room in our house. His head is cocked back, his mouth open as if he's still gasping for air. Services for Dadoo are held at Brewer's Funeral Home, in a rococco two-story brick building that is supposed to look like a medieval church. For months afterward, my devastated mother instructs my father not to drive past the funeral home.

All I remember from the funeral is "The Old Rugged Cross," sung by a lady with big breasts who serves as secretary at the place. The song strikes me as very religious, but I know Dadoo never went to church or said a blessing at mealtime. Mama wants it sung, because she is religious and wished her papa had been. She goes to the Episcopal Church of the Incarnation every Sunday and takes my brother and me. My daddy only goes at Easter and Christmastime. Mama tells me I was baptized there when I was just a baby. Lou-Reine is my mother's name, a name meaning "queen," I am told. She feels ashamed that her daddy had been a gambler, a card shark, who moved from boom town to boom town as new oil fields were discovered in East and West Texas. He worshiped his little queen and told her so in letters kept in boxes tied with yellow and pink ribbons I find years later in the attic.

Brewer's Funeral Home is on Ross Avenue, a three-lane street going downtown with streetcar tracks in the middle. Now, since Mama can't stand to be reminded of her daddy's death, she has Sam take us home by driving up San Jacinto, a parallel street. I'm in the back seat, bored and scared. Each night Mama drives home from Sam's Good Eats to fix dinner for my brother and me, and then we go downtown and pick Daddy up, dead tired. I'm scared because our money is running low, and my parents look sad. Daddy has used up his bonds from Army service to buy the eating place, and he's making just enough money to keep food on the table. I hear my mama worrying about this every night at dinner. One day my mother tells me she knows that if my father has to, he will take the .38 caliber revolver in their dresser drawer and hold somebody up before he lets his family starve. I feel scared when she talks that way.

Mama feels ashamed that Daddy has to do this kind of work because he used to be an office manager in the Santa Fe Building and wore neckties to work. She's also ashamed that she has to make big pots of soup at home to take downtown to sell. She has had to quit her chapters, her women's groups, at church where she played bridge and heard about living in Highland Park and belonging to a country club. I learn shame from her and start feeling I'm not good enough to be around playmates whose fathers still have white-collar jobs and wear neckties.

The shame carries over to my being obliged to sell magazines and have a newspaper route. I turn the magazine bag on my shoulder so the words *Saturday Evening Post* and *Ladies' Home Journal* are hidden against my body, where they don't show. I deliver newspapers so early in the morning that I don't worry about anyone seeing me. There's nothing wrong with working to help your family, but somehow I transfer Mama's shame to myself. I keep remembering that *reine* means "queen" in French, and I'm told she is doing work beneath her. Her papa, Dadoo, let her know that she should never work, that she should have servants and be taken care of. Instead, she ends up working and caring for two kids and a husband. In my boy brain, I take an oath that someday I will make it all up to Mama and Daddy.

Before the Depression, my father would decide he ought to go see his papa and mama in Mountain View, Oklahoma. My father's daddy moved up there to open a general store in the little country town. He moved from a small town outside of Dallas, where he had the same kind of merchandise business. I guess my daddy got the idea of waiting on the public for a living from his daddy. His father and brother, Pierce, are big men. My father is average height. I am small. One time on the way to my grandparents, our Chevrolet got stuck in red clay. We were pulled out after awhile, but when I hear of Oklahoma, I think of mud. Many of the roads weren't paved.

Pittman learns about the Depression from his daddy, whose own father lost his grocery store in the hard times that ensued. J. B. McGehee's ambition had been to become a lawyer. He was a freshman in a small college in Arkansas, where his family lived, when he was told that because of the Depression he would have to come home and get a job to help make ends meet. Instead of going to law school, Pittman's daddy ends up delivering bread in small towns in western Arkansas. He marries and becomes a traveling salesman in Oklahoma for the DX Oil Company with a statewide chain of filling stations.

J. B. McGehee's young bride never quite gets over being taken to "Indian territory" and moving away from her beloved mother, who herself was half Cherokee. Just as painful, she also leaves behind six brothers and sisters and all the other people who remember how great a preacher her father was. He died when little Ruth was just three years old. The Reverend Nathan Hanks was renowned throughout Arkansas as a charismatic, itinerant, Bible-thumping, fiddle-playing man of God.

Young Pittman hears about the stained-glass windows in country churches dedicated to his grandfather. The reverend was a man of many talents. In addition to being an ordained Cumberland Presbyterian minister, he was a master brickmason who could build a church, preach the gospel from the pulpit and entertain the congregation with his fiddle playing. He saved his parishioners a lot of money with his broad range of valuable skills. His youngest daughter idealized his memory. And her mother favored her more than any other of the children in the big family. Mrs. Hanks also was very impressed with the town doctor, James Pittman, who delivered all seven of her children. Her youngest daughter, Ruth, hears so much about the good doctor that she ends up naming her younger son after him, James Pittman McGehee.

In Drumright, with her husband on the road five and six days a week, and with two young boys to look after, Ruth becomes lonely and depressed. Pittman spends many hours with his mother, who puts his head in her lap, talks of her father the preacher and tells her young son that when he grows up, "I hope you will help people with their sadness."

Nonetheless, Ruth doesn't let her depression keep her from being as good a mother as her own mother was. As winter comes on, she decides that Pittman needs a good pair of outing pajamas to keep him warm. Their little town can get frigid in the winter, Ruth learns, because "there's nothing between Pikes Peak and Drumright to keep fierce winds from sweeping down across the Plains out of the Rockies." So she takes Pittman thirty miles to Tulsa to buy him pajamas. He picks a pair of Roy Rogers outing flannels because they have a picture of Roy's horse, Trigger, on the front. He's so proud of them he asks his mother if he can wear the pajama top to school the next day. She agrees, and thinks it is a grand idea. Pittman's brother, only two years older chronologically, but "eons" ahead of Pittman in maturity, thinks it's stupid. Pittman calls him "the colonel" because his brother has a military manner and orders the younger boy around so much. The brother's real name is Jarrett—after his paternal grandfather—and he does love the military way of doing things.

The McGehees live in a rented two-bedroom, one-bathroom frame house at the top of a hill. The very next night after the trip to Tulsa, there's a big snowstorm in that part of northern Oklahoma. The blizzard shuts everything down, and Pittman thinks it is going to be a perfect day. It's a Monday, and Mr. McGehee normally takes to the road, working the territory, selling oil and car products to filling stations in his two-state region. Today, however, there's too much snow even to get the car out. The hill the McGehees live on is frozen solid with ice. So Pittman can't think of anything better—his dad will be home instead of gone, there's no school because of the snow, and he can wear his pajamas underneath his regular clothes to go out and make a snowman.

So everything is snug and cozy for a six-year-old boy looking forward to a Monday like he has never enjoyed before. His father is reading the paper at the kitchen table, his mother is cooking oatmeal and cinnamon toast, and Pittman is in the bathroom waiting his turn at brushing his teeth. The colonel, as befits his rank, is using the sink first. Pittman is warming himself in front of the small, open-faced bathroom stove turned up high. He backs his Roy Rogers flannels too close, and in a flash he is on fire. His screams startle the toothbrush out of his brother's hand. The colonel, already cool-headed in crisis, remembers a safety film recently shown at school on what to do in such an emergency. He grabs a throw rug on the bathroom floor and rolls Pittman up in it, putting out the fire searing his little brother's legs and waist. Mr. McGehee comes rushing in from the kitchen when he hears his little boy screaming. He snatches sheets and quilts off the bed, bundles his young son up and, like a paternal pietà, carries him to the parents' bedroom. Pittman goes into shock from the pain, and they send out an emergency call for Dr. Orange W. Star.

The hill is so icy that the doctor can't get his car up the incline. The back wheels can't get any traction even with the help of Mr. McGehee, who comes slipping and sliding down the hill, begging him to hurry. Having no choice, the two men struggle on foot back up the long hill to the McGehee house. Dr. Star remembers to bring a water bag and a line to drip fluid into Pittman, who is badly burned over half his body. The doctor knows that loss of fluid kills as quickly as the injury itself in third-degree burn cases. Mercifully, the medicine man/medical doctor also brings morphine, which he shoots into the boy and which leads Pittman later as a "revisionist" preacher to say, "I found redemption in a syringe." After three scary days, Dr. Star tells the McGehees their little boy is going to live but will have scars on his legs the rest of his life that could cripple him.

Through the winter, Pittman lies in a rented hospital bed by the big front window in the living room and watches his friends go by to school. It's very painful for him to get out of bed and try to walk; so painful that he tells his mother he can't walk and stops trying. The danger of not walking is that the ligaments and cartilage behind his burned knees will shorten and disable him or cause him to drag his foot.

Dr. Orange comes by each afternoon to check on his young patient, taking scissors to cut off the "proud" flesh and burst the blisters. One afternoon the time for him to come passes and there is anxiety in the house about his not showing up. Then the phone rings and his mother answers. In a minute she turns to Pittman and says, "It's Dr. Star. He wants to talk to you." Without thinking. Pittman gets out of bed and walks to the phone to talk to the big-chested medicine man who saved his life. Before long, his elders begin telling him he has been spared for something special. His destiny is to be a wounded healer. Young Pittman, with his love for the Indian doctor, learns his first lesson in the power of faith.

In Dallas, I sit in my backyard and watch school chums walking to and from Vickery Place Elementary, ten blocks away down Glencoe, the unpaved side street by our house. I have my left ankle in a cast, broken from a twisting fall I suffered sliding into home base on the playground at school. My mama is gone, helping my father at Sam's Good Eats. I am lonely. I have to watch life go by on the other side of our backyard fence. My only company is Rags, our black little mongrel whom I bathe in a big #10 washtub when I can walk. I love him dearly, but I want to run and play at school. Instead, I sit and make up games, such as turning my old tricycle on its side and using one wheel to pretend I'm driving a big bus. (Years later, when I am depressed and I feel that I am watching life through a leper's slit, I remember this boyhood immobility).

Nobody laughs in our house much anymore. My brother, John Hugh, is serious by nature, like my father. The celebratory drink of whisky my parents take on New Year's Eve no longer raises their spirits or softens my father's frown. My mama is known for her cheery, lilting laugh, which can be heard by the Sandifers across the street. But it's muted now. She has this mask of a smile and her mouth moves as if she is laughing, but her heart isn't in it. I don't know how to cheer her up. I just become more like her.

In the sixth grade, Pittman stops having to try to cheer his mother up. She becomes "joyous" on her own. Ruth and J. B. McGehee are going to have another child. Pittman is embarrassed because his friends at school know what his parents have been doing to get his mother pregnant. The colonel never mentions her pregnancy. He spends time alone in the bedroom building model airplanes. Pittman listens to his mother for hours as she wonders whether the baby will be a girl or boy. Together she and her younger son consider names for both. He marvels at how changed his mother is. She tells him it is "astonishing" to be pregnant. Her face has brightened all over, and Pittman delights in his mother's happiness.

During this glad time, Pittman and his brother play ball in the yard and fight make-believe wars, getting as dirty and hungry as frontline troops. Ruth periodically steps out onto the porch and calls to them, "You boys come in now and wash up; it's time to eat." This becomes a ritual of playing hard, getting dirty, being hungry, washing up and eating.

It is like the primary sacraments, young Pittman comes to recognize, that a mother church offers—a bath (baptism) and a meal (eucharist). All fulfilling.

Not long afterward, Pittman wakes up to find a neighbor woman in the kitchen. She tells him and his brother that their father has taken their mother to the hospital in Cushing, ten miles away, to have her baby. Pittman is excited. The colonel doesn't say anything. Pittman has learned that, when visitors come to the house, he is to be social and talk to them. His brother, meanwhile, is in charge of domestic duties and rules. So on this morning Pittman is busy talking with the neighbor and the colonel is in the bedroom building model airplanes, having finished his duties. The phone rings and the neighbor goes to answer it. In a minute, Pittman sees a startled look on her face as she calls to his brother and says, "Your father wants to talk to you." The colonel listens on the phone, then hangs up and says to Pittman, "Our mother had a baby girl, but the baby girl died."

A few days later, on the outskirts of town, there's a gathering at a small country cemetery. Circling a freshly dug grave are Mr. McGehee, the retired Methodist preacher, the mortician, Pittman and his brother, standing at attention. Pittman is behind his father, and as the ceremony ends, he sees his father's shoulders shaking. It's the first and last time he is to see his father cry. The sound shaking his shoulders is deeper than just a cry coming out of the throat. It's a lifetime cry of sorrow, frustration and failure—a cry of quiet desperation. The young boy goes up, kneels on the damp earth and holds on to his father's leg, wishing he could make it better. Pittman cries and looks down at "the red clay pretending to be dirt."

A few weeks later, Mrs. McGehee has recovered physically, but Pittman can see in her face and manner that though she is carrying on her family rituals and household duties, her heart is not in them. When Mr. McGehee is home on weekends, one of the rituals calls for Pittman to go in and tell his parents goodnight. From the time he was a toddler, he would kiss both his mother and father before going to bed. One night, Mr. McGehee stops his son and says he has something to tell the boy: "You are old enough now for me to tell you that men don't kiss or hug each other. They shake hands." So father and son shake hands and Pittman, hurt and embarrassed, goes to his room and cries and cries. Mr. McGehee, a kind man and good father, tells his wife he is simply teaching his younger son the way the world is.

I never see my father cry. I never hug him or say "I love you." That's not what men do, I learn early, no matter how many years there are of quiet desperation in their lives. I even stop holding my mother's hand. She tells people, "He's all boy." She also tells them how I used to be a fat little boy so friendly he "never meets a stranger." My grade school auditorium teacher picks me to lead a little band she has assembled among the third graders. My mother comes on parents' day to hear the band. I announce our favorite number, the "Blue Danube Waltz," although I pronounce it "the bue Danoo." My mama thinks my baby talk is cute, so she never corrects me, and it isn't until an older neighbor boy across the street named Belton teases me that I become aware that I am mispronouncing words. I am telling him about playing two blocks down the street along a creek that runs through the neighborhood. Only I call it the "treek," and he laughs in my face. I go home ashamed.

Pittman, now grown, married and a graduate of the Virginia Seminary, accepts a call to become the Rector of Christ Church in Tyler, Texas. He and his wife have two small boys. His mother is ailing and his father retired, so Pittman convinces them to move to Tyler to be near him and their grandchildren. Ruth McGehee is proud of her two sons, one a rising officer in the air force and the other a popular preacher and priest, but she has never really recovered from the loss of her baby girl. She's never regained the radiance Pittman remembers in her face during her pregnancy. "It was a like a light behind her eyes was on a rheostat that kept growing dimmer," he recalls years later. J. B. McGehee, a kind-hearted man, "couldn't muster enough hope or meaning or peace to assuage" his wife's grief and help relieve her depression, which at times became dysfunctional.

Ruth McGehee dies one Thanksgiving after the traditional holiday dinner with her family. At her funeral, Pittman has to tell his military officer brother that he, the priest, will be in charge of the service and determine in what order the family will go into church. J. B. regrets not having done enough to make his wife happy. Pittman is sad she never regained the radiance that came to her only too briefly. However, life with this family, as with all families, goes on. Pittman does well in Tyler and his reputation as a spellbinding preacher and caring pastor grows. He's courted by bigger churches in bigger places, and he accepts a call to become dean of Christ Church Cathedral in Houston. Mr. McGehee, who has adjusted to the life of a widower, chooses to stay in Tyler. Always disciplined, he follows a strict daily routine of reading the newspaper early each morning, taking a long walk every afternoon, showering and then pulling up a folding chair on his driveway and drinking two cans of Pabst Blue Ribbon beer. On special occasions, such as his sons coming to see him, Mr. McGehee pulls out a bottle of Weller's bourbon for some real drinking. There's special reason now to celebrate, because Pittman is now a dean, no less, the rector of a cathedral rich in Texas history and boasting a congregation that includes some of the biggest movers and shakers in the booming city of Houston.

On one such visit, Pittman has what turns out to be his last conversation with his father. In many ways it is also his first—the first in terms of ever getting to know what his father really feels about the life he has lived. It is a night when both father and son take off their ties. Pittman learned how to tie his tie from his father, as many boys may still do, if they ever wear a tie. Pittman thinks they are lassos around our necks, cutting us off from our hearts and keeping us strictly in our heads. Men, the ties are meant to remind us, are about logic and loyalty, he says. Jarrett Bryan McGehee had lived his life that way—loyal to his family of origin and to his wife and sons, hardworking at every job he had and loyal to the company that kept him on in economic slumps as a traveling salesman. Without ever thinking of being otherwise, he was automatically loyal to the male credo of not talking about feelings and thus avoiding intimacy. Nonetheless, on this night, during a long conversation that is both first and last, this father and son do spend their time together talking about feelings.

Pittman's father confesses how it feels to live a lifetime of "quiet desperation," borrowing his favorite line from Thoreau, whom he had read across the years. His father knew the hard life of his own father—Pittman's grandfather—who had worked as a boy in the coal mines of Greenwood, Arkansas. At home, there were kerosene lamps and Saturday night baths in a big tub heated with water out of kettle on the stove. Pittman's grandfather grew up to own a small grocery store, which failed in the depression. J. B. McGehee, now seventy-nine and a survivor of prostate cancer, recounts the pain of leaving a small-town college to make a living. He tells of giving up dreams of "studying the law," of never succeeding financially, of long, lonely nights on the road, of the stillbirth of the baby girl his wife wanted so badly, of feeling helpless in the face of his wife's chronic depression. Father and son talk through the night until early in the morning. When it is time for Pittman to leave, he tells his father, "Despite what you once told me, I'm going to kiss you on the lips and hug you goodbye." And he does, ending the first and last heart-to-heart talk he ever had with his father.

Not long afterward, Pittman is in Northport Point, Michigan, to preside at his "summer parish." He receives an urgent call from a doctor friend in Tyler. The physician is calling to tell him that Mr. McGehee has had a massive stroke, "a bad bleed in the left hemisphere of his brain, causing the right side to be swollen with blood." A neighbor came into his house and found him unconscious in the shower, the water still on. Mr. McGehee can be kept alive, the doctor says, only by life support equipment breathing for him. Pittman directs the physician to pull the plug. He feels his father died a sacred death, immersed in water—a holy sacrament symbolizing birth, baptism and love—in this case the love of two men who finally took off their ties and let their hearts speak.

My father dies of a stroke on the concrete slab that passes for a patio outside the backdoor of the frame cottage he and my mother built sixty years earlier. Ten years later my mother dies in the back bedroom, which had been the room my brother and I shared as boys. She dies in the arms of a loving black "nanny," as Mama called her, a caretaker named Fairy. It's the room I once came back to as a young man, suffering my first depression despite success as an award-winning newspaper reporter. Counting Dadoo, my grandfather, who died in the living room, the old house has seen enough death. The occupants of this old place were good people who cared for one another. Yet what its walls never heard, to my great regret, is the good people in this house saying to each other, "I love you." They felt it, but, strangely, could not say it.

THE SCIENCE

The science of who we are is a theme of this book. Our corticolimbic loop carries our story, which is written into our very synapses and neurons by all who shape us as we grow up. Jung said that the greatest burden we carry is to live the unlived lives of our parents. However, trying to make up for what our mothers and fathers longed for, but never got, often runs counter to what a deeper and older legacy calls us to do—or be.

Archetypal theory tells us that we carry in our cells and synapses the legacy of two million years of human striving and selfhood.[1] What motivates and moves us can be found in a panoply of ancient images and myths from long before the Greeks. The story that our childhood encodes in our brain as to what we should be is sometimes out of sync with who we are. When we fail to rewrite the story and reshape our neurons, the body will tell us we are living a lie and rebel against us. The test for who we are is found in whether our doing is in harmony with our being. Trouble comes when it isn't.

No one has ever seen either archetypes or the collective unconscious, the arena in which they reside and exert their power. Depth psychology is aptly named because it does attempt to explore what's universal in us, regardless of cultural influence. The universal, collective unconscious that Jung discovered is beneath the personal unconscious, which is the subterranean region claimed by Freud. Jung's archetypes help to explain our true nature. When we become too much of something we are not meant to be, we are asking for trouble. Imbalance or disharmony may occur when we seek to satisfy the need to control at the expense of the need to connect. Attachment-autonomy, affiliation-achievement, speak to the same archetypal needs and phylogenetic steps, which Eric Erikson addressed in his stages of development.[2] A common error, which I know well, is to try to use achievement as a way to attract attention and be loved. But the Self, which is our soul and essence, permits no substitution or cheating.

While we cannot see them, both archetypes and the unconscious are known by their affects.[3] My teacher, quoting Jung, talks of archetypes as being dry riverbeds waiting to be filled by life experiences.[4] The metaphor has some correspondence to that of our neuronal axons and dendrites as roots and branches of a tree constituting connecting pathways to countless other trees in a dense forest. When certain experiences occur to us they may flood, trickle into or just fill the archetypal riverbeds waiting for them, depending on the power of the experience. When we encounter experiences that we learn from and remember, often from the emotions we feel, we send electrical and chemical forces into the synapses and circuits of our brain's "riverbeds" and deepen them. Both the structure and functioning of our circuits change, giving our neocortex a new story to tell. Archetypes have long been symbolized as Greek mythological figures. As legend has it, the high-and-mighty gods would swoop down and wound certain mortals, giving them the assignment to heal fellow sick and afflicted humans. Olympian logos, no doubt, told the gods that the best healer is someone who has been wounded himself. So Pittman gets burned within an inch of his life, and I end up resected, ostomized and partially disemboweled after various lesser wounds.

I was tending to the sick and dying before I consciously became acquainted with archetypes. I never knew I was a wounded healer until so described by my analyst, the priest. Pittman knew he was one much earlier. He wears deep scars on his legs from near-fatal burns, a constant reminder of what his elders told him: "You must have been spared for something special."

In terms of neurobiology, Jung saw archetypes as inherited modes of functioning, predisposed patterns of behavior.[5] Pittman views them as being "hardwired" in our brain patterns and functioning. Wherever the truth lies, they represent the archaic legacies with which we are endowed; through their "instinctual images" in our collective unconscious, they pack a punch. Some common archetypes are Mother, Father, Nature, God, Priest, Physician, Wounded Healer and Home. Through the feelings they evoke, they have emotional power, so it behooves us to become acquainted with them. When what we try to do or become is out of harmony with our archetypal imperatives, affliction of one kind or another is inevitable.

"Hardwired" doesn't mean we are impelled to behave or believe in accordance with whatever archetype or archetypes we may have under our skins and in our psyches. Neuroscientists are now telling us that God is hardwired in our brains.[6] When we connect with what we call "God," certain parts of the temporal lobe and limbic loop "light up" during a PET scan. We can scoff and disbelieve and never darken the door of a place of worship. Our "God circuits" won't turn on, but the wiring is still there. We still have a "riverbed" waiting to be filled with the "idea" of God, and we have neural connections just waiting to light up when someday we see the Light.

Jungian "acorn" theorists remind us that the nature of an acorn is to become "the best oak tree it can, given the nature of the soil, the condition of the climate, the proximity and height of the surrounding trees.... Deficiencies in any of these environmental conditions will result in stunting or susceptibilty to disease."[7] Thus, the physical and social environment we start with and gravitate toward will play a decisive part in the development and blossoming of the human acorn in us. It's possible for us to twist this way and that to adapt or even succeed in some pursuit, occupation, relationship or setting, but if that isn't our true "calling," then our "archetypal intent" has been thwarted and we are likely to end up unhappy, unhealthy and unwise. The good news is plasticity, the brain's capacity to change with a change of mind, or, as my therapist the priest calls it, "metanoia." Of all the "noias," he fondly adds, "metanoia is my most favorite and paranoia is my least."[8] Metanoia is changing our outlook, how we see ourself and the world.

Anthony Stevens, a widely recognized Jungian psychiatrist and author of *The Two Million-Year-Old Self,* has formulated "laws of psychodynamics" in recognition of the power of archetypal imperatives and intent.[9] They include a law that states, "Archetypes possess an inherent dynamic, whose goal is to actualize themselves in both psyche and behavior." Another states, "Mental health results from the fulfillment of archetypal goals" or intents. This law's negative counterpart is: "Psychopathology results from the frustration of archetypal goals." To the psychobiologist I am and to the patient in me, the laws insist that trying to become what we aren't is a surefire way of suffering ill health—physical, mental or both.

Archetypal intents and imperatives can also be understood as expressing the need to balance the dichotomies in our nature. "Two million years" is the figure Jung gave to the psychobiological legacy we live with in our brains and bodies. We have inherited a reptilian brain, the earliest in our legacy; a paleomammalian (emotional) brain, which brought us closer to being human; and a neomammalian brain, which rests on top of and loops over the other two and presumably makes us more rational. The archetypes represented in all three, however, demand a balancing of complementary needs. On one hand, we need attachment just to stay alive in early life. On the other, we need autonomy after we have become erect enough to answer the call to explore our world. Parallel to the attachment-autonomy dichotomy is the drive to connect and to control—to love others and to control enough of our life and environment to adapt and achieve as well as belong. Because of the materialistic goodies that our culture values and the fame it bestows on champion achievers, we can go control crazy to the point that power is our god.

Aristotle's wisdom not only may have foretold discovery of the DNA molecule two thousand years later (see chapter 4). It also posited three kinds of life in which we find strong archetypal pulls, depending on whom we are meant to be or what we end up becoming. He said there is [1] "the hedonic life, governed by pleasure; [2] the political life, devoted to honor and the exercise of power; and [3] the contemplative life, devoted to wisdom and truth." The first two, Anthony Stevens tells us, "are extraverted...while the third is introverted and in accord with the Jungian orientation."[10] Does this mean we have to be either entirely extraverted if we are into [1] and [2], or completely introverted if we are into [3]? No, almost everyone is a mixture, but at our core, we are more one than the other, and we know it. And yes, period or stage of life does enter the equation, but getting older doesn't turn an extravert into an introvert or vice versa.

I have tried all three of Aristotle's kinds of life. Only now am I coming to terms with my innate core or acorn, which means I not only don't deny my introversion, I embrace it. In pursuit of honor and power, I have won journalistic prizes and awards, I served as the right hand of the mayor of the fourth largest U.S. city,[11] I had a big office and staff in the private sector, went to posh hotels and lush resorts, and wined and dined with some of the rich and famous. I also have had the privilege of being a dean in academia. Finally, I became sick of it all. Who I am cries, "Enough!"—enough pretending, masking and ignoring the pain at the deepest reaches of my psyche and soma. The wisdom of my body has been trying to tell me the truth, but I am either deaf or a slow learner. So that's why I have teamed up with my partner in the belly of the whale. He learned a lot faster.

On Pittman's part, he enjoyed for a time being big-shot dean and administrative head of a historic, well-endowed cathedral. There were more invitations to important publicized dinners, dances and dream vacations than he could accept. All the while his introversion kept gnawing away at him, and the Jungian call became louder inside him. So for years of weekends and summers he studied to become an analyst, all the while wearing the white collar of an Episcopal priest. He told one of his training analysts about his idea of leaving the priesthood and going to Zurich to finish his Jungian degree. His supervisor, Dr. Robert Johnson, told him to "learn to be a priest first." Pittman learned that he had been wearing the garb and acting the part, but he still wasn't yet a priest from the inside out. So he stayed a priest until he felt he truly was one, from the inside out. Then he left his church, but kept his white collar.

In Pittman's words, "I couldn't stand living in a fishbowl any more, always on display. I was losing myself in a life that wasn't mine—or should I say, isn't who I am. I don't even like going to church or being around a lot of people. I like everything about being a priest but that." So my teacher left the cathedral to be who he really is, a complete introvert who writes poetry, "chases the truth" with words and sits hour after hour, week after week, listening to the expressed and repressed travails of souls like mine.

What has all of this to do with the science of our story? First, human nature is still alive and well in natural science. Science realizes that it can't explain human beings and doings strictly by genotype, phenotype or objective observables without factoring in two million years of archetypal inheritance rooted in human nature.[12] Second, the unconscious is powerful; its archetypal intents and other imperatives cannot be ignored; and science—not just Freudian analysis or Jungian psychology—is becoming increasingly interested in the collective unconscious, its memory and neural organization.[13] Third, neither the body, psyche nor soul can be fooled, and that is becoming more recognized as a scientific fact—meaning an objective, empirical, replicable truth. We can suppress, repress, deny, rationalize or project whatever and whoever we really are, but the body, psyche and soul of who we are will agitate and pain us to the point it gets our attention. It will demand that we listen to what it is saying, namely, "Stop acting like a fool and start being who you are." Who I am may still seem to be a fool to others, but then, I'm the one I have to live with.

Dr. Orange W. Star

CHAPTER 6

CHASING DREAMS, EMBRACING SHADOWS

It is amazing that we can make incredibly accurate predictions

about the movement or composition of stars in galaxies millions of light years

away while much closer to home, many crucial processes in our own

heads remain shrouded in mystery.[1]

THE STORY

It's Palm Sunday, March 24, 1991: The Very Reverend J. Pittman McGehee, Episcopal dean and priest at the historic Christ Church Cathedral in downtown Houston, straightens his robe and hood and mounts the high pulpit to deliver his sermon. The death of his father in recent months is still fresh in his memory and, as it turns out, his unconscious. After a disclaimer about the inadvisability of disclosing publicly the contents of one's deepest inner world, the priest tells his listeners that "some dreams demand to be told."[2] His justification is that such dreams "evidently belong to the collective," meaning that they emerge from that part of our psyche that is universal in all of us.

Pittman tells of his father coming to him in a dream. "He appears as if he has just gotten out of bed. He looks like I have seen him for so many mornings in my span of life. His hair is white and silken, slightly tousled. He is wearing his robe, always too short of sleeve, and those house shoes with the backs ridden flat by years of clopping down dark hallways.... He looks at me and twinkles his eyes which always, under thick brows, looked soft and slanted. He smiles a knowing smile and speaks."

Up to this point, everything the son remembers about his father—every detail from bushy eyebrows to worn-out slippers—is the same as it was in life. This is the man, the son will never forget, who quoted poetry to his boys in the family's two-bedroom, one-bathroom rented house on a hilltop in Drumright, Oklahoma. As Pittman well knew, J. B. McGehee particularly liked Thoreau's poetry and the line, "The mass of men lead lives of quiet desperation."[3] This is the man who struggled his entire life against "his own sense of failure, having sat each weekend at his desk in the dining room… posting his books and trying to squeeze out of his expense account enough extra to make ends meet."[4] This is also the father, his son remembers, who "couldn't muster enough hope or meaning or peace to assuage my mother's chronic and, at times, dysfunctional depression."

So here and now, years later, in the son's dream is the man he had always known, but the words the man says come from a new person. He has the same looks and manner as

Pittman's father, but he has an entirely different message to pass on to his son: "All of the things you are worried about don't matter." Pittman would never have dreamed of hearing such a message from his father, but dream he did.

Dr. McGehee reminds his congregation that the Christian Holy Week, particularly the Passion of Jesus Christ, has its own "nights of quiet desperation for the human masses: betrayal, denial, anguish, horror, death, and yet"... at the end Easter comes, bearing the same message of hope and peace that Pittman believes his father is conveying in the dream. What counts are things of the heart, not the head. Nothing else matters in the big scheme of things. "So the father's voice begins to utter an Easter dream." And though he didn't say so from the pulpit, Pittman knew that his own "rebirth" would start with ceasing his efforts to make up for what his parents never had.

Is the dream "true"? Is it something to take to heart and to believe? Of the states of mind, consciousness and unconsciousness included, that science is now seriously investigating—thanks to advances in neuroimaging and other technology—dreams are still often dismissed. Pittman tells his listeners that "it doesn't matter whose voice" was in the dream or whether the dream was "real." As a Jungian just beginning his training, he recognizes that the voice and dream could have come from any number of sources. But "if it was my father complex, an archetypal image of the Self, or God, or some chemical reaction to something I ate, those words are mine. Hume asks, 'Did you dream God spoke to you, or did God speak to you in a dream?' Finally, the distinction makes no difference, for the words come."[5]

Though new to the study and analysis of dreams, Pittman is learning to take them seriously. Because they come from a psychic level deeper in us than our ego, they speak the truth of the Self, the core of who we are. Pittman's calling comes from his mother. And through her, he walks in the shoes of her father, the Cumberland Presbyterian preacher so well known and loved that churches all over Arkansas had stained glass windows dedicated to him. Pittman will never forget being taken by his mother to see one of them as a boy. So in becoming a preacher, the son honors not only the wishes of his mother, but also the memory of his grandfather. He remembers, too, that his mother charged him to "grow up and help people with their sadness," which Pittman has ample opportunity to do as a priest.

Being a priest suits Pittman completely, apart from becoming what his mother charged him to be. From his first day at Virginia Seminary he has been "like a golden retriever born to dive into the water and retrieve ducks." He revels in religious readings, hermeneutic challenges and mystical divinations. So he doesn't hear anything in his father's voice that is saying he shouldn't worry about being a good priest and pleasing God. The message is more personal than an Easter promise of hope. It is telling him to stop trying to please his dead mother or to live the unlived life of either of his parents.

Verification comes later in a second dream. In it, Pittman is sitting in his office at the Cathedral and sees vapor sliding out under the door. The vapor is streaming forth from his very chest. He recognizes it immediately as the shadow that has been pushing him toward acquiring more and more ecclesiastic power, to become the Anglican equivalent of the pope. He had been approached about becoming a candidate for bishop of the diocese of Texas. At the same time, he receives an invitation to go to a New York City church. The vestry there flies him up to see if he would like to become rector of the oldest, and one of the wealthiest, Episcopal parishes, Trinity Church. It's in the heart of Wall Street and is where General George Washington worshipped. Now all that is going up in the smoke of a dream that comes to him. Dr. McGehee feels great relief as the vapor drains from him and slips through the crack under his office door. His driving ambition is suddenly gone. He will stop trying to make up for what his parents longed for, but never had—the awards and rewards that power and prestige bring.

Meanwhile, during the same Easter season, my chest is issuing forth not vapor but blood. A line of basal and squamous carcinoma skin cells, resisting repeated treatment, continues to circle my heart and to bleed. I am bleeding not only from the cancer cells but metaphorically from my heart, which weeps for our daughter, Liz, and her continued failure to break her cocaine and heroin addiction in New York. I can have surgery for my chest but not for my heart. Liz has been in and out of the best treatment programs. She's out again and back on dope and a life on the streets.

So now I find myself in a small operating room adjacent to a cytology laboratory and am undergoing Moh's surgery. It's a procedure that keeps cutting a wide enough swath to make sure all the cancer cells have been excised. By the time the laboratory tests assure my surgeon that she's gone far enough, I am left with a circular hole in my chest three inches in diameter, but, fortunately, less than an inch deep. For the next month, I get to view nature at work as it faces the task of building bridges across the edges of the hole and generating tissue to fill it in. At home Rita helps me twice a day to change the shoulder harness dressing and apply antibiotics to my wound. We watch what is going on in the hole. What we quickly learn is that the repair work is very sensitive to the ups and downs I experience with regard to our daughter.

Liz reenters St. Luke's-Roosevelt Hospital in uptown Manhattan. Her own heart has been so compromised by cocaine addiction that she has congestive heart failure and an acute infection. I am on the phone twice a day with her doctors, with whom I established personal contact during her previous hospitalization there. Some days the news is better than others. I can see my capillaries making progress laying down connections between the edges of my chest wound. On those days my collagen tissue, which helps fill the hole, seems brighter, as I am.

There is hope in Easter after all. Liz recovers enough to be discharged and is told she has two more years to live if she stops doing drugs. She doesn't, but she still beats the odds. She doesn't die until three years later, which gives Rita and me time to sit with her during yet another—and final—stay in the ICU and say our goodbyes. We read poetry aloud, listen to Mozart on a pocket-sized tape player, express feelings of mutual anger, disappointment and failure, but mostly love. We look at Liz's last watercolors and agree to scatter her ashes at the places of beauty we had taken her to that she remembered best. My heart still weeps, but it has stopped bleeding. The hole in my chest is now more of a shallow indentation. And life goes on.

And so do my episodes of depression. Here I am, nearly five years later, searching for my demons in the deeper realm of dreams. Pittman, meanwhile, has buried his demons with the deaths of his parents and seven years of analysis. I am slowly identifying my shadows in all the shit I am sharing with him, the shit being the base material that we are trying to convert to gold in our alchemical container.

I am as skeptical of the idea that dreams are the key to healing as I am about all else I have tried. I tell Pittman, "I have written one book on how to keep from getting sick and how to recover when you do, I have written another on finding well-being despite illness, and I teach the healing effects of finding benefit in illness. But in my depression, I practice nothing of what I preach. I get up late, I go to bed early. I don't seek people out. I know people heal people, yet I avoid people. I fail to walk my talk in everything."

My therapist just listens. He doesn't tell me until much later what he is thinking: *Blair minimalizes the shit he has had to deal with—a severely depressed first wife who tried to kill herself, a schizophrenic son who tried to kill him, a daughter who died from addiction, and his own three colon surgeries, the effects of which he is still feeling. He is so sick. I wish I could pick him up and carry him home to wash him, feed him and parent him. He's totally depleted, without even the strength to lick the roof of his mouth.* Instead of doing any of this, Pittman resorts to a little humor, knowing that humor is the one thing I can usually respond to even when I am down.

"Lawyers die without wills, doctors don't get checkups, and clergy don't do everything they tell others to do," Pittman says to me. "You're in good company. I went to a psychiatrist once when I was having writer's block on sermons and a hard time living up to what I preached. He told me something I'll never forget: 'Don't think you will ever practice everything you preach.'"

Pittman knows by now that I perceive faults, failures and phoniness in myself as part of the shadow I keep only one step behind me, reminding me that I am no good, just a piece of shit. My gut got tired of holding all the crap that I had in my life, real and otherwise. So it exploded. Now my dreams are full of crap. I have a dream of a toilet that has brown wrapping paper, instead of a bowl, to collect deposits. It gets peed on and shit on. But it holds. This is the point Pittman makes to me when I tell him the dream. I'm holding together, despite everything.

I continue to have shit-related dreams, but soon my shadow takes on other features. I'm in a stairwell, and there's a big, fat man on the steps above me, acting as if he is going to jump on me. I identify him as bosses I have known and feared. Suddenly I turn around and spit these words out at him: "I have a knife. If you jump on me, I'll kill you." My shadow takes other forms, foreign to me. I'm in a tennis tournament playing against a Russian. My serves are good and accurate. In the middle of the match, the Russian walks off the court silenty, beaten. To my therapist, it's a turning point. My alien self is backing off.

Instead of trying always to please powerful people in my life—from my mother to my "masters" on the various jobs I've had—I am trying now to be true to my own nature, to being an introvert who doesn't have to keep performing for applause. My dreams suggest that I am beginning to encode in my neocortex a new and truer story of who I am. As both a priest and a Jungian scholar, Pittman tells people to "pay attention to your dreams, listen to them; the god within speaks. They have important information to give you. They should be honored." The first assignment Pittman had upon graduation from seminary and being ordained an Episcopal cleric was at a church in inner city Kansas City. "I was so new," he recalls, "I kept smelling the first black shirt I wore as a priest. Late one day, when just about all the staff had left, a secretary contacted me and said a woman in her office had to see a priest. The secretary let me know that I was the only one around, so she was going to have to refer the visitor to me—a subtle reminder of just how new I was."

The visitor was a large, earthy woman who had recently arrived from South America, her native land. She had to see a priest because she had a dream she needed to tell the *sacerdote*. She told it, and promptly left, no questions asked. She knew that dreams are to be honored by sharing them. According to her tradition, a person is to take the dream to a priest. The point is to tell the dream and listen to what's in it, Pittman learned. It makes good Jungian sense, he decided. "It's the voice of the unconscious, the Self, where the *imago dei* resides."

Pittman's belief that God's voice comes in dreams is not new. John Sanford, also a Jungian analyst and Episcopal priest, wrote a book years ago on *Dreams: God's Forgotten Language*, which is still widely quoted.[6] Jung himself noted that the Catholic Church acknowledged the occurrence of *somnia Deo missa*, dreams sent by God.[7] Jung added that "most" of the church's "thinkers made no serious attempt to understand dreams." Jung doubted, though, "whether there is a Protestant treatise or doctrine that would stoop so low as to admit the possibility that the *vox Dei* might be perceived in a dream." As to my therapist, the iconoclast who "colors outside the lines," particularly ecclesiastical ones, he not only emphasizes the voice of God in dreams, but declares that institutional religion is one of the "barns" that keep people from seeing the moon and experiencing God. Ever a "re-visionist," he ends up giving this "heretical" advice: "Burn the goddamned barn down so you can look at the moon." He translates this as meaning, "Don't let institutions, even the church, get between you and the source of light." Institutions, as well as people, have their shadow sides, he believes.[8] More recently Dr. McGehee uses barns as a metaphor for ego defenses needed to protect us from feeling overwhelmed or abandoned, particularly in the first half of life. But in the second half of life they can keep us from being that which we are created to be, from being our true self.[9]

Many nights my "dream machine" is in such low gear or is so incoherent I have little to record. So I sit opposite my therapist and say nothing. I bring my dream book to report my meager night work, but instead we just sit and shoot the bull in between stretches of silence. That seems as therapeutic as stalking my shadow. Insight is necessary, but not sufficient. I keep reminding myself that the information that my implicit self and limbic brain absorb in the experience from our relationship is the factor that changes brain chemistry. Today I learn that I don't have to keep writing books or coming up with new talks to present to audiences. Pittman tells me that he himself has been giving the same sermon for twenty years. He just changes the beginning and end.

"What's in the middle?" I ask. "What is your one and only theme?"

His answer: "Jesus loves me, this I know. For the Bible tells me so."

"Is that all?" I ask.

"That's all," he says.

We look at each other, saying nothing while I process this weighty ounce of wisdom. Finally, I say, "My shadow thinks it's funny."

"Good," Pittman replies, "Embrace your shadow."

Meanwhile, another realm that I am learning to embrace gladly lies somewhere between or beyond my shadow and my elusive true self. It includes daydreams and experiences that take me out of the realm of *I-It* to *I-Thou*. Philosopher Martin Buber said no one can live without the *I-It* realm, where—as physicist Chet Raymo observes—"we put on our shoes, go to the bank, change the oil in the car" and embrace all the other *Its* of the everyday world in which we "win our bread" and try to keep from bogging down in the quotidian of life.[10]

"Without *It*," Buber said, "man cannot live. But he who lives with *It* alone is not a man."[11] At least, he is not a person who is in touch with his soul—or dreams. *I-Thou* experiences touch the soul in the sense that when we connect with people or things at a deeper level, we feel a resonance. Raymo says it is "the kind of experience that is relational, mutual and transcending."[12] Raymo, for example, has long been drawn to herons:

> I see the heron as a sheet of feathers in a shock of light, a splash of blue shot through with silver, streaming droplets of gold. I perceive it as movement: wings heaving against air. I classify it as a species and study... its anatomy and mode of life. I subsume its presence into physics, chemistry and molecular biology.... In all of this the heron remains an object.... In all of this the heron is an *It*. But it can also happen, *if I have both will and grace,* that in experiencing the heron I become bound up in an unbidden relationship. I am struck through by a power that resides in the bird that finds a resonance in me—a power that is nameless, all-inclusive. I address the bird as *Thou*. I enter briefly, ecstatically, into spiritual union with the bird.... no longer *It*.... This relation—unasked for, unexplained—is the primordial religious experience.[13]

All this comes from a scientist who is the author of *Skeptics and True Believers*, a professor of physics who aligns himself with the skeptics. So, I ask myself, where or when does physics end and metaphysics begin; or where does an analytic mind merge with a poetic heart? The answer, it seems, is when our *Thou*, our soul, penetrates to the essence of an *It*—or is penetrated by it—and transforms our relation into a *Thou*. At that point of mutuality we get inside the other and feel one with it. Pittman does this with his poetry. The closest I come to doing it—when my inner deadness lightens a little—is with occasional daydreams and night dreams that transport me beyond my shadow to a realm where I remember my soul used to sing. It's where I had *Thou* experiences with the world of *Its*. The *Its* I connected with included dogs and trees, which would elicit in me an experience of synchrony and empathy and a sense that my *Thou* touched theirs.

Even now, my reveries sometime come with a sense of reverence, as though I am in the presence of an unseen god or something holy. With our dogs, I hold their heads and look into their dark eyes as if expecting to find what their "Thou-ness" is like. The Jesuit scientist and priest Pierre Teilhard de Chardin, a field paleontologist, could find *Thous* in fragments of fossilized bone, perceiving in them the hand of God. His evolutionary vision saw God's creation as "the preordained unfolding of life and mind from primordial matter," the alpha point, to an omega of cosmic consciousness and redemption.[14] Pittman can follow Teilhard de Chardin, another favorite of his, to these lofty heights, but the closest I have approached omega is experiencing a *Thou* in alpine peaks, Douglas firs, wildflowers and Tibetan dogs.

I am convinced that, when we have close encounters with "the thin places" where the physical and the spiritual meet, where the visible and the invisible come together, we get a taste of the transcendent.[15] It is the experience I have had in depression-free days in the mountains and is the kind of poetry and music I long for again. There is a place in the brain— a region called the rostromedial prefrontal cortex near the center of the forehead— that links short-term memory, long-term memory and emotions and gives us the spine-tingling endorphins and dopamine that nurture body and soul with the feeling of healing that music and poetry can evoke in us. This is what alpine mountains, wildflowers and Douglas firs can do for us. My sense of "transcendence," then, is not found in otherworldliness, but in the immanence of the beauty, mystery and grandeur of this world. The Irish Catholic priest John O Riordian calls this perception of God in all there is, here and now, "The Music of What Happens."[16]

An unusual dream of distinct imagery comes to me six year's after Liz's death, on the night of our older daughter Cindy's wedding on the deck of our Colorado house. In the dream two dogs the color of our black-and-white Tibetans come toward me with flowery plants in their mouths. As if by some deeper knowledge, I immediately perceive the plants as having medicinal properties, suitable for treatment of schizophrenia and depression, the two terrible diseases I know best. I tell the dream to Pittman, and he sees it as another early sign that better days are ahead for me. In his end-of-the session custom of anointing my forehead with oil and asking for God's grace on both of us, I silently pray that he is right about more light at the end of the tunnel.

However, the tunnel is even longer and darker than I imagine. I stumble into stormy shadows not long after Cindy's wedding. It happens in another mountain setting. I go with Rita to another wedding, this one a lavish affair in the Black Mountains of western North Carolina. The son of friends is marrying a young woman from an uppercrust family of Asheville, the site of the historic Biltmore Estate of Commodore Vanderbilt, where out-of-town guests are lodged and the rehearsal dinner is held. Both the bride and her husband-to-be graduated from Princeton. Her name is Elizabeth Ann, the name of our younger daughter, who killed herself with drugs in New York. This Elizabeth Ann writes for a newspaper in New York City. Our Liz attended a boarding school near Princeton and later sought to be an artist in New York. This Elizabeth, also boarding school bred, has traveled worldwide. Liz studied in France and Spain and traveled widely with Rita and me.

This Elizabeth has hair the same color as our daughter's. She has the polished good looks Liz once had. She also has the manners and stylish appearance Liz lost. Rita is well aware of these similarities. I am blind to them. I am unconscious also of the amount of wine I am drinking as I sit at our dinner table watching a long video of the storybook bride and groom across their growing-up years and into the present.

I proceed to drink so much of the Biltmore Estate wine that I have to be helped onto the shuttle back to the inn. I black out after that. I vomit in bed. Rita summons help, and two strong-armed staffers come to lift me up out of my own vomit so fresh bed linens can be installed. I resist waking up the morning after, dimly aware of what happened, but unconscious of the gory details. In trying to reconstruct the events, I am still unable to see any connection between the wedding Liz and our daughter Liz, who ended up walking the streets of Manhattan seeking her next fix. Rita tries to tell me, but nothing penetrates. Finally, back in Houston, my therapist breaks through to me.

"Getting drunk and all the mess you made are passive-aggressive behaviors, straight out of the unconscious." It's some of the most straightforward talk I've heard from a Jungian. With Pittman's help, I come to recognize that my passive-aggressiveness was directed, in part, at the circle of privileged people I was around in Asheville. It's a circle from which my family of origin was excluded, although my mother aspired to belong. The Depression killed even her hopes. Nonetheless, most of my buried anger is at myself. I feel I failed Liz, and self-forgiveness comes hard for me. I don't know how I could have saved her, but my guilt tells me I didn't do enough for her. The voice I hear inside insists I was never a good father. No treatment program we tried for her—some entailed many months in residence—had more than temporary effects. I kept researching and calling new ones until time ran out. Once she took to the streetlife of an addict, I gave up. I disowned her, and never acknowledged it, even to myself.

All of my training told me her addiction was a disease. I taught the precursors and features of the illness. But because hers was so degrading, I could only feel shame instead of compassion. Her shame was my shame. I stuck her like a skeleton in the closet and never told anyone the kind of life she was living. When people asked about my daughter Liz, my stock answer was, "She's living the life of a struggling artist in New York." I buried all the love I had for her along with my anger—at her and myself. Some soft part of me died when she died, and I knew it when I recoiled at the sight of her waxen face and shrunken head sticking out from the coroner's blanket that covered up her autopsied body parts.

Pittman says to me, "If either of my sons had become addicted and died, I know I would never have gotten over it." However, Pittman has greater capacity to forgive, including forgiving himself. I can live with the holes I still feel in my chest and beneath my sternum, but I am forever haunted by a speechless voice that pronounces: "Guilty." I am "guilty." But of what? I'm told we did all anyone could to save her. Nonetheless, the voice tells me I violated an unspoken code that fathers don't give up on their daughters. They certainly are never glad that their daughters finally die. I hear a sharp censure out of the distant past: "You should be ashamed of yourself for feeling like that." It's my mother's voice, berating me. Again with my analyst's help, I have learned to accept, if not embrace, some of the other wrongful, "not-good-enough" shame that I have locked inside. Yet even as I feel my brain start to free itself from some of its depression, my soul is still heavy.

I tell Pittman, "I'm back in the belly of the whale and I feel more psychic storms coming on."

He nods and says, "We'll ride out whatever comes. There's still light ahead."

"Whatever" comes the next night in a dream packed with emotion. I am with Rita at a racquet club, and we are below the first floor, looking outside through narrow basement windows. It's growing dark, but I can see a funnel cloud forming and yell, "It's a tornado coming down the tracks!" Next to the club are railroad tracks, and a large locomotive is stopped on them not far from where we are. The tornado sweeps down, tearing up the tracks and demolishing the heavy steam engine. The scene shifts, and we are in a large room occupied by old, poor people and cots. We're looking for an exit. Finally, a wizened, white-haired woman in tattered clothes appears. It's a Sophia, a wise woman, and she is showing us a way out of the rubble.

Awake, I don't need to be told that the fierce wind is the storm in my "basement" unconscious, and the steam is the anger in my engine.[17] If I look closely, Pittman suggests, I will find in the rubble, including my drunken mess and vomit, something of value. Maybe it's not gold, but it is a shiny coin of some promise. Perhaps I can redeem it for more consciousness.

THE SCIENCE

On April 6, 1959 *Newsweek* magazine featured a cover story on "The Science of Dreams." As elaborated upon in a book three years later by the same name, the magazine's science editor, Edwin Diamond, was allowed to become an experimental subject in a dream laboratory. Small disc electrodes were attached near his eyes and on the scalp. Long lines connected the electrodes to an electroencephalograph machine (EEG) in a small room next door, separated from the sleeping subject by a plate glass viewing window and wall. The machine's pen traced a record of brain waves and eye movements on a slowly turning drum.

As soon as the sleeping editor's eyes began moving back and forth under his eyelids a telltale pattern began taking shape on the moving graph paper, indicating that the curtain was about to go up on a dream. Just as the dream was starting to unfold its plot, the scientific investigator watching all this from an adjoining cubicle sounded a bell, waking his subject. Over an intercom, Diamond was asked, "Were you dreaming?" A tape recording was made of his answer. Four more times during the night the procedure was repeated, with the dream subject reporting more than an hour of detailed and vivid dream episodes into the intercom.[1]

Neuroscientists have learned much about the sleeping brain and its habits in the decades since *The Science of Dreams* appeared. They know that dreaming occurs not only in the REM stage of sleep, in which rapid eye movements occur under the eyelids, but also in non-REM stages (designated as descending stages one and two) that occur shortly after going to sleep. In an attempt to better understand where in the brain dreams originate, they have done studies on people with damage in the brainstem, in the limbic loops and in the neocortex, covering all three strata of evolutionary development in our inner world. Two noted neuroscientists, Allan Hobson and Robert McCarley, reported that their experiments demonstrated that the pons, a part of the brainstem, is the dream generator. The brainstem is "mindless" and devoted to basic physical instincts, such as feeding, fighting and fornicating. Alarmed Freudian analysts saw the Hobson theory as the end of the road for their long held belief that dreams are the "royal road" to understanding the unconscious mind.[2]

The analysts were told that dreaming was caused by the chemical acetylcholine reaching critical levels in the pontine brainstem, causing a discharge of random electrical impulses and waves. Not only were there no unconscious wishes or repressed complexes involved, but also there was no motivation of any kind expressed in dreaming. The forebrain, our thinking part, is left with the job of making sense out of the inchoate images, devoid of intrinsic meaning.[3] The stories, events and dramas we report as dreams, then, are products of confabulation, according to this theory. Freud himself had a term for such a theory: "Dreams are froth."[4]

But soon science righted itself, in the eyes of clinicians, and new evidence showed that dreams, in fact, are mindful and do involve strata of the brain above the reptilian level. The primary driving force behind dreams, as now reported, is the mesocortical-mesolimbic system, which includes both our limbic, emotional brain and the neocortex, our thinking brain. It is the "seeking" system of the brain that is activated.[5] In dream sleep this system gives us a way to explore and investigate whatever our unconscious throws before us without worrying about time, space and other constrictions and inhibitions waking life imposes upon us. In other words, "when you sleep, you cannot go about exploring or seeking what you are motivationally interested in," but in dreams you can do so.[6] There are still scientists, however, who insist that dreams are nonsensical, if amusing, byproducts of chemical changes; any meaning is incidental mythmaking while the real function of dreams is to run a check on the different parts of the brain's machinery.[7]

It's true that in dream sleep, random PGO (pontine-geniculate-occipital) waves, representing three ascending areas of the brain, do occur, producing a "chaotic cacophony of brain stimulation."[8] But along with the "nonsense" jumble of images and sensations that may be produced, our "story synthesizer" in the cerebral cortex is stimulated and fits the dream into a narrative. What comes out may be a new or confirming way we look at ourselves and our lives. In my case, instead of the old "I'm not good enough" story, my neurons start encoding a new version of who I am. Dr. Susan C. Vaughan, research psychoanalyst affiliated with Columbia University College of Physicians and Surgeons, has written extensively on changing the neurons in our "story synthesizer."[9]

Dr. Hobson of Harvard, the sleep science authority and longtime critic of Freudian dream theory, now notes that "by paying attention to our dreams" we may learn more about our "instinctive/emotional" nature. He believes that the "emotional salience" in dreams, as well as in waking life, is linked to "associative thinking."[10] Hobson holds that, like "neutral word list stimuli," dreams may trigger important trains of thought, having emotional relevance. Because in dreams the brain is activated by cholinergic, rather than aminergic, chemicals, Hobson believes that in dreaming "we restore the most fundamental aspects of our cognitive capability—the capacity to order our memories in a way that serves survival." Dreams, then, promote "emotional competence" and sharpen our skills in recognizing "when to approach, when to mate, when to be afraid, and when to run for cover."[11]

If we agree that dreams are more than just silly "froth," having no bearing on our waking lives, then are there functions other than the chemical ones that Hobson reports? Some writers on the subject see dreams as a source of information that may help us solve specific problems. Mona Lisa Schulz, both a neuroscientist and psychotherapist, learned to pay attention to her dreams while working simultaneously on her Ph.D. and M.D.[12] At first, she ignored what her dreams kept telling her, namely, that she was so strung out that she was courting bodily danger. Then she began having trouble moving her fingers. An MRI showed two discs had collapsed in her spine. She finally had to undergo spinal surgery. Dr. Schulz now listens to her dreams, which she uses to deepen her intuitions and sharpen her diagnostic skills with patients. She has concluded that "the soul speaks to the human consciousness through sensations of health or disease in the body"—and through intuitions. In the case of disease, she believes that leaks, holes or other abnormal openings—such as in the bowel, in my case—are apertures the soul uses to tell us what needs to change in our lives.

Other scientists have historically reported that a dream helped them solve important technical problems they were working on. The chemist Frederich August Kekule attributed his discovery of the ring structure of benzene to a dream in which he visualized a snake-like chain of atoms grasping its own tail.[13] Otto Loewi "dreamed the experiment which proved the chemical basis of neurotransmission."[14]

A second function dreams may perform is precognitive. Dr. Larry Dossey learned to honor his dreams in his first year of medical practice in Dallas. He had a dream about Justin, the four-year-old son of a physician colleague. In the dream the boy was "yelling, fighting" and trying to remove a gadget that a white-coated technician was attempting to place on his head. "I awoke," he said, "in the gray dawn with the sensation that the dream was the most vivid I had ever experienced—numinous, profound, 'realer than real.'"[15] The next day he was having lunch at the hospital where he practiced with the boy's father. Then Justin's mother appeared with the boy in her arms, crying. The mother was distraught. They had just come from the electroencephalography laboratory, where a technician had unsuccessfully tried to perform a brain-wave test on the boy, using an apparatus like the one Dossey had seen in his dream. Justin had developed a fever, followed by a brief seizure, which was justification for having the test. All the details from Dossey's dream the night before were now being played out in front of him. Within a week he dreamed two more times about events that would occur the next day. "In all three instances, time seemed to be reversed, with effects appearing before their causes."[16]

Some years before Dossey was born, an aeronautical engineer named J. W. Dunne found that he dreamed about events that were about to happen. One night, while in the

British Army in South Africa, he dreamed of a volcanic eruption that led to the death of 4,000 people. When a newspaper arrived in a few days from London, a front-page headline told of a volcanic eruption killing 40,000 people on the island of Martinique.[17] The newspaper estimate was later revised to 4,000. Dunne began developing a technique that required writing a dream down immediately upon waking from it. After discovering that this method led to more prophetic dreams, he taught it to others and wrote a book, *An Experiment With Time*, which describes, as Dossey did, the phenomenon of time running in reverse.[18]

Mathematicians who have looked at prophetic dreams explain them as coincidences. For instance, "people will dream, say, an earthquake or a plane crash, only to read in the paper the next day that it actually happened. But given the fact that roughly 250 million people in the United States spend several hours in dreamland each night, 'we should expect as much,' [mathematician John Allen Paulos] says. 'In reality, the most astonishingly incredible coincidence imaginable would be the complete absence of coincidence.'"[19]

My dreams have not been prophetic, but, in recent months, they have at times been instructive and, on occasion, semi-scientific. In almost a didactic fashion, they sometimes give me ideas about how the physical and psychological come together, how mind and body join, how brain and soul relate. I lose sleep by making myself get up at night, go into the bathroom where I can turn on the light without disturbing Rita and record what the dream part of me dictates—meaning I write almost by rote, as if "automatic writing" overtakes me in dream sleep.

What strikes me most, however, is the frequency with which I have dreams about dreaming. Maybe this is a variant of lucid dreaming, which is the state of being aware in a dream of dreaming. Mine are more dreams within dreams. An example: At 4:15 one morning, I write: "I am paired up with another man, someone like Pittman, to demonstrate two ways for dreams to affect the body. One is by direct action on the autonomic nervous system, sympathetic branch, by way of the amygdala. This is a 'top-down' mechanism. The other is a 'bottom-up' action, starting in the unconscious, silent part of the self moving up to the amygdala and on to the hypothalamus." At 6:00 a few mornings later, I write: "A dream machine sinks into the soil of my brain and gets stuck. We get it out, and I tell the operator that it's not necessary to use the machine. Dreams can be generated on their own without danger of getting stuck." What strikes Pittman as I report my dreams in therapy is that they have a functional, practical quality to them, nothing burdened by shadows. I still have dreams of elimination, but they, too, seem free of darkness. In one I develop a method so that dogs take care of their "business" with fewer "accidents," such as pooping or peeing inside the house. The interpretation I offer to my therapist is that I seem to be spoiling my own nest less. He nods. Another good sign is that I occasionally have a humor dream. After attending a symphony orchestra concert featuring a world-renowned young pianist, I have the following dream: A famous young pianist named Yin Yang is invited to play with a very prestigious symphony orchestra. When asked by the conductor what he would like to play, he says, "Chopsticks."[20]

Occasionally, I stray out of the scientific arena (and sometimes the humorous one), into the moralistic or theological. Again, it's as if some unknown part of me is doing "automatic writing," which I am surprised to read when I awake the next morning. This is the "dictation" I took down in the bathroom light one early morning:

> I am instructing the young on the proper response to life: "You are privileged to be here, to be alive," I tell them. "Respect the earth and honor God, the Creator. Help the poor and sick. Behave in ways that bring credit to humankind. Be kind to animals, which are our kin in creation. Be grateful for the beauty of the earth and nature. Nurture and respect it. Give thanks for the gift of life. Make your life a work of art."

If this sounds more like a homily than a dream of someone committed to science, then I must be taking on some of the character of Dr. McGehee. My dream writing often surprises me, but my biggest jolt didn't come in "automatic writing." My biggest emotional charge in REM sleep came when I had the tornado/locomotive dream.

Pittman gives talks on Jonah, the Biblical prophet, finally "coming to himself" in a storm after trying to flee from God.[21] I now am beginning to see that coming to myself is a message that I keep getting both in and out of my dreams. I am waking up to what I am meant to be; honoring my Self, my soul, rather than my ego. I am learning that dreams, including daydreams, do speak to our souls and can tell us about our essence, our core archetypal "acorn."

Pittman learned something from the dream message of his dead father. I have learned from my dead daughter. I see Liz sometimes in my dreams, as if she is assuring me that she will come to me on occasion. Shortly after midnight one Wednesday, I record this: "I check all parameters for sleeping and dreaming. Then I go to sleep and, as I expected, Liz comes up, or the dream command for Liz lights up. I feel secure in the knowledge that there is a dream command for Liz, and I am grateful she will reappear."

Although I am still learning from dreams of shit and from shadows, I am also becoming aware that shadows can be positive and awaken us to truths as much as dreams can. The shadow of sickness is an example. It may point me to finding soul. In addition to Dr. McGehee, my teachers on this particular theme have been neurologist Oliver Sacks, Jungian Jean Shinoda Bolen and author/medical director Rachel Naomi Remen.[22] Since prehistoric times, soul, dreams and debility have been associated. Early philosophers regarded dreams as activities of the soul.[23] Primitive people, anthropologists conjectured, "were greatly troubled by two biological enigmas: the difference between a living body and a dead one, and the human-seeming shapes in dreams and visions."[24] The soul was seen as the key to understanding such mysteries. On death, the soul leaves the body for another realm. In dreams, the soul wanders away from the body visiting places and performing acts the dreamer dreams.

What soul and dreams have in common neurologically is that they are represented in that implicit part of the brain deeper than words. More than a decade ago, Oliver Sacks coupled "neurology and the soul." In the deep limbic brain, and its multiple connections to other areas, the soul will animate us even when disease or injury have immobilized and silenced us. As in a dream, we can again gain the wholeness soul represents. In fact, in dreaming we may experience once again what it's like to be whole, to feel free of disease or injury.[25] Our old friend the amygdala seems to make the impossible possible in dreaming.

Music, acting, performing, or worshipping can activate the soul and brain in the very presence of Parkinsonism, sleeping sickness, post-encephalitis syndromes and other neuronal lesions. Sacks tells of a patient with Korsakov's syndrome, a profound impairment of memory due to alcohol-induced damage to the brain, who would be totally disconnected and disoriented until he participated in the rite of Mass. He would then "come together" completely. The Mass would enable him to regain coherence and meaning and to recover for the time being "his own continuity of soul."[26] The neuroscientist Rhawn Joseph looks to the amygdala, and its place in the inferior temporal lobe, for such re-experiencing of the soul. Joseph also states that "the right hemisphere and limbic system which are responsible for dreaming dreams 'speak different languages,'" which "cannot always be transferred to and understood by the left hemisphere." Although the left hemisphere "observes the dream," it may forget it upon waking. The images and impressions thus "remain unconscious."[27]

Many patients with Tourette's syndrome had been musicians, athletes or actors, Sacks observes. This disease causes violent compulsive tics and compulsions. But in the very act of "making music, of batting, of acting, of performing, they completely cease to be Tourettic." Concentration of movement, in a creative task of driving, playing, acting or making love could provide a temporary "cure" for Tourette's as well as Parkisonism.[28]

Sacks had one patient with massive frontal lobe damage, "rendering him completely 'flat' emotionally. But he loved music (country music especially) and when he sang, as he sometimes did spontaneously, he would come alive in the most remarkable way." Through the music, his soul—deeper than his cortical damage—had the power to transcend his disability and give him back what his cortex had lost.[29] As long as our amygdala and caudate nucleus are free of damage, we often retain the capacity to reexperience our deepest loves and be moved—literally—by them.[30]

The noted Italian neurologist A. R. Luria once defined science as "the ascent to the concrete."[31] For all of us who have suffered injury, disease and disability, our case history is recorded by our physicians and healthcare providers. However, above, beneath and beyond case histories, we have an essential personal biography which is closer to who we are or are meant to be. Sacks recognized that it is at the intersection of biology and biography that we find clues to the soul, our source of animation and full life. The taproots of who we are and are meant to be come from the soul's neuronal companion, the amygdala, a fairly large aggregate of small nuclei hidden inside the temporal lobe. The "essential personal biography" of Sacks is more recently relevant to the "narrative medicine" developed by Dr. Rita Charon of Columbia University.[32]

Paradoxically, disease and disability may be the way we connect with soul, as well as with the deepest parts of our personal biography and narrative. Dr. Bolen, a physician who is also a Jungian analyst, says that illness can "bring us close to the bone, to the essence of who we are and what we are here for at a soul level."[33] She also notes that "what we believe or feel in our bones are matters to do with soul." Soul, then, speaks to us in ways deeper and stronger than words. Archetypes, representing images and symbols full of numinous energy, speak the language of soul, as dreams do. Soul uses the amygdala to voice our essence. Dreams, intuitions and "funny feelings" often have important messages to give us about ourselves if we pay attention. Sometimes it takes serious injury or disease to get our attention. I have been a slow learner on this point. However, I now have had enough happen that I am listening to what's being said to me on a level deeper than words. Dreams speak the deeper language of the unconscious, as do our shadows and soul.

If soul is in the deep part of us that is verbally silent, it is far from quiet. The "acorn" that is the core of who we are will keep pushing and punching away at the hard soil of our consciousness until it can break through and be noticed. In both Jungian theory and neuroscience, consciousness is not just a state of being awake and aware, but also one that is "evaluative. It imparts value."[34] My therapist, well versed in all that is Jungian, says, "Consciousness is a knowing integrated with value and meaning."[35] To have such consciousness requires becoming fully acquainted with the unconscious, which includes dreams.

The research neuropsychoanalyst Mark Solms notes that the evaluative function of consciousness tells us whether something feels good or bad to us. In so doing it monitors us viscerally and presides over the "delicate economy of the internal milieu of our bodies," letting us know when we have exceeded set-points having to do with such vital things as temperature and blood sugar level.[36] As we have seen, dreams reflect some of our feelings about what is going on in our bodies and lives. An example is Mona Lisa Schulz and her dreams.

Antonio Damasio, another widely published neuroscientist, is convinced that emotions and feelings "were crucial to the evolution of consciousness and, along with it, a sense of self."[37] His theory is also body-based, holding that emotion is a change in body state in response to a stimulus, while a feeling represents that change in the brain and leads to mental images and readout of one's "life state." Body and brain, then, through consciousness, provide us with what Damasio calls "the feeling of what happens."[38]

Damasio looks for the homeostatic dynamic and value of feelings, which can be so extreme that all balance is lost. Sadness, "a form of crying out for comfort and support with few tears," he says, "can be protective in the right circumstances, for example, when it helps us adapt to personal loss."[39] But Damasio also recognizes that the "malignant" sadness or sorrow of depression is self-destructive. "In the long run," he notes, "it is cumulatively harmful and can cause cancer, in this case, of the soul."[40] The hubris of a demanding ego may drive our self-destruction by mocking and belittling us for our losses and failures.

So soul, whether battered or whole, is now commanding the attention of both research and clinical scientists. Elio Frattaroli, a psychoanalyst affiliated with the University of Pennsylvania, sees soul as "the place where experiencing happens."[41] In fact, he sees the "soul as the experiencing self, the 'I'"—with "thoughts, feelings, images, sensations" being part of what we experience.[42] Jungians capitalize the "S" to refer to the Self that is synonymous with soul and doesn't become subordinate to ego. The Self's neuronal connections extend to higher layers of the brain, such as the medial prefrontal cortex near the top. Here a sense of self, with a little "s," is experienced. When this portion is damaged by disease or injury, a person may no longer seem to be himself or herself—as in the famous neurological case of Phineas Gage.[43]

Our visceral sensations may speak to us in terms of a dream or a gut feeling and what we sense in our bones and soul.[44] Visual imagery, as in dreams or daydreams, may also speak deep truths that "mere mortals" overlook. Einstein could "visualize" his equations. Mozart would go on a walk and "see" as well as hear a symphony or concerto as a whole in his mind's eye and ear.[45] The somatosensory regions of the brain are triggered in such experiences, as well as feelings of "chills," "thrills," "trills" or tingling resulting from aesthetically pleasing art and other forms of beauty. There's no teasing apart sensation, dreams, hunches, intuitions or other feelings in terms of where in the mind and brain they originate. The truest and most profound seem to involve the amygdala nuclei and represent the soul, but other areas are involved due to the interconnectivity of brain modules and regions.

Jung spoke of "feeling" as knowing the value of something from the perspective of sensation.[46] In his lengthy investigations of consciousness, he became convinced that there is consciousness in the unconscious. Certainly in many dreams, we experience being conscious, although the dreams come from the unconscious. Edward Edinger, a "classic Jungian," discussed both in his classic work, *Science of the Soul.* He says, "All we know about consciousness is what individuals experience; it's a term describing an experience" and the reflection on it.[47] The soul is at the seat of it. And the amygdala gives it color.

Body, mind and soul, then, are inseparable. The brain and the biology of consciousness are coupled with the psychological to give us a way to "feel in our bones" and sense whether we are being true to who we really are. When our shadow drives us to wear masks and use our personas to pretend we are something we are not, then we have problems. There is, then, a painful, gnawing conflict between what our consciousness tells us in our bones and soul and what our masks keep presenting to the world—a misrepresentation of who we really are.

I can speak from experience on persona. I started wearing a mask when my mother insisted I was a little boy who never met a stranger, the extraverted little guy who became leader of his grade school band. My history since then became a twisted tilt toward achieving and acquiring power and prestige, garnering plaques and awards to display as trophies on the wall. In the process, I was defying some principal archetypal laws of dynamics, which tell us that when we get too carried away with position and power, neglecting close connections with others and something bigger than ego, we are skating on thin ice.[48] Our body and brain, through consciousness and soul as well as dreams, keep ringing an alarm we hear but ignore. They may be urging us to embrace our shadows. Sooner or later, the ice breaks and we sink into dark, cold waters. In near drowning, illness or disability may be what rescues us and importunes us to seek archetypal parity.

Until we do achieve balance, our dark side and negative shadow will remain perched on our shoulders like a raven, mocking our masquerade and belittling our performance, which is full of sound and fury, signifying nothing. Our dreams will keep trying to teach us.

However, if we ignore them, what we have repressed—whether it is our true nature or our brokenness or our deceit—will come back to haunt us, usually in very painful ways. What I carry in my shadow bag is shame-based, driving me to try to substitute achievement for affiliation with too little attention to my two daughters and son. With my younger daughter and one son, I tried to override their shame and my own by "becoming somebody," somebody who would also make up for what my parents never had. My ambitious mother and faithful father would have been proud enough to continue seeing my byline on front page newspaper articles and cover stories in magazines. But my shadow, driven by ego, demanded more. So I kept climbing until finally my belly broke, my neuronal tree withered, and my ego defenses collapsed. There's no way to hide from myself and others a major depression or a colostomy bag. What I have continued to hide inwardly is anger at my own guilt and weakness.

Shame and guilt are twins, lodged in deep parts of the brain. The insula, which houses them, is visible only when the overlying cortexes are retracted.[49] James Hillman, a well published Jungian psychologist, says the "cure" of the shadow is loving all of ourselves, our inferiorities, defects and self-loathings so that we come to appreciate "the paradox that rotten garbage is also fertilizer."[50] To transform my shit, Pittman is helping me recognize that under all the manure there is a pony. The only ponies either of us had in our lives as children were stage props for our mothers to have pictures made of us, dressed up in cowboy outfits.

Baseball is still the image I like most. My analyst, the star athlete in high school and college, reminds me again of baseball's archetypal power. On one level are the grime and grit, sweat and tears—the profane. On another is the sacred, the hero's journey and the sublime feeling of running the bases and coming home.

Pittman, impressed with the power of darkness, reminds his audiences that those who suffer and dwell in darkness are being given an opportunity for soul-making. And what good is that? I ask him. By soul-making, we connect with wholeness and the true health behind and underneath our mask. The more soul we have, the more abundant our life. Dr. McGehee promises that "the abundant life is about finding… the quintessential element, which we are not going to find anywhere but in our own little simple life…. The thing we seek is who we are"[51]—all of which takes me back to finding my "acorn" and knowing what I am here for.

With that discovery, our amygdala sings and our limbic system experiences a social synchrony with others and the world. In the central nucleus of the amygdala are the biochemical mechanisms for many connections,[52] rich in opioids, which contribute to our capacity for "almond joy," warmth in relationships and connecting to God. The Jungian science on the subject of soul, then, complements the neuroscience.[53] Both speak of something deep, complex, substantive and symbolic, charged with numinous energy, waiting to infuse all those who are true to who they are. For me, as I edge closer to the light, it will be more of a transmutation confirming the alchemical formula of turning dross into gold.

CHAPTER 7

SEX AND SHAME

THE STORY

The intuitive I have as a therapist and priest gives me a new mantra today. I am to repeat inwardly: *Brain chemistry, stop fucking with my head. I love you, but get in balance.* Pittman is well acquainted with both the conscious and unconscious mantras stuck in my cortex. On waking, I still find myself thinking, *There's no point to the struggle, but to struggle.* The silent voice of my unconscious mantra is terser and more to the point: *You're not good enough,* it tells me. On bad days, the litany becomes, *You're no good,* and during the darkest hours that still haunt me, the default message is, *You're shit.* Depression recedes slowly, like a glacier.

The vulgar new mantra, I realize, is a prescription that is in keeping with neuropsychiatric findings, based on advances in brain imaging. Talk is not "just words," but biology, meaning it can change neuronal connections and transmission.[1] Strong, "affect" words are needed to displace the present mantra I have. For the story synthesizer in my frontal lobe to change its tune, new pathways must be laid down in my neuronal tree. The words Dr. McGehee has given me to repeat should be powerful enough to help dislodge my negative script. They constitute packets of archetypal energy constellated around basic functions of elimination and reproduction.

Pittman feels that my "mind is okay" and my behavior appropriate, but my brain machinery has some crossed wires and this throws the electrical transmission and chemistry out of whack. Convinced that shadows are to be embraced and not rejected or repressed, my teacher tells me to love the fuck-up in my head. Such paradoxing would have seemed senseless to me a few months ago, but now I am beginning to see that good and bad, light and dark, positive and negative are archetypal poles inherent in nature, human and otherwise. My job is to let the light absorb—embrace—the dark, and not try to obliterate it, which is impossible. In Jungian terms, "light" is synonymous with increased awareness and consciousness.[2]

My priest the therapist has put a new emotional charge into our analytic container. "Fucking" has a stronger emotional valence than embracing, although I am told to love what my "fucking brain chemistry" is doing to my head. If there is another paradox involved here, then I recognize it as more of that big word Pittman likes to show people he can still spell: "enantiodromia." Jung said that "this characteristic phenomenon practically always occurs when an extreme, one-sided tendency dominates conscious life; in time an equally powerful counterposition is built up, which first inhibits the conscious performance and subsequently breaks through the conscious control."[3] And, from personal experience, I would add that when the counter characteristic or tendency crashes into our awareness, all hell breaks loose.

The discovery that I make today, as our therapeutic dance builds up steam and I listen to the new mantra in my head, is that there is still more anger I haven't dealt with. "Fuck" and "shit," any good Anglo-Saxon dictionary tells us, are offensive terms to express anger (see exceptions in The Science below). Depression and anger are literally bedmates. I know this from the rage I have felt toward myself for being impotent for long periods, unable to perform "like a man." Rita has always been understanding, not demanding. She has had the wisdom to know that once my brain chemistry does stop fucking with me, I will be myself again. Meanwhile, my wife's understanding extends to sharing a bed where her husband wakes up lying in his own shit. If the seal on my colostomy bag loosens during the night, leakage occurs. And so does my rage.

I am just one of the more than 70,000 people a year in this country and Canada who have to undergo colostomies and have to wear "The Bag," as Richard M. Cohen termed it in his series of fine essays in *Science Times* of the *New York Times*, and more recently of a book.[4] Cohen, a 55-year-old television journalist and producer, notes:

> There is no human walking the earth who does not share this function of the body. Yet we seem to regard it with shame. I was sentenced to see, indeed to stare at, what my body was producing. I wondered why this plastic bag had to be transparent. This seems a cruelty, as if our faces must be rubbed in our bad behavior, like pushing a dog's nose into his overnight misconduct.[5]

As to the sexual shame that I have felt, Cohen's experience parallels mine. He comments that "The Bag" is like a "sissy pouch for transporting that which everyone else turns a back to.... As for a sense of my own sexuality, forget it. I instantly became asexual." Cohen's adversity is compounded by multiple sclerosis, which is making him blind. His travail makes mine seem small, although clinical depression seems to have escaped him.

So now is the time for me to recite my litany of shit, anger, sex and shame to my therapist. It begins with the following body blows: four times my belly is sliced open across a span of months, leading first to a sacrifice of most of my sigmoid colon. Next I give up a hernia in my crotch, followed by a reconnection of the remaining parts of my lower colon. Then, one midnight, adhesions from my sigmoidectomy start strangling my upper colon, the ileum, and I sacrifice another foot of bowel. Twice I nearly died, according to my surgeons. More than twice I have been feeling dead in every fiber of my being except for a twinge of slow locomotion, which barely gets me out of bed.

The reason I am confessing all this to my partner the priest is that I feel so betrayed by my body for failing me. I am full of unacknowledged rage, which has been a deep, dark shadow for years. The revenge it has taken on my inflated ego has been through the body that is now mocking me in my frailty: I'm the professor who never declared a sick day for twenty-nine years; I'm the guy who climbed mountains with my young wife of thirty years, led by our Tibetan dogs, who can go higher and faster than either of us. I'm the ball of fire who talked my wife, asthmatic as a child, into marathon running, refusing to stop until we had done New York City three times and Boston once. I'm the adventurer who went to the Antarctic and returned to persuade Rita—who loves the balmy beaches of Acapulco and Maui—into camping out in the snow at 8500 feet in the Rockies, on acres we ended up buying.

There is a madness in all this that I need to acknowledge. It's a mania that has driven me in between depressions. Its purpose has been to keep me so preoccupied with frantic activity that the pain in my belly becomes secondary. It is overshadowed by sheer physical movement. "Multitasking" is too weak a word to describe all the performing I have made myself do. The ache in the belly long preceded the explosion of my gut. I discovered that only sex gave me temporary relief. Sex meant a momentary surcease. Otherwise, I couldn't sit still: I jiggled my feet, I fidgeted and I paced floors as part of the madness. I made my persona appear calm, but underneath was a storm. My house of cards crashed down with my emergency surgery at Mount Sinai.

Now, in keeping with the old "not good enough" mantra I have sworn to give up, I'm a shadow of myself who can barely drag my sore belly and stiff legs out of bed each morning. As my therapist sits and listens, in his customary posture of feet on the coffee table between us, I remind him of the promise I made before embarking on this long, dark night of the soul and our journey in the belly of the whale.

"I promised that I would never lapse into self-pity. What I'm telling you today is not out of pity, but anger and shame. I'll give you an example: I'm with Rita, her mother and stepfather at the symphony. We couldn't get our usual seats, which give me easy access to an exit, because we have Rose Alma and Ed with us. The only seats available turn out to be smack in the middle of center orchestra; this means I am trapped between thirty or forty people on each side, before there's an exit I can take to go to the toilet. I start feeling my colostomy pouch puffing up. There's a noticeable and typical intestinal growling and a popping sound of the stoma from a build up of gas. I know what's coming, but feel helpless. Shit starts filling up the bag. There's a stink I can't hide. Meanwhile, Rita, her mother and Ed try to keep their eyes and ears trained on the soloist playing Mozart's Piano Concerto No. 21, a favorite of mine under more auspicious circumstances. As the last chords of piano and orchestra are played, I start stumbling over pairs of feet excusing myself clumsily as I head toward the exit. Once safely inside a men's room stall, I dump the contents of my pouch into the toilet, feeling relief only in the belly. In every other part of psyche and soma, I feel deep anger and shame."

Pittman nods and says nothing. He learned a long time ago from Dr. Robert Johnson, his wise training supervisor, to keep his mouth shut. "Pittman," Dr. Johnson told him, "if you will just sit and listen and keep your mouth shut, patients tend to get better."

As Pittman thinks of the healing power of silence, I am thinking the words, *Fuck you, Blair. You were the guy so full of self-righteous ego that you would never allow yourself to think, much less say, the fucking word.*

Finally I decide to make myself speak what I am thinking and say out loud the ego-forbidden words. "I've never even had 'fuck' in my vocabulary. I went through the navy without it. I heard fuck this and fuck that every hour. I heard it repeatedly in newspaper city rooms where I worked for many years before becoming a professor. I even hear it on occasion in the cloistered halls of academia. But my ego has kept feeding me the line and lie that I'm above such language. I lost a good friend in the navy because of such hubris. Our ship was in port and my friend had been ashore and came in half-drunk and shook my bunk. He wanted to tell me of his sexual excursions fucking women. I righteously reprimanded him, and we were never close again."

So now I have been given dispensation by the priest sitting with me in the whale's belly to tell my ego to go fuck itself. Pittman is not above profanity, because he thinks the profane is camouflage for the sacred. He's also not above anger and hatred. "Did I ever tell you," he says, breaking silence, "that when I left the church payroll and stopped being a cathedral dean and parish priest, I was left with making a living as a full-time Jungian analyst, teacher and lecturer. The vestry and other parishioners gave me a big retirement party. After a few rounds of drinks and conviviality, I was jovially buttonholed by a senior partner in a big law firm, who makes sizeable donations to the cathedral."

Half-tight, this power broker put his head and breath a few inches from Pittman's face and bellowed, "Welcome to the real world, Pittman. Now you will learn what it's like to make a living like the rest of us."

Already allergic to being viewed as a navel-gazer who sits around praying, Pittman lifted himself up to his full basketball star height of six feet, four inches and, sticking his face into that of his taunter, he growled, "Listen to me, you goddamned son of a bitch, and I'll tell you about the unreal world I have been living in all these years. Have you ever baptized a dying sixteen-ounce infant in an incubator with a Q-tip, as sobbing parents look on? Have you ever knocked on a front door at 2 A.M. to inform a mother that her beloved teenager and only child has been killed in a car crash? Have you ever gone to the bed of a dying colleague and not just held her hand, but got in the bed and wrapped your arms around her as she died?"

It is my turn just to listen and let our mutually attuned limbic systems and souls do their silent communication in a language deeper than words. I get the impression that my angry priest also bestowed a "fuck you, mister" on his speechless, real-world aggressor. So Pittman lets me know that even an agent of God doesn't stuff all his anger in a shadow bag. But does that mean my analyst has no shadow? The only one he is willing to acknowledge to me is a fellow preacher, Jimmy Swaggart. This television star on the God circuit was the antithesis of the dignified and stately Very Reverend J. Pittman McGehee. It's my teacher's belief that the Reverend Swaggart wore two pounds of hairspray on his head to keep his giant coiffure held together. But to save the Reverend McGehee from ego inflation, God mercifully gave the priest a lesson in humility.

For years, Pittman transformed the faithful with his spellbinding, consciousness-expanding (or altering) sermons. A white-haired widow soaked up every word each Sunday from a front pew. And every Sunday after the 11 A.M. service ended, she went promptly home and drank herself into an alcoholic stupor. It was a weekly ritual until one Sunday, in the stupor, she began channel surfing and landed on the Reverend Jimmy Swaggart. He peered over his plexiglass television lectern, looked her square in the eye and said, "God loves you, and don't even try to understand it. It's all grace, all grace." The widow left her bottle and chair and went straight to the telephone. She called a friend whom she knew was in Alcoholic Anonymous. She told her she was ready to join, thanks to Jimmy Swaggart and his two pounds of sprayed hair. The fundamentalist television preacher succeeded in doing what the Reverend Dr. McGehee, with his polysyllabic pronouncements and hypnogogic words, failed at. Pittman has never since questioned God's autonomy to use even a priest's own shadow to puncture hubris.

Now the ball is back in my court to confront—that is, embrace—some of the origins of stuffing anger into the bag of shadows that is now literally attached to my body, my shit/shadow, inescapable and omnipresent.

The day my anger was bagged and caged was unforgettable. I was nine years old and sitting at the breakfast table on a warm summer morning. My father was in the kitchen making coffee. My grandfather, Dadoo, was sitting across the table from me pouring some Post bran flakes into my bowl. My brother was still in the back bedroom where we slept. My mother was in the front bedroom recovering from surgery. She had been brought home by my father two days earlier from the hospital, where nonmalignant lumps had been removed from her breasts.

Dadoo told me, as he often did, to sit up straight, drink my milk and eat my breakfast cereal. Suddenly my father stood in the open doorway between the kitchen and small breakfast room. His face was red, his knuckles white. He shouted at my grandfather, "Stop correcting my son! He is my boy, not yours! You're always telling him what to do. That's my job, not yours. I'm sick and tired of it!"

I had never seen my father express anger verbally. I heard my mother screaming from her bed, "Please, please, stop it! Stop it!" I was terrified by what was going on. My grandfather got up, walked past my father without a word, went to the back bedroom, where he also slept, and began packing his one suitcase. Within an hour, he was gone. The man all the neighborhood kids loved, the man who carved the wooden figures I played with, the man who entertained us with stories of playing in circus bands. Gone. My mother cried in her room. My daddy was no longer red in the face. He held Mama's hand for a little while as she cried. Then he put on his coat and tie and left for the streetcar a block away. It was before he loses his job in the Depression, so he went to work.

That was the first and biggest lesson I learned about the terrible power of anger. The second occurred on the playground at my grade school. I said something mean to my best friend, Stephen, and he punched me in the stomach. It was a blow that pained me for years. Eventually we made up, but I learned that anger is awful.

Third lesson: My brother and I were roughhousing in the back bedroom, wrestling around, as we had done before. I accidentally kicked him in the crotch. Mama came home and he told her I had kicked him in the balls. It sounded as if I had done something dirty, because in our wrestling, my foot hit his testicles. She was horrified and spanked me. I learnt that even playing like I was mad is dangerous. So into the bag anger goes, only to come back years later in a chronic aching in the belly and, finally, a full-blown explosion.

Sex, shame and anger get all mixed up in my shadow bag. Because the Depression teaches me that being idle like my father when he is out of work is also to be feared, I decide early that I must always keep busy. Not working makes me feel guilty. Even pleasure has this effect. The only play I permit myself after my discharge from the navy and graduation from college is sex. I end up marrying my first wife for sex. After that, my desire for sex as a release leads to a series of clandestine affairs with many women. My ego even encourages it. It tells me I not only can hold down two jobs at once, I can even fuck two different women on the same night. The meaning of sex to me, however, is more than a feeding of the ego. It also provides a physical escape, fleeting as it may be, from the pain in my belly.

My first episode of depression follows a railroad trip to El Paso, an assignment given to me as a reporter for the *Fort Worth Star-Telegram*. En route I write a feature story on the retired conductors aboard who are being given the trip by the T&P Railroad in appreciation of their long service. I join the two public relations agents in the group for a night on the town in Juarez, across the border. They take me to a seedy bar and strip joint, where the highlight of the evening features two big-breasted young women, wearing only G-strings, going through sexual maneuvers, with one strapping on a large wooden penis to fuck the other. I vomit on the train back home, have a bout of diarrhea and start a slow, steady descent into depression. As soon as the dark slide hits me, my ego goes into hiding. I am left with guilt as a companion, joined by shame and a reminder of all the lies and deceit that were necessary to live the kind of life that my depression put an end to.

I look up to see if I have put Pittman asleep. I have been looking down all this time while sharing all these never-discussed secrets. A head-down posture is appropriate for shame. My therapist hasn't been sleeping, though. He's been listening and remembering what Dr. Johnson told him.

THE SCIENCE

The science of affective language is evolving out of the neuropsychiatric revolution in medicine and the advanced technology that allows us to watch the brain change as a function of "just words"—and the meaning we give to them. That talk is biological in its effects means that words are not mere abstractions having no bearing on physical health. Both the unconscious parts of who we are and the conscious areas of the brain listen carefully to what we say to ourselves and to others and respond in chemical terms.[1] While the words we say to others may deliberately mask what we are feeling, our internal dialogue is what the brain and body respond to. It's what we are saying to ourselves that reflects the true meaning of our experience.[2]

Although the "forbidden" in American English has shrunk considerably since the "Free Speech" movement of the 1960s, there are still enough "taboo" words to justify a book on the subject.[3] In both Spears's *Forbidden American English* and the time-honored *Oxford*

English Dictionary, scatological terms—namely, shit and all its derivatives—head the list of "taboo" words, followed by sex and its countless neologisms. An example is "abso-fucking-lutely," which is classified as "typical male-to-male talk."[4] As to creative uses of "shit," the navy taught me that only a dummy "doesn't know the difference between shit and Shinola;" a staple chow line breakfast offering is "shit on a shingle."

Our brain, then, gets daily doses of language that light up the prefrontal cortex and its close connections with the limbic system. The amygdala, in the emotional second layer of our evolving brain, is a "first responder," in 9/11 language, to what we experience inwardly and express outwardly in primary emotions, such as anxiety, anger, shame and humiliation.[5] It transmits the information that appears on its radar screen to a vast network of other nuclei. The hypothalamus, a control center in the middle of the brain, comes on line and directs chemical and electrical activity in both the central nervous system and the hormonal system. Memories begin to be laid down first in the non-declarative part of the self and later in the hippocampus, the verbal part. The center of the soul, our invisible essence, feels the reverberations of all this spoken and unspoken, conscious and unconscious, neuronal activity.[6]

When the brain uses strong words to express an experience, the body reacts accordingly and turns on a panoply of stress chemicals to meet the challenge. However, the challenge is not usually a physical threat. It is the meaning we give to nonphysical events, situations, failures and frustration that produces distress and causes the body to react as if it is being physically threatened. If we and our ego appraise the words and symbols as awful, terrible, catastrophic, the body turns on high levels of norepinephrine, epinephrine and cortisol, which over time turn against us, causing damage to arteries, brain tissue and the gut.[7] If our shadow bag is full of complexes, the ego is almost certain to react strongly and try to keep them stuffed out of awareness.[8]

To understand more fully the powerful effect that language and symbols have on psyche and soma, we must turn to specific words and their images. One word that captures the forbidden feelings behind piss, shit and "The Bag" is "yuck." The science of yuck is no more of a joke than the scatological archetypes constellated around shame, sex and anger. The premier science journal, *Nature,* bestowed recognition on "the yuck factor" in a "science update," which focused on the universal nature of disgust.[9] "Yuck" has been reported as possibly the only word that requires no translation across cultures and nationalities.[10] Its very sound conveys disgust, which is only a few steps removed from shame[11] and clustered in the same part of the emotional brain.

The feelings of disgust and shame have been subjects for social psychologists to probe. Jon Haidt of the University of Virginia, an "intuitionist," has given people fried grasshoppers to eat in his study of disgust. Observing people's reactions when asked to try on a T-shirt allegedly worn by Adolph Hitler falls under Haidt's category of "moral disgust."[12] Although such sleazy subjects as shame and disgust are shadows that require exploring, if not embracing, they do not preclude expressions of the "higher" side of human behavior, which Haidt calls "elevation" emotions.[13] While our core sense of self, our soul, seeks transcendent meaning, our material self, anchored in the body, strives for comfort and freedom from pain.[14] As I well know, sex can deflect attention from bodily pain, though anger and shame later aggravate it.

The study of anger, sex and shame is closely linked with the science of the gut. One of the points at which neuroscience and Jungian psychology converge is where both physical instinct and psychic instinct come together in the anatomy of the bowel. As indicated in chapter 3, neuroscience has found that the gut, like the heart, has its own brain.[15] Michael Gershon, M.D., of Columbia University College of Physicians and Surgeons has observed, "We have more nerve cells in our gut than in the entire remainder of our peripheral nervous system. The enteric nervous system is also a vast chemical warehouse within which is represented every one of the classes of neurotransmitter found in the brain."[16] Thus, when Candace Pert, Ph.D., then chief of the section on brain biochemistry at the National Institute of Mental Health, said in 1986 that "emotions are not just in the limbic brain, they're in the body," it portended recognition of the new field of neurogastroenterology.[17] Having a gut feeling, Pert added, is more than a figure of speech. I should know. I ignored what my bowel was trying to tell me until it finally ruptured and nearly killed me.

Jungians have recognized that the metaphors for which the gut is famous carry such power because they are archetypal—standing for symbols and images that both attract and repel us. Examples: "spill our guts," "haven't got the guts" or "gut it out." The powerful, primary emotions of anger and shame are played out in the gut, which is one of the body's advanced sensors for reflecting what the brain and mind are feeling. Just as the gut carries out signals from the head, the bowel often senses trouble or truth before the cerebral brain does. It's called "gut instinct," the subtitle of Gershon's 1998 book *The Second Brain.* Gut instinct is related to the function of intuition in Jungian typology.

Dr. McGehee prides himself on working almost exclusively as "an intuitive." He intuits, he tells listeners on occasion, what quantum physicists and theoreticians like Stephen Hawking require blackboards of equations to explain.[18] It seems that Hawking's no-boundary hypothesis corresponds with my teacher's intuition that God and the universe continue to evolve.[19] It follows, then, Pittman believes, that our job as mere mortals is to contribute the best we can to this cosmic expansion by at least endeavoring to increase our own consciousness and awareness of what's going on both around us and inside us. I need to ask my teacher if his colossal intuition of where all the stars, satellites, galaxies and universes are headed comes to him intestinally. It hurts my own gut just to imagine such prescient power.

On a more earthy plane, one of the emotions that the gut feels and expresses early on is anger. Anger has been the subject of medical and psychological science since early-day diagnosticians, both here and abroad, recognized that men can get so red in the face with rage that they drop over dead from a heart attack.[20] Repressed anger can also be dangerous. It becomes a shadow, hidden in the invisible bag we drag behind us. The only difference is that its poison takes longer to kill us than overt rage does. Female anger, expressed or repressed, is often more subtle, but just as potent. Studies by Janice Kiecolt-Glaser of Ohio State, who holds academic appointments not only in psychology, but also in medicine and immunology, show that levels of the stress chemical cortisol can predict divorce two years ahead of what newlywed wives prefer to admit about their marital "bliss."[21] What a young wife is willing to acknowledge may be the opposite of what she is holding back and what her stress measures show. Cortisol is a sentinel chemical that the body uses to tell the truth of what the ego denies.

The science of my anger, more so than that of my mentor's, was telling me for years what my gut already knew too well in its brain. I had suppressed, repressed and projected this highly unacceptable part of me, which I learned early on gets me in big trouble. Meanwhile, my belly kept trying to awaken me by chronic abdominal aching. My ears refused to hear the alarm bell my amygdala kept ringing. Where does such anger avoidance start? Developmental neuroscientists say that it begins in the early, face-to-face, preverbal language and rhythmic dance that occurs between baby and mother.[22] The baby's limbic loops are on the lookout for signs of disapproval, which, if present, are encoded in the developing brain and remind a child that his job is to please the parent even if it cramps his belly. A relationship that looks storybook good and loving from the outside may have a different tale to tell from the inside. The shadow bag starts filling up early when failure to please transactions keep recurring outside while forbidden anger is experienced internally.[23] Shame is a lowly handmaiden of the anger generated by failure to fulfill powerful needs to grow and separate as well as to please parents.

As for sex and its organs of expression, babies become fascinated with these curious body protrusions and orifices early on. "That's not nice" is the command heard for explorations of such openings and extensions. More graphic is a baby's first encounters with feces. The "science" of shit at this point is very simple: touching, smearing and smelling the stuff is a form of play to the baby. To horrified adults it is a forever forbidden no-no. The external demand is quickly translated in the autonomic nervous system so as to ring the stress chemical alarm bell if the transgression doesn't stop. Even if the behavior does stop, it may not be extinguished. It is simply transferred to the unconscious and its appendage, the shadow bag.

Along with anger and shame comes disgust. Charles Darwin recognized disgust in his studies of faces and features.[24] The great English naturalist wrote scientific treatises about the facial features of humans and animals showing different emotions. Disgust, like other primary emotions, produces characteristic expressions of the eyes, mouth and nose. Expressions of disgust mean something is so distasteful that it is poisonous or dangerous. Yet disgust is not only biological, it is also moral in its functions. William I. Miller of the University of Michigan Law School, in his book *The Anatomy of Disgust,* notes that when enough people in a society brand something as disgusting, laws are made to prohibit it.[25] Egregious examples of sexual acts or art end up in the courts. Society is saying to perpetrators: "Shame on you." Shame is about a personal feeling, while guilt is attached to acts or behaviors that a culture frowns on or forbids by law, according to Professor Miller. We come with innate social emotions, both positive and negative, upon which our survival as a species depends. Included are shame and embarrassment, as well as kindness and compassion.[26]

Psychologists and sociologists, who have struggled for decades to define the difference between shame and guilt, are now in general agreement that, as lawyer Miller indicates, shame focuses on self while guilt is about behavior. The empirical evidence indicates that shame is more pathogenic; that is, it is strongly associated with depressive disorders.[27] Attribution styles are another way to distinguish between shame and guilt. Explanatory or causal attribution is another name for these styles. The cause of shame to the person feeling it is himself. As he sees it, the shame pervades everything in his life and is permanent. The shame and self-blame, then, are internal, stable and global—known as the ISG style or PPP, for personal, permanent and pervasive.[28]

For one who has such as style—me, for instance—the recurring tendency is to say, when bad things happen, "It's my fault, it always happens like this, and it's ruining everything in my life." With guilt, the attributions are also internal, but more specific to one occasion and are non-global. The person feels the guilty emotion, but it is tied specifically to a single act and doesn't tarnish everything else. My therapist, Pittman, makes the distinction simple: With guilt, the internal dialogue is, *I made a mistake*. With shame, it is, *I am a mistake*. The feeling of "I am a mistake" is the very opposite of a sense of "good enough," which analyst D. W. Winnicott recognized is lost through trauma.[29]

Sex, shit and piss are subjects that can arouse shame among those who feel they are "not good enough," which includes persons with depressive disorders and PPP explanatory styles. People whose bodies require "outdoor plumbing," as my wife calls it, characteristically feel shame. They are among the thousands who have to wear external colostomy bags to catch their feces. They are called "ostomates." I know from having been an ostomate in the "Ostomy Society." Ostomy refers to a bodily opening that is not natural or normal. Surgeons created an opening in my belly to collect excrement while my remaining colon healed and remained separated in two parts. Colostomies and other ostomies are made necessary by surgery for such disorders as cancer, ulcerative colitis, diverticulitus or Crohn's disease.[30] Other people have openings for urine deposits. Some unfortunate individuals are born with malformations that require bags to be worn to collect human waste for a lifetime. Ostomate groups form to give mutual support. The shame experienced from ostomy loses some of its sting or stigma if a celebrity emerges with the same problem and goes public with it. Actress Barbara Barrie, a Tony and Academy Award nominee, has become the poster person for the tens of thousands of people in the United States and Canada who undergo colostomies every year.[31] Her book, *Don't Die of Embarrassment,* helps to dampen the shame an ostomate may feel.

The characteristic posture of shame is holding the head down, the very opposite of beaming with pride and looking up. The danger shame presents is death. Dr. David Hawkins, who has developed a calibrated scale for measuring various emotions, considers that "the level of Shame is perilously proximate to death, which may be chosen out of Shame as conscious suicide or more subtly elected by failure to take steps to prolong life."[32] Hawkins capitalizes the "s" in shame to emphasize its lethality. He comments on the pain of "'losing face,' becoming discredited, or feeling like a 'nonperson.'" "In Shame, we hang our heads and slink away, wishing we were invisible."[33] I have felt dead without the ritual of suicide and have wished for invisibility. However, Spinoza's conatus, a saving life force, has refused to let me give up.

The scientific principles of support groups suggest that shame and embarrassment may be ameliorated by "downward comparision."[34] If I feel sorry for myself, if I feel shame and embarrassment because I wear "The Bag" or feel dirty, then put me in a group with people who *really* have reason to be embarrassed because of what their disease or surgical treatment has done to them. Alice was a patient who progressively lost her nose and eyes to an insidious inflammatory process that literally ate up her face. Even one of the physicians who attended her said, "Looking into the cavernous recess of where her eyes and nose had been, I felt my stomach clench and my heart break."[35] So, I tell myself, *Get a life, Blair. Your body hasn't* really *betrayed or failed you.* Nonetheless, even unwarranted embarrassment can't be banished by positive self-affirmations alone.

Embarrassment is one door into the neuronal caves of disgust and shame. Evolution equipped us with such chambers to regulate human behavior and keep us from ingesting something toxic or embracing some creature that could do us harm. When brain damage occurs to nuclei bodies known as the insula, the cingulate or part of the prefrontal cortex, basic social manners and ethics vanish. As indicated in chapter 6, the classic case of Phineas Gage is still cited in neurological textbooks. Gage went from being a respected, hardworking, well liked foreman of railroad crews to a "social lout."[36] He became so unpredictable, untruthful and obscene in speech and behavior that the railroad company that had employed him for years had to fire him. As we saw, Gage's damage came from a railroad blasting cap accident that sent a piece of iron bar through his head with such force that it landed some distance away. Incredibly, the foreman stayed conscious and required relatively little treatment. However, it was soon apparent that Gage was no longer himself. The iron bar had removed Gage's frontal brain tissue as well as his social neurons and their inhibitions.

Other evidence suggests that early shaming can do functional damage to the prefrontal cortical neurons by pruning them, thus stunting the development of arborizing axons and dendrites in lower parts of the brain in charge of defense.[37] It follows that a shamed child needs neuronal equipment to defend against a world that can't be trusted. Gage escaped early pruning of social brain cells only to lose them later.

Had Gage's indecent language and crude behavior been confined strictly to macho male groups, nothing much might have been said. The social biology that regulates brain parts that keep us reasonably sensitive to our environment operates along gender lines. Men who pride themselves on toughness and "tell-it-like-it-is no-bullshit" can find not only acceptance, but even popularity in groups of males who have such an attitude and demeanor. Macho male chest-thumping encourages scatological and sexual syntax as well as hostile gestures, which go beyond raised middle fingers to include mocking movements meant to portray fucking or sodomizing anything that walks and wiggles. Fortunately, female *Homo sapiens* have tended to contain and constrain the degree to which male counterparts are allowed to be "dirty" in speech as well as manner. However, females are neither omnipresent nor omnipotent. Out of the presence of women, some men immediately revert to the vulgar in speech and behavior round the clock.

I was in the Antarctic when women were still prohibited from being at "the bottom" of the world. Men proved their manhood physically—by how long they could withstand cross-country traverses facing blinding snows and treacherous crevasses, by how many hours they could work without sleep, by how much money they could make at a perpetual game of poker, and by the number of obscene neologisms they could mouth in an hour. One other test of toughness consisted of negotiating, without falling, an ever-growing glacier (actually a huge mound) consisting of the urine draining out of the latrines outside our huts. Perfect performance admitted one to "The Yellow Glacier Club," to which I was proudly admitted after many tries.

Shame, embarrassment, disgust and humiliation are powerful weapons used to reject, stigmatize or keep from the inner circle persons who are different. The stigmatizing differences that brand the outcast across the ages include religion, color, sex, age, infirmities and looks. Lepers have long suffered from these weapons of discrimination. In the past even houses of worship used leper's slits in concrete walls to keep the outcast at a distance from the faithful on the other side. Rita and I belong to the Order of St. Lazarus, an international organization more than 900 years old. It is dedicated to helping lepers, who suffer from a disease still found in this country and more so in less developed regions of the world. In Mexico, we visited leper clinics and colonies we help support. In passing the peace with patients at worship services and looking into their eyes, I felt an affinity at some deep limbic level. I feel the same empathy in the presence of my schizophrenic son. He carries the stigma of a mental illness that causes him to look, act and think differently from all the "normals" who shun him. My "madness," though different from his, seethes with anger at his rejection.

Adult authority figures, as well as groups and societies, misuse the powers of exclusion and inclusion. When I was barely six years old and proud of the words I could spell, I learned a joke that I made the mistake of passing on to a dour, middle-aged male friend of the family. I was with my mother visiting one of her best friends. They were in the kitchen while I was in the living room with the man, a brother of my mother's friend. I asked him what the first two letters are of the word "spring." He peered down at me through thick bifocal glasses that pinched his nose. Then he answered, "S, p."

I replied innocently, "Es don't."

I was immediately reported to my mother, who was humiliated. "You should be ashamed of yourself," she scolded. And I was.

While I have longed to be accepted, even as I keep trying to tell the right kind of joke and use the right obscenities to gain admittance to a group, my partner Pittman has played the game more successfully. Locker room language and scatological and sexual references are not foreign to him. It's not possible to become the captain of even a high school football team without some proclivity for profanity. Certainly one cannot play basketball for a legendary coach and nationally ranked team without mastering athletic rituals that may include, off the court, goosing an unsuspecting teammate bending to tie his shoes or, on the court, fondling and hugging the same player for a great point. Pittman's social brain is so finely tuned that he can break rules and "color outside the lines," a favorite expression of his, leaving him free to be a "re-visionist." He offers interpretations of the Bible not found in any standard book of hermeneutics, and produces frowns on the faces of the orthodox.

Meanwhile, I struggle with my ego and a lifetime of episodes that have caused it to blush and go into hiding until I get my act together and allow hubris to reign once again. As to the brain structures that nature has bestowed on us, they quietly go about their business of lighting up in limbic regions despite what the ego dictates as forbidden. The untouchable, the unspeakable, the unsightly and, ultimately, the unseen, which results in making a person unrecognized and invisible, all register in the collective neurons of a culture.

Richard Cohen has been caught up by diseases that the culture turns away from. Cohen writes that he wants his "old swagger" and "boundless self-confidence" returned to him.[38] They were stolen by colon cancer, three colostomies and "The Bag." Yet the most crippling confederate in this theft of swagger and confidence has been his steadily debilitating case of multiple sclerosis, which has left him legally blind and weak in the knees. People like Cohen— and those like me, who have suffered far less—resist being regarded as "wretched refuse" consigned to a "hidden population."[39] In a society that equates self-worth and esteem with youth and good looks, it all comes crashing down when you lose both. When you no longer look good, smell good or perform well, fear of becoming refuse overtakes even shame.

At this point I hear Pittman telling me once again that the profane often camouflages the sacred. What starts out as profane may lead us to the sacred. God and/or evolution shaped humans so that, in the words of my therapist the priest, we come into the world between "shit and piss." The line between the sacred and the profane becomes invisible when a father watches the birth of his own child. "It was one of the most sacred moments of my life," Pittman says, commenting on witnessing his sons being born. In any other context, the sight and smell of bloody tissue, mucus, entrails and placenta strike most people as disgusting. When it's your own flesh and blood coming into being, it's a gift from God, a sign of grace, a sacred experience encoded into the deep nondeclarative part of our brain and being as well as the conscious, verbal part.[40]

However, there is another context in which the profane seems to signal nothing but barbaric brutality: A bloody, headless torso was found on a backwoods road outside of the deep East Texas town of Jasper. It attracted the media worldwide and illustrated how an event involving shame and disgust both repels and attracts us. James Byrd, Jr., an African-American, was chained and dragged by three white men in a pickup truck late one Saturday night until his swinging body hit a concrete bridge abutment deep in the woods and severed his head and shoulders. His assailants unchained the remaining torso and abandoned it on a dirt backroad. The following morning, when the Sunday sunrise sent shafts of light through the piney woods, the horrible maiming awakened the Huff Creek community outside of town. As if we needed to be reminded of the juxtaposition of the profane and sacred, the bloody remains were found outside the white, wooden, one-story Huff Creek Community Church, whose congregants were black.[41] It was from this church and low point that Jasper slowly repaired itself, spiritually and ethnically, to the point of redemption, as portrayed in a documentary by that name.[42]

My partner and I include this episode in our story as a reminder that the anger, disgust, shame and guilt built into our psyches and somas to serve our survival can be horrendously hijacked to produce the profane. In such extremes, only the sacred offers redemption. Pittman remembers that redemption for the pain searing his six-year-old badly burned legs came in the form of a syringe filled with morphine and held in the hands of a full-blooded Cherokee Indian named Dr. Orange Star. My redemption is still evolving. The scalpels and skills of four surgeons who cut me open from the heart to the genitals have left me with a scar that I touch every night in bed. I lie there and silently pray the doxology; this gives me some sense that I may slowly be redeemed. I get the same feeling when Pittman anoints my forehead with holy oil at the end of our weekly séances. He asks God to heal us both.

CHAPTER 8

HARMONY AT NEW HARMONY

THE STORY

My first real glimmer of new light comes unexpectedly in New Harmony, Indiana. By now I should know that the unexpected is the way that synchronicity and mystery come to us. In this historic little town, I glimpse a harmony inside myself that I once knew, but lost in my deep dive into darkness. Before entering Dr. McGehee's analytic container, I would have resisted the word "mystery." As for synchronicity, I am still more comfortable with serendipity, which much good science depends on. Whichever it is, I am here because my wife, a mystic in her own right, signed us up for a weekend conference on shamanism and healing. Rita has been searching for some magic that will pull me out of the pits. Shamanism, she hopes, may do the trick.

However, even before the first full session convenes, something different is happening to me. I'm not fighting against waking up. I'm not asking what the point is. It's been many months since I have actually looked forward to a new day—a feeling that went down the toilet a long time ago with my shit. I climb out of bed, quickly put on my jogging clothes in the crisp, predawn chill, and head down the dark, treelined narrow street. Its silence is something else I am aware that I am noticing. Another good sign. I haven't enjoyed silence for a long time. On many occasions when I have been alone and even the city streets quiet down, I have feared the silence, equating it with death. I embrace it as an old friend.

Depression deadens the senses, which, I quickly hear Pittman telling me, are the inlets of the soul, as his favorite eighteenth century poet, William Blake, intuited. Since my senses feel more alive this early morning than in many a moon, I say to myself, *Maybe now I can even savor the taste of wine again and the sound of music.* I smile at the thought that the spark lighting in me seems willing to guide me across a threshold from numbness to movement. I smile also because of where this liminal experience is happening.

New Harmony is a prototype of the experience of crossing from one reality to another. Father George Rapp and approximately 1,000 German-born followers established a close-knit religious community here in 1814. The Harmonists, as they called themselves, sold their village, its "manufactories, farms and buildings" in 1824 to Robert Owen, a Scotsman and a "liminist" in his own right. Owen, having made a fortune from cotton mills in Scotland, saw New Harmony as nothing less than a "seedbed for Utopia."[1] Owen insisted that "man's life and character could be changed and elevated by improving the environment and through education."[2] "Man," in this case, meant men, women and children. Owen was

years ahead of the rest of America in advocating the rights of women, equality, free school-
ing and a self-government that invited all to participate.[3] Owen's vision has been passed
down through the years; Jane Blaffer Owen, who had married into the family, could be seen
in her eighties, at the beginning of the century, delivering welcoming flowers in a golf cart
to the cottages of visitors.

With that optimistic and enlightened beginning, New Harmony has become a haven
for scientists, scholars and educators, as well as the site of conferences such as the one that
my wife and I are attending. Knowing this about the place where I find my glimpse of new
light, I can only be thankful for the gift from whatever god there is in charge of both synchronicities and liminal experiences. Since my senses seem to be showing some surprising
signs of life, I am letting them guide me this early morning. I find that their destination
is an outdoor labyrinth.

I walk briskly, even jogging at intervals, down North Street and pass Tillich Park. I
know from Pittman, who has preached and lectured in New Harmony, that a green space
is named after Paul Tillich, who came here for the park's dedication some years ago. I immediately think of *The Courage to Be*, a book that brought fame to this already noted theologian and philosopher.[4] My translation of what Tillich says is that the courage to be is the
will to live even when faith is dead and hope is gone. I wonder what Tillich thought about
Spinoza's "conatus." What's hardest for me in finding "to be" courage is the "doing" that
I use as justification for "being." Depression has taken from me any sense that what I do is
worthwhile. Therefore, if my doing is worthless, how can I have the courage just to be?

On one of the rare occasions when Pittman reverts to the biblical, he reminds me that
grace does not depend on good works. It's a gift. I have never felt comfortable with material, much less spiritual, gifts. I must earn them. So sitting around being depressed, or trying to do something worthwhile and failing, generates great anxiety, which is why I need
Ambien to put me to sleep. What grace does require, if I remember correctly, is faith. My
faith at this time is not spiritual or religious. It is a trust that the neurobiological effects
of talk therapy will change my brain chemistry, particularly if the talking takes place with
my bonded partner the priest. The glimmer of light I experience this dawn encourages me
to believe that my trust in scientific evidence may be well grounded.

Putting an end to my musings, I look around and see that I am across from the Roofless
Church, a creation of the noted architect Philip Johnson. Hanging on the walls in this top-
less structure is a picture of the Reverend J. Pittman McGehee, on the occasion of his round
of sermons and lectures here. It is a coincidence—perhaps a synchroncity again—that Pittman spoke then on the love of letting be—not in an apathetic way, but in the empowering
sense—which he sees as the way to finding one's true self.

I have now reached my destination, not far from either Tillich's courage-to-be park
or the Roofless Church with memories of Dr. McGehee's resounding words in its walls.
The outdoor labyrinth, forty-two feet in diameter, is made of inlaid granite stones with a
path of eleven concentric, spiraling circles and thirty-four turns that eventually lead to its
center. As I take my first few steps, I am surprised that I find no need to repeat the new
mantra Pittman has given me. Instead, I am repeating the four-syllable Aramaic word that

I learned from another priest, Dom Laurence Freeman of London, when Rita and I attended a retreat he led in Canada. "Ma-ra-na-tha" is the mantra Dom Freeman taught us. It means, "Come, Lord." I adjust my cadence to the rhythm of the syllables. It's a meditation that Rita and I used on long climbs in the Colorado Rockies at a time when we felt helpless and distraught over the trials and tribulations of our daughter Liz. On our descents, with our dog leading the way, we would go for hours silently saying the word. Neither the word nor the Lord saved Liz, but it sustained me. Having it come back to me now may be yet another sign that I am crossing the line to better times.

This is not the first labyrinth I have walked. If I divide my life into BC (before colostomy) and AC (after colostomy) periods, my experience with labyrinths has all been BC. On a visit to Chartres, France, Rita and I first discovered there was such as a thing as a labyrinth. The one there, in the ancient Chartres Cathedral, dates back to 1200 when the faithful needed a vicarious way during the Crusades to make a pilgrimage to the Holy Land. The labyrinth provided the means to enact the pilgrimage and complete it safely. In more recent BC years, we have stopped at Grace Cathedral in San Francisco to walk the outdoor labyrinth made from terrazzo stone in the church's "Interfaith Garden," overlooking the city below. Only now does it occur to me that I am approaching the New Harmony labyrinth of concentric spirals, turns and loops with a different set of eyes. In France, the visit for me was ego-building, giving me something to quietly brag about. In San Francisco, I fed my hubris with the pride of beating Rita to the center, a six-petaled rose-shaped area. In neither place did I have a clue as to what a labyrinth is for psychologically and spiritually. To me, it was simply ego-inflation.

Now, I am better prepared to accept with gratitude what my senses have done for me in leading me here. I'm aware that I am in the presence of an archetypal pattern, a mandala, symbolizing wholeness across cultures. More specifically, the labyrinth represents the central archetype of wholeness, which Jung called the Self. Rather than approaching it as a challenge to my athletic prowess, I am more respectful of the experience it can give me. Now that archetypes are being acknowledged by neuroscientists,[5] I am glad to have the opportunity to have a direct experience of one—meaning that I can see it, touch it, and feel what it has to give me. What I am beginning to sense for the first time is that this labyrinth is offering me a liminal experience. Celtic Christianity and mythology identified certain places where the immanent and the transcendent meet at a border between two worlds, such as the visible and the invisible, the mundane and the divine. The Latin word for such a threshold is *limen*. Such sites are also considered "thin places," where the usual walls between physical and spiritual melt away. So my steps here take on new meaning.

I recognize for the first time that the winding path to the center, with all its twists and turns, is a metaphor for life, for my life, with its unexpected reversals. As I follow the clockwise direction going into the center, I suddenly remember that this part of the journey is called "purgation."[6] Purging, for me, is a shadow experience that comes with my colostomies, along with the gallon of "Colyte/NuLytely," which members of the Ostomy Society have to drink before surgery and preparatory to subsequent reexaminations of the remaining sections of colon. My wise wife told me, as I sat for hours in the bathroom watching the purging effects of the drink, to be thankful for all the shit I am getting rid of in my life.

As my feet slowly pass over the inlaid stones, I am grateful that I am slowly learning to release enough of my ego to let my soul begin to stir. I also associate "purgation" with purgatory and silently thank my teacher for telling me that, based on legend, I freed our daughter from that state of the underworld (see chapter 2). The labyrinth is helping me accept the mystery of that experience, which must have occurred at one of those borders, or limens, between life and death. I pray that on the brink of my near death, Liz was given some sort of new life.

After pausing several times and having my left brain tell me how "illogical" the turns are in the labyrinth, I renew my determination to let the path lead me rather than trying to impose my will on it. My trust pays off: I have come now to the rosette, the rose at the heart of the labyrinth. I wonder whether by standing here awhile I will feel more in touch with my own center and soul, the archetype of who I truly am. I am aware that the cleansing stage is over and I have entered one designated as "illumination." I have no immediate, blinding insights, but I feel some kind of doxology is in order. So I express thanks for being here at all and sensing a glimmer of rebirth.

Then it hits me: not a blinding light, but a clear image of two figures side by side, one depicting a lateral view of the brain and the other a top view of the labyrinth. As I mentally juxtapose the brain over the labyrinth and marvel at the similarities in their shapes, I begin probing for a deeper meaning. I immediately recognize that before the juxtaposition, the brain was on the left, for logic, and the labyrinth on the right, for eros. I had not only put logic above love, but also the linear over the circular. With that fact before me, I replay the impatience I felt in following "illogical" turns in my path to the center. With mental effort I had made myself stick with the path. My mind vetoed what my left brain was insisting on, namely, being logical and taking a straight, linear course to the middle—which would have never delivered me a rose. "Illumination" is the stage of the rosette, and I am satisfied that the center has been aptly named.

From here back to the perimeter and starting point I should experience union, the third and final stage of labyrinth walking. The yoke I seek is with myself, the soul I hope to find behind the persona and underneath the roles I have played in quest of fame and fortune. I am now seeking more connection and less control, more affiliation and less achievement. In Jungian terms, I need more eros and less logos. The illumination I had at the center points toward scientific ways I can gain both balance and union.

"Eros" and "logos" are the terms my analyst has spent much of his Jungian career probing into. They also were the subject of a sermon—it may have been billed as a lecture—that Pittman gave at New Harmony. His thesis is that eros is the religious principle of the psyche, that its energy is one of reunion, of bringing together that which has been split. Since the word "religion" itself is derived from *legare* which means to bind or connect and from which we get the word ligament, which joins bones and muscles, I have had some experience of the connection between eros and religion. I experienced eros in action in the surgical wound that removed cancer from my chest and in my body's intrinsic power to heal. As for religion, I feel that I may once again experience God.

Pittman strives to combine eros with logos, because from that combination, he believes, comes the rare experience of what he calls wise love.[7] Logos stands for suffering and for the understanding that relieves suffering when people like me come to understand the meaning of their distress.[8] So putting the energy of eros next to the power of logos, one gets wise love. This is what Pittman seeks to practice and to prove. Since the day he envisioned his thesis on the subject, he has been committed to showing that wise love produces healing. I know all this from having read it, heard it and experienced it at my teacher's feet—literally. I also know that wise love stands for "letting be"—letting people be who they are meant to be by leading them to recognition of their essence or true self. It is not a permissive "anything goes" letting be, but an empowering one.

With all these reflections on union coming to me as I complete the final stage of union in my walk of the labyrinth, I feel it has been a fruitful journey. I immediately flash on the surrounding trees, branches and roots and wonder whether my clockwise journey in and counterclockwise path out have arborized my own dendrology, my neurons and their rhizomes. Something in the chill of the air and the song of birds greeting the new day tells me the answer is "yes."

Rita is at the exit to greet me. It hadn't escaped her notice that I had gotten myself out of bed without encouragement. As a reality check, I ask if she can hear any birds singing. She says, "Certainly. Aren't they lovely," and points to a pair in one of the old, still sturdy trees. She reminds me that Dr. Clarissa Pinkola Estes, the Jungian conference speaker and author of *Women Who Run With the Wolves*, is talking this morning on "El Rondo: Curanderismo."[9] Without asking if my Rip VanWinkle sleeping soul is seeing any light, Rita finds it interesting that my sign of new harmony, slight as it may be, comes in a town by that name, and at a meeting featuring a healer whose energy is feminine. The suggestion here is that maybe my own anima, feminine soul, is feeling safe to make her voice heard over the heavy logic that dominates my internal dialogue. Doubting Thomas as I am, I answer that I want to see the speaker's own wounds before acknowledging her healing power. "Logic tells me," I point out to my mystic wife, "that any woman who runs with wolves has got to get hurt sooner or later." With that, Rita sighs and takes me by the hand to go and see for myself.

THE SCIENCE

Does walking a labyrinth and experiencing its mandala demonstrate that archetypes are real? Until very recently, the scientific answer would have been no. Jung astutely observed that regardless of time or space, cultures seem to be moved by images of the same kinds of forms, shapes, figures or narratives.[1] It was believed that there was something inherent in these things that caused people to respond to them in similar ways. Along the same lines, something innate in *us* seems to respond to the energies that certain images, shapes, forms and stories present to us. Nonetheless, science has remained skeptical. What's new is that neuroscience is now offering some confirmation of the reality of archetypes.

Three standards that phenomena must meet to be considered "real" and "objective" are they must be empirical, stable and public. This means they must be measurable, stay the same across time and space, and be judged the same way by trained observers. With the advances that are occurring in neuroscience, the neuronal effects of archetypal images seem undeniable, as established by functional magnetic resonance imaging (fMRI), positron emission tomography (PET) and single photon emission computed tomography (SPECT).

But wait: These are measures of effects of experience, not the imputed archetypal causes. True, but science commonly makes inferences of causation from observing effects. Many physical phenomena—such as elementary particles and force fields—are not directly observable.[2] Quantum physics recognizes "the power of mental effort and mindfulness to alter neuronal connections." Mental effort is an invisible phenomenon.[3] But again, its physical force is inferred from its effects. It is proposed that "archetypal structures exist in the genotype independently of the individuals that trigger their innate releasing mechanisms. That is, the archetypes are autonomous; they exist independently of human psyches in the same sense that the human genotype exists independently of individual humans."[4]

Jung early on argued that "the existence of the instincts can no more be proved than the existence of archetypes, so long as they do not manifest themselves concretely."[5] In other words, in the presence of an archetype, we provide the concrete evidence of its existence by our psychological and physiological responses. Just as there are archetypal words that pack a punch, there are parallel archaic images that are equally "affective" or emotional. The amygdala is the sentinel in our limbic brain that is exquisitely sensitive to shapes and forms. Archetypal theory tells us that across the millennia, humans have responded most deeply to the same designs in nature and manmade art and objects. An example: The spiral, a shape that is well represented in a labyrinth, is "literally encoded into the universe" and found throughout nature—from the patterns of pinecones to the nautilus shell, from the vortex of draining water to the whorl of our hair at the crown of the head.[6] Such forms or images often take us to liminal spaces—the "thin places"—where we get a glimpse of the transcendent. I had some nascent experience of this in my labyrinth walk, which is another sign that I may be seeing better times ahead. From the spiraling form of our DNA to the labyrinths of stained-glass windows in cathedrals, we are given the opportunity to glimpse what is both immanent and transcendent.

I was in the audience at the Texas Medical Center when the director of the National Cancer Institute, Dr. Andrew von Eschenbach, put on the screen pictures of two patterns side by side.[7] He asked the learned professors and skilled clinicians what the two slides depicted. There was a consensus that one was the DNA molecule coiled up in a spiral pattern. The other, which contained in its circle six rosettes not dissimilar to that found at the center of a labyrinth, turned out to be a stained-glass rose window in the west wall of the National Cathedral in Washington. In hindsight, I believe I perceived in both the thirteen-pointed "invisible" star that seems to radiate out from the center, connecting the outer points with the inner rosette.[8] This same pattern shows up in the microscopic image, magnified 2,000,000 times, of a tungsten atom.

So, given that archetypes are ubiquitous in the patterns of nature and human artifacts, what are they for? Why did God and/or nature build them and us in such a way that certain forms, figures, images and stories affect us in deep parts of the brain and may stir us right down to the soul level? More specifically, since the labyrinth that I just walked is archetypal in its shapes and form, what purpose does it serve?

One answer is that it gives us a blueprint for transformation.[9] It may be a tool, in other words, for us to use to change ourselves for the better or to discover who we are and are meant to be. One walk around "the track" is not likely to transform a person, although there are testimonies to that effect. I believe that I experienced new insights and felt their effects in the "illumination" stage at the center. Even short of transforming, a labyrinth can reconnect us to deep, universal forms and images, represented in both nature and our very brains.

It is regrettable that "transformation"—a perfectly legitimate concept—is being advertised as something we can order on demand like a product. On the commercial front, "transformation," along with "transcendence," is being co-opted by "enhancement technologies." The promise is that we can experience "transformation, by pill or scalpel," to use the words of a headline in the *Science Times* of the *New York Times*.[10] Just as Prozac was initially touted as not just curing depression but giving us a sparkling, new personality, we have now entered a new era of self-fulfillment where we can be "better than well" through Botox, liposuction, eyelid alterations, nose jobs, breast sculpting, sex hormones and the latest generation of SSRIs.[11] "Medical enhancement" is another name for the "pursuit of perfection."[12] In reviewing this dubious cultural craze, Sherwin Nuland, physician and best-selling author, writes:

> The definition of "human suffering" has gradually changed. We now find ourselves faced with the reality that it is no longer sufficient to prevent or treat sickness of the body or mind, but that physicians are expected to address increasing attention—and society's dollars—to the millions who are dissatisfied with what nature and their own DNA have given them.... Not sick in any usual definition of the word, such discontented people would like to be better than they are, better than merely well.[13]

Personally, I am one depressive not pursuing pills or surgery to make me more outgoing and lively. I seek to overcomine my illness "the hard way"; that is, to "earn" my recovery, with the help of a teacher/therapist. The science that I trust to bring me to that end is not only providing empirical evidence in support of Jungian analysis, but also is demonstrating that "mental effort," along with resonance in relationships, can reshape neurons and balance brain chemistry.

Mental effort is illustrated by what I discovered from walking the labyrinth. When my left brain was demanding that I give up the illogic of spirals and turns that seemed to lead me back to the starting point rather than the rosette in the middle, I resolved to refocus on "trust in the process" and keep my feet on the path. This mental effort is no different from that which keeps me sitting in the belly of the whale with my therapist the priest and trusting that we will be delivered to high ground soon. It is also no different from the effort I once experienced in going to support groups, faced with the sad knowledge that our daughter had chosen heroin over life itself. I resolved to keep the "soles" of my feet—as well as the soul of my being—in the room, no matter how futile it all seemed. It didn't change the inevitable end Liz suffered, but it helped me, in the words of Isaiah, to walk without fainting.

Jeffrey Schwartz, research professor of psychiatry at UCLA School of Medicine, has demonstrated the power of "top-down" plasticity to resculpt the brain.[14] This is the power of the mind to alter brain circuitry by mental effort and refocusing. Schwartz's program is designed to change the brain chemistry of obsessive compulsive patients who learn to refocus. In my case, while walking the labyrinth, I resolved to refocus on the path when logic told me, "That's crazy." Another example is refocusing on a positive mantra, even if it is crude and vulgar. A third is to keep repeating a meditative prayer that has me asking the Lord to come even though my experience of God is still moribund.

What this technique does is to break up "brain lock," the compulsive repeating of self-downing or self-defeating thoughts or behavior. In depressives like me, it's called "depression interlock" to distinguish it from the "brain lock" of patients with obsessive-compulsive disorder. In both cases, it's as if we are stuck in a gear that keeps the striatum in the brain using the same output pathway to the thalamus, regardless of how excitatory and upsetting it is. By refocusing, shifting attention or sheer mental effort, a second, more quiescent pathway is taken to the thalamus, a major player in the limbic brain just above the amygdala.[15]

Much of this has come to me as I keep the labyrinth image in my mind alongside a lateral view of the brain. Just as my limbic loop, starting at the amygdala, curves around the motor cortex in the center like a cochlea, the spiraling circuits of the labyrinth envelop the rose at its heart. The experience I get from this twin imaging is assurance that with practice in walking the labyrinth I can move closer to contact with that part of me that is deeper than words and includes my unconscious. If I am lucky, I may even experience my essence.

Practice requires repeating something over and over. I can do this to an unhealthy extreme. Perseverating is repeating a thought, a self-demand, over and over and is not uncommon among depressives. It can bog us down over trivia. More than once, I have perseverated over what belt to wear with dirty dockers, as if people will look at my belt and ignore my pants. Pittman asked me early on if I am compulsive. I lied and said no. I didn't want my compulsiveness to detour us from my depression. Now I know they kindle and inflame each other to produce neuronal detriments.

However, the labyrinth and limbic loop images have also reminded me of an innate persistence that is more positive. It is "conatus," which is "the relentless endeavor of each being to preserve itself."[16] Conatus was the favorite subject of the Dutch-Jewish philosopher and theologian Spinoza, who intuited that this striving to persevere "is nothing but the actual essence" of one's being. But what does seventeenth-century philosophy have to do with the current millennium's striving for perfectability through enhancement technologies? Only this, according to Antonio Damasio, professor and head of neurology at the

University of Iowa Medical Center and author of the book *Looking for Spinoza: Joy, Sorrow, and the Feeling Brain*. It is conatus "the essence of our beings," that is "called into action when we are confronted with the reality of suffering and especially the reality of death, actual or anticipated, our own or that of those we love."[17] That's the sorrow part. This striving and yearning are also found in pursuit of joy and the dance of our limbic loops when they find attunement and synchrony with another. Conatus is involved in authentic transformation and genuine enhancement, from the inside out, which is the opposite of being a "more perfect me" through technology.

In Pittman's New Harmony presentations, across the street from where I walk the labyrinth this morning, he talked about the dance that connects doctor and patient. It is a dynamic relationship involving the conscious and unconscious of both partners and leads to a feeling of "a spirit that connects, yet frees."[18] "Perichoresis," Pittman repeats, "is the play of psychic energy that translates eros and logos into agape." The dance builds up healing energy and succeeds when eros, the innate yearning to unite, is balanced with logos, the striving to understand, to find meaning and preserve autonomy.

In the *Tao of Physics*, Fritjof Capra tells of his own experience as a scientist sitting by the ocean one late summer afternoon watching the waves roll in and feeling the rhythm of his own breathing.[19] Suddenly Capra becomes aware of a "gigantic cosmic dance," from vibrating molecules and atoms to the high energy of cosmic rays. My therapist understands dance as being the universal, aboriginal art and fundamental energy. When we learn the steps and sense the rhythm of separating and connecting, we experience joy. In talking about "the abundant life," Pittman always includes dance, even if it is a dance, as he says, with a fly swatter in the kitchen to the tune of a buzzing fly.[20]

I haven't yet mastered the deep rhythms of perichoresis. I can see that the circling and perambulation that are inherent in the labyrinth evoke an archetypal energy that Sufi dervishes carried to ecstatic extremes. I am still at the stage of just congratulating myself on moving my body out of bed and following a labyrinth path to a modicum of illumination. I am still stepping on my analyst's toes in our analytic container. However, with mental effort, I am refraining from mantras of self-blame. After all, if I step on Pittman's toes, I can blame his big feet: Size 13D.

CHAPTER 9

SERVING TO HEAL

THE STORY

I ask her if there is anything I can do to help her, the same question I enter each room with. She looks up at me and holds out a swollen, black hand: "Say a prayer with me." Now it's my turn to comfort, to be present for someone sicker than myself. I take her hand, feeling the cold and calluses through my plastic gloves. I ask if she would like to see a chaplain, thinking she might want a prayer professional instead of a doubting amateur. "No, I don't want to be seen like this." She is sitting on a portable toilet at the side of her bed having loose bowels from chemo and the contents of one or more of the other bags hanging on the steel treatment tree to which she is tethered. I ask if she knows the Twenty-third Psalm. She nods, and we begin saying it slowly together.

I know Psalm Twenty-three well enough so that my mind starts drifting in the middle of walking through the valley of the shadow of death. I'm thinking, *Here I am back to what's familiar, the stench of shit and a mantra affirming the Lord as Savior.* We barely finish saying we will dwell in His house forever before she looks at me and asks, "You believe in the Lord?"

I surprise myself by answering without equivocation, straight from the cardiac brain, "Sometimes I do."

She smiles and slowly withdraws her hand, now moist with sweat, "Me, too. My mama made all us kids believe. But she's dead, and I guess I'm just a sometime believer now."

Mabel is this lady's name. At least, that's what she instructed me to call her. I have no reason to question it, because it comes close enough to the name on my roster for the patient in this particular room on the stem cell transfusion floor. The roster says she is Madeleine, but when I ask her about it, she says, "I've been called Mabel all my life, all sixty years of it." I say to her that I prefer not to call patients by their first names unless they tell me to. "I'm telling you to," Mabel replies.

I help her get off the potty and back into bed, with the back inclined so she can breathe easier. Her legs and ankles are swollen like her hands, all part of the lymphoma—and the treatment, and some heart trouble. Mabel is waiting to see whose stem cells will be harvested for her transfusion. "I've got a lot of brothers and sisters," she says, "so one of them ought to come close to matching me."

Mabel is from Muleshoe, Texas, and is surprised that I know where it is and how it got its name. "Sure, I know about Muleshoe," I tell her. "They thought so much of mules, they put a statue of one right in the middle of the town square. It's in the Panhandle."

I like the way I can break the ice with patients by some recognition of hometowns. "Home," I'm thinking to myself, is the mother of all archetypes. Pittman is the authority on archetypes, but there is something about the combination of the words "home" and "town" that conjures up warm, old-fashioned, Norman Rockwell feelings. When it comes to hometown geography, I've been enough places to have a fair memory of where they are—not only in Texas, but also elsewhere. Even people who don't like their hometowns like for other people to have heard of them. Home is the place they've got to take you in even when they wish you would stay away, is what my mother believed. I find out that Mabel has not lived in her hometown for many years. "I still call it home," she explains. "It was a place everybody knew my name. Big cities don't know anybody's name."

I'm struck by how many patients I see who seem to know how to make lemonade out of lemons, which is a down-home expression that you can find in even some scientific literature. It happens to be the theme of a long-term Harvard study on successful aging.[1] There are a lot of men and women who have lived anonymous lives in big cities, and it isn't until they get cancer or some other serious illness and have to go into the hospital that anybody pays them much attention. Even then, too many hospitals know them mostly by a number or diagnosis rather than a name. This isn't true at this sprawling cancer center, M. D. Anderson by name, where I do volunteer work. I've been doing it now for more than four years, which means I started making myself do it when I was still deep in the pits. At some level of knowing, I am certain that I have to keep scrambling up the spiral staircase—using tooth, toenail, whatever my body will give me—to free myself from the mire into which I have been sinking.[2]

At first, it was hard work, physically and emotionally, for me to stand at the bedside of so many people struggling with their own life-and-death issues. In making myself do it, I resolved to practice "Fordyce's law," which states that "people who have something better to do don't suffer as much."[3] So my motivation to serve is to help myself as much as to be of help. I know that in addition to doing Dr. McGehee's periochoretic dance in the analytic container, I have to find my own ways of turning dross into gold.

Now, after some time on the job, I find I like this work. It's gratifying. It is rich in psychic income; good practice in egocide, which is what a Jungian authority at nearby Texas A&M University, David Rosen, calls whittling down one's hubris.[4] As a patient advocate, I do whatever I can to help people like Mabel as long as it isn't medical or religious. I leave those areas to the professionals. But, like Mabel, some of the people may need a fast prayer and don't want to bother a chaplain, particularly if they can't control their bowels. Patients don't put on many pretenses around volunteers like me. I may go into a room and have a man or woman stick a foot out for me to rub. I do it. Some want a magazine. I get one. Many want to see the newspaper. I carry a few copies in the black shoulder bag I take with me from room to room, leaving it just outside the door. In the bag I also keep a toothbrush or two, toothpaste, shampoo, combs and talcum powder. A number of patients with advanced cancer have to come back into the hospital in the middle of the night by way of the emergency room. They don't have time to bring toiletry articles with them.

Carrying the bag I have also keeps my ego under wraps. I'm right back to delivering newspapers and magazines as I was doing in the Depression, and Mama felt it was a shame I had to do it. "Well, Mama," I say to her in my morning meditation, "you can still be proud of your 'baby' boy. I'm helping to meet the basic needs, 'lowly' as they may be, of the high and mighty along with the poor and powerless." Cancer respects neither income, race, sex, creed, color nor position in life. It's the ultimate equalizer.

I have to smile about the mask I wear over my nose and mouth and the gown over my clothes to keep from passing on any germs to the patients, who have had all their white cells knocked out in preparation for stem cell transfusion. The reason I smile is that now that I have good reason to wear a mask, my persona doesn't much matter to me any more. I don't have any ego to puff up on this job.

I look across Mabel's ample frame to the top of the small bedside table on the other side of her bed. Much of her constricted world is there: glasses for reading, a *Reader's Digest*, a Bible, a water glass, a television log. Not long ago I was where Mabel is, though not in this hospital. The boundaries of my world were just as contracted. I would read as long as I could, then stare up at the ceiling tiles, study their shapes and number, and then go back to practicing becoming an optimist. I know the steps, because I still teach them and believe in the research on them. However, like Martin Seligman, the grand master of learned optimism, I'm still a dyed-in-the-wool pessimist. It's the default position that has long been in my bones, maybe before I was born. Rita, my cheerleader wife, knows this. She tells people I'm a pessimist who knows how to be optimistic. That's true, and optimism is what I practice when I'm privileged to enter the private worlds of the very sick people I see.

Sick people I can identify with. They seem realer than people outside the hospital. You can get right down to the basics in short order. Small talk is fine, but holding a hand or rubbing a foot is better. Humor helps. It connects people in an affectionate way. I've had some of my best laughs with people who have died by the time I came back the following Wednesday, my volunteer day. I particularly enjoyed Arnie, a man from the Bronx who didn't die, but suffered from a big spiritual, as well as physical, struggle. He had a New York City sense of humor. The first time I met him he asked what my roster shows for him in the column under "religion." I said, "N-s-p," for nonspecified. "That's wrong," he replied, "tell them to change that to "N-O-N-E," and he spelled the word with great emphasis for me. This avowed agnostic or atheist, it varied from week to week, graduated in electrical engineering from NYU and went on to make millions in real estate in Florida and Arizona. "Transformers bored me," he explained when I asked how he went from engineering to real estate. His wife also had cancer and was a patient on a different floor. He bought an expensive highrise condominium at The Spires, a few blocks away, to cheer her up and give her a place to stay on weekend passes out of the hospital.

One day I came into his room, and he said he was worried about his wife. "Her cancer is spreading, and she's getting more and more depressed. I don't know what to do to help her."

I said, "Have you thought about praying for her?"

To my surprise, he answered, "I have thought about it. But I don't know how." I gave him a quick lesson in just talking to God, then taught him a few short prayers.

A week later, when I saw him again, he told me he had been praying for her, and she was better. However, the following week, he reported she was worse again. "How much have you been praying for her?" I asked.

"Two or three times a day," he said.

"That's not enough. You've got to up the dose," I told him, and he did. To our surprise, both his and mine, his wife not only got better, she became clear of almost any sign of cancer. So what started as sort of a playful game between Arnie and me had this unexpected happy ending. Then I remember what my priest the therapist likes to tell people. "Never underestimate the autonomy of God," Dr. McGehee says. "He'll use Jimmy Swaggart or a plastic Jesus on a speed freak's dashboard to get people to see the light." I think Pittman is also telling me that God has a sense of humor.

The people I see on the bone marrow transplant floor have had just about every treatment there is—chemo, radiation, surgery, even previous stem cell transfusions—and they are still inspirations I stand in awe of. Spinoza had it right about conatus, the striving to preserve essence. Essence shines through when everything else inside and outside the body goes down the tube. I saw it in the faces of people I met delivering mail in the mud of deep South Dallas during rainy Christmas holiday seasons when I worked at the post office on college breaks. I've seen the same look working for the mayor in the part of Houston called "the Bottom" because when you live there you are on the bottom. It's where people take pride in just making it through another day. High in the Bolivian Andes, where Rita and I have done mission work in the summer (their winter), the same strong faces were apparent in the Quechua Indians, many of them subsistence farmers using a wooden plow pulled by oxen to till the soil. Their god is Mother Earth, so they won't use a steel plow, even if it is given to them. It would hurt their god. In the work we did down below at the Amistad orphanage in Cochabamba, we saw the look in the faces of the devoted staff and the happy, dancing boys and girls. In the Himalayas of Tibet, we encountered an almost beatific expression as we passed schoolchildren, farmers and monks on the winding mountain trails.

Back in the Texas Medical Center, at Methodist Hospital, I've seen the depressed face of an aphasic Hispanic-American woman light up and glow in an encounter with our Tibetan dog, Tashi. Rita and I went through animal-assisted therapy training with Tashi.[5] Then we took his younger sister, Bodhi, through training to become a certified "Caring Critter." Now, with photo IDs in place, they go on Friday afternoons to practice their "magic" on patients whose limbs or brain cells have been paralyzed by strokes, injuries or surgical mishaps. On this occasion, the middle-aged woman was rubbing Tashi's rich fur with her hand as a physical therapist kept asking, "What does he feel like, what does he feel like?"

Quietly but distinctly, the woman finally said, "Soft." It was her first word in three months. The woman's countenance was transformed. Everyone in the rehabilitation room felt they had witnessed a transcendent experience.

So the look I am describing can be found in the faces of many people, the poor and the infirm, including those in hospitals such as M. D. Anderson and Methodist. Their expression says, "I know how to survive and I'm glad just to be alive."

Now I'm back in Mabel's room, and she's telling me about her marriages and kids, her ups and downs, and her many jobs. Mostly she's worked in Laundromats. "People like me used to be called a washwoman, which my mama was. But you don't hear of her kind anymore."

I tell Mabel that in my day, people who could hire a washwoman had her wash clothes in a big, black iron tub over a fire built in the backyard, which is what the Justices did before the Depression. I tell her I know a man (Pittman) whose father as a boy got Saturday night baths in a tub heated with hot water from a kettle on the kitchen stove. Hot water out of the tap was something they didn't have. "You know something else," I add, "studies show people were just as happy then as those living now with all the modern conveniences, not to mention more money." I may be overstating, but Mabel nods and makes an "uh-huh" sound in agreement.

Mabel knows about life's vicissitudes, many of them painful. She says she doesn't know if she is going to die or not. She doesn't know if those stem cells, no matter how well they match, will save her. Nonetheless, she's going to take it one day at a time. I say, "Good," and tell her the old Chinese saying about the way to journey a thousand miles is one step at a time.

"I tell the Lord," she says, "I'm ready to die if he's putting me next in line. I'm not volunteering to be next, but if that's what he wants, I'm not going out crying." She pauses, then asks if I will say the Shepherd prayer with her again, starting at "yea, though I walk through the valley of the shadow of death, I will fear no evil." I answer that I will. When we finish, she asks me again, "Do you believe it?"

I say, "Sure," which again comes from some part of me other than my head.

My analyst the priest tells me that life is not a mystery to be solved, but an invitation to an experience. That's something I do believe in my head. I would like to quote Pittman to Mabel, but I don't, because I'm afraid I would lose her. I'd like to tell her that we all come trailing clouds of glory, as Wordsworth said, and my partner believes. We get plucked out of eternity, Pittman says, and invited into this spatial-temporal box called the human experience. So when we die we leave the box, but we're still in eternity. Nothing lost, and a whole lot gained if we have lived "the abundant life" that Pittman believes is gospel truth.

The rub comes, as Mabel knows, from the pain inherent in the experience. Pittman thinks pain can be palliated with pills. It's suffering he focuses on. That comes from something we can't quite metabolize spiritually. I've had both suffering without pain and pain without suffering. From talking to Mabel, I'd say she has, too. Pittman, with Jung's help, sees suffering as a struggle in search of a meaning. Once we understand the meaning, what the suffering is pointing us toward and what it's trying to say to us, we stop suffering. When I stopped trying to figure out the physical cause of my colon rupturing without pathology, and started focusing on the "teleological" cause, I got somewhere. I quote

Aristotle as Pittman quotes Jung. In this instance, Jung's teleological cause is Aristotle's "final cause," the main one, the one that stops the hurting.

In either case, it's a cause that rings the alarm on my amygdala, which starts waving its axons at me as a traffic cop would do and yelling, "Turn, turn, see the sign, it says turn!" So I turn and find it's a long, narrow, rocky road marked "Authentic Avenue." No more persona, pretense, pursuit of power or pleasure. Just sitting with people like Mabel and being real—a very gratifying experience. I tell her so. She smiles and holds my hand, then closes her eyes as I leave. I make a mental note to tell Pittman that I feel lighter. Another good sign, as good as harmony in New Harmony.

A few weeks later, though, I feel my depression creeping back on me as I finish my monthly "living room" talk with patients and caregivers at M. D. Anderson in a unit called "Place of Wellness." I go into the reception room to leave and see sitting there a man and his wife who had been in my just-concluded session. They want to talk some more. As it turns out, they lift my spirits. The husband, who is a retired physician, stands and announces to me, "You're a holy man." It catches me by surprise. I've been called various names, but none of them "holy." His wife, a breast cancer patient, nods in agreement.

Thinking I may have misunderstood, I say, "Spell it."

He does, "H-o-l-y."

We sit down and talk a little, and then I ask, "What do you mean when you say I am a holy man?"

Without blinking an eye, the doctor replies, "Loving, caring, knowing what people think and feel, being kind and doing for others."

I thank him, then say, "That's quite a bit to live up to."

I'm feeling a little embarrassed to be called holy, so I change the subject back to them. I remark that they seem to be quite spiritual or religious (I have learned to use both words, since some people insist that they are spiritual, but not religious). The wife confirms that they are "very" religious. The husband then relates an experience during Eucharist at their church of tasting "blood" in the chalice. "I'm a doctor and know what blood tastes like. But when I looked down into the chalice, the color of the liquid was amber. I know I sipped blood."

Then the man asks me, "Do you consider yourself a healthy person?" He is referring to the discussion I just had with patients and family members on "finding well-being despite illness," the subtitle of a book that I wrote on cancer. I surprise myself and say without hesitation, "Yes." The answer comes straight from the limbic brain, meaning that my lost soul may be showing signs of returning, and my amygdala feels safe enough to sing sotto voce. Without knowing it, the husband and his wife have helped me to reverse my sense that depressive feelings were overtaking me once again. In helping them, I received a benefit in return.

I define well-being as a "core" wellness, which is deeper than physical health and comes from connecting with something bigger than self. The couple in the waiting room affirmed that both of them felt healthy in this sense. In the session just concluded, another man, who had liver cancer, and his wife, with breast cancer, told of their deep involvement in scouting. They had recently taken a group of Girl Scouts on an outing to Valley Forge. "I've been sick," the wife said, "on a number of trips and have been in the ER in hospitals all across the country." This confirms again my conviction that sickness and health can exist concurrently.

I directed a randomized, controlled study at M. D. Anderson on women who had completed treatment for breast cancer.[6] Two years later I followed up with in-depth interviews with many of the women, a number of whom were showing signs of metastasis and experiencing pain.[7] They reported to me that they were healthy as "a person," meaning they experienced well-being at their core, but not in the physical part of the self. The common expression they used was, "I have cancer but the cancer does not have me."

So science and spirit meet once again, as I keep reminding Pittman. Connecting to something larger outside the self comes easy for my partner. Pittman preaches and teaches on ways that he recommends for experiencing God and "the abundant life." Such experiencing, by definition, means attaching to something larger than one's self. He is convinced that such transcendence is all around us, but we fail to see it because we wear blinders. A Zen poem that Pittman likes to quote says, "The barn's burned down. Now I can see the moon." His point is that whether it is blinders or a barn, we often can't see something bigger even though it's right in front of us.

According to my teacher, the place where we can "experience God most profoundly is in Nature.... The dance of all creation is exemplified in the simplicity of sitting for a cycle of seasons and watching a tree in one's own yard, to see a tree as a metaphor and as a living experience of our own life, the reality of death and loss and the hope of transformation in new life." A second way to transcend and tap into the abundant life is "in our own creativity," Pittman says. "To use the tree as a metaphor for the beginning of consciousness in Eden and the transformation of consciousness at Calvary... the beginning, the end and new beginning. I like human beings and their ability to be creative," he goes on. "Through our creativity, we use the tree to build a house, to keep warm by the fireplace, to make the paper for the book we read."

A third way is through the intimacy and love of relationships, and feeling free to disclose our feelings, fears, fantasies and failures. My analyst and I have tried to practice this step in our relational therapy. We are mutually self-disclosing, but I am bigger on fears and failures than he is.

Pitttman's fourth way of experiencing God and the abundant life is through daily rituals. In this step Pittman includes daily ablution, elimination and adornment in a "sacred" space and "sanctuary" of one's house, which is for me the bathroom. We encounter the sacrum there, a word derived from the same root as "sacred." So once again we are reminded of the fusion between the profane and its opposite.

Pittman's fifth way to experience God and to become part of something bigger than self takes us back to suffering. "I'm not talking about physical pain," Pittman explains, "but suffering of the soul, where we have a conflict or difficulty we must carry until we can find its meaning." How does this lead to experiencing God? If we suffer long enough, as I myself discovered, we are taken to our knees, where we end up praying for relief and/or forgiveness.

In any case, we seek a closer relationship with God. Some of the women in my cancer study had this experience. Others found something bigger in their life through service. I remember Marilyn in particular. After her own period of baldness from chemotherapy, she began studying the best ways to tie scarfs and wear headdresses. She toured countries abroad to find the right dyes and fabrics. The program she offered to women patients back in Houston was her way of serving and attaching to something bigger outside the self.

Pittman, though, has found that "the most convenient way" to experience God and the abundant life is one that is "undervalued" and overlooked. "It is our body," he says. "Blake described the five senses as the inlets of the soul…. All the sacraments of the Church are around the senses—sight, sound, smell, taste, touch." Holy Communion, he notes, engages all the senses for connecting with a larger life. Many of the men and women with whom I volunteer at M. D. Anderson Cancer Center see their service as connecting them more closely with a higher power. Most are cancer survivors.

At a three-day conference on "the spiritual path," my therapist asked his listeners what keeps us from the abundant life and experiencing the transcendent. Nature is all around us, creativity is everywhere, suffering comes to everyone, we all know the value of loving and serving others, dreams are commonplace—so why don't we appreciate the abundance that is inherent in life? As we saw in chapter 6, Pittman delights in posing as a heretic, particularly at conferences on spirituality and religion. He closes his remarks in a typically iconoclastic manner. "My strong admonition to you," he tells the audience, is to "burn the goddamned barn down and see the moon."[8] In other words, institutions and authorities can get in the way of a personal experience of something bigger. There will always be "barns" to blame, but there's also the matter of cleansing the doors of our own perception, which the poet Blake suggested.

THE SCIENCE

Much of what Pittman says about finding something bigger in life parallels what the new science of positive psychology is now calling "discovering signature strengths."[1] According to research on the subject, when most people do something that is truly satisfying and helpful, they feel good—"authentically" happy in most cases. While exercising a "signature strength" in the service of something bigger than ego, people lose track of time and self-consciousness. They become totally absorbed. These are some of the effects I experience in my volunteer work with cancer patients. Helping is now recognized in validated studies, such as those by Midlarksy and others, as a form of coping.[2] It helps relieve pain. It lightens mood.

Martin Seligman, who has done groundbreaking research in using the positive in people to reverse the negative, calls this the way to achieve "authentic happiness." Pittman is convinced that purpose in life has to do with being "real," with being oneself, with being that which one is created or conceived to be. When we are, it shows—we feel it, others see it in us. Seligman says our signature strengths are identified by their effects. "Gratification" is one signature effect. It is more than pleasurable. It is an experience, I have found, that speaks to our essence—our purpose in being here. It "tingles" the amygdala, as Kandel would say.

I don't have to ask Pittman what his signature strengths are. They include speaking and preaching and feeling the voice of God channel through him when he really gets into a state of flow. "Flow" fits Pittman because he takes to holy waters and Jungian polysyllables "like a golden retriever swimming back with a duck, doing just what I'm born to do," to quote him. So my partner has no problem feeling authentic. The "real" Pittman is the same behind the pulpit or in the analytic container. No subterfuge, no persona. He wears the white collar of a priest only when he baptizes, marries, buries people or is a guest preacher at some church that dares to invite him; his clothes change but his essential self does not.

Whether it's "the real" me that I express in service or whether I am using helping as a way to cope, the evidence is clear that "dross" can indeed be transformed into something valuable. The Study of Adult Development at Harvard has tracked three separate cohorts totaling 824 individuals from all walks of life for the last half century. They were selected for different facets of mental and physical health and studied from adolescence into their old age. Those who have fared best psychologically and physically and have survived the longest are characterized by the ability to "turn dross into gold." Dr. George Vaillant, the psychiatrist director of the project, repeatedly uses the metaphor, along with "making lemonade out of lemons," to describe the power of this kind of alchemy. It applies to all three cohorts—to the highly advantaged, economically stable Harvard men; to the inner-city-Boston area males, coming out of broken homes as children and many going into manual-labor jobs; and to the "Terman women," whose families were somewhere between the other two groups economically, but who were selected for their high IQs. Vaillant comments that "the lives of all three cohorts repeatedly demonstrated that it was social aptitude—sometimes called emotional intelligence—not intellectual brilliance or parental social class that leads to a well-adapted old age."[3] In other words, "the language of the heart," as expressed in relating to others, is more important to aging well than left-brain rationality. The "real self," the data suggest, seems to prefer the right hemisphere.

The real self seems to be expressed when we exercise what Seligman calls our signature strengths and Vaillant identifies as "mature" coping styles. These serve us when life plays hardball with us. In Vaillant's long-term study, the coping modes or defenses that best predicted happiness at age fifty and health at ages seventy-five to eighty were altruism, sublimation, humor and suppression (in the sense of stoicism).[4] I have tried, in particular, to use altruism and humor, but I recognize that the determinant of coping mechanisms is largely unconscious and may resist deliberate attempts to use one style or another.

And there is something else to consider: The "hard science" of biology also helps in discovering the keys to the "real self." Antonio Damasio, in the prestigious journal *Nature*, suggests that some, if not many, scientists would say the self is "what the immune system identifies as belonging to the body."[5] This highly complex system is sensitive to recognition of "non-self" invaders, including needed kidney or heart transplants that are given to help a patient. But what does it mean when the immunological self starts a lethal battle with the rest of one's self?

I know of a bone marrow transplant patient whose "donor" stem cells were harvested from his own body. The match was perfect, better than it would have been if the cells had come from a brother, sister or other close relative. The man died a painful death. His body reacted strongly to his own tissue. Psychologically, one could speculate that when there is a fierce inner battle going on in our lives, as if two parts of us are at war, then "the real self" may become the victim. On the other hand, many heart transplant patients are certain that they have taken on the distinctive habits, tastes, and even temperaments of their donors. Even the immunological self, then, may be influenced by the hearts, perhaps the "real" selves, of others.

On a less speculative note Seligman, at the University of Pennsylvania, has taken concepts such as authenticity and gratification into the laboratory and dissected them to understand how they work. More than a quarter of a century ago, Seligman came to my attention because I was depressed, and he was demonstrating how depression is a form of learned helplessness and pervasive pessimism.[6] I can relate to Seligman because he, too, acknowledges that he is a pessimist who has learned how to be optimistic. Seligman has taught me and thousands of other depressives the techniques for curbing pessimism and acquiring optimism. I learned and taught them, but one crucial step was missing. I failed to internalize them. To change neurons requires learning that is anchored in relationship.

I am using my experience with Pittman to complete that crucial step of internalizing. The most powerful form of learning is modeling—finding a teacher who models the behavior you wish to make your own. Pittman is a good teacher because he sits patiently with me on this long journey in the belly of the whale until I "metabolize" such morsels as meaning, optimism and authenticity.

The science on such subjects is straightforward. As we indicated in chapter 7 on shame and guilt, pessimists, being the opposite of optimists, are convinced that, when something bad happens, it is always their fault, it is bound to keep happening, and it is ruining their lives. If someone walks out on a lecture I am giving, it is because I am boring, it always happens this way, and I can never be happy because of it. By contrast an optimist like Pittman would think that whoever walks out during one of his lectures must have to go to the toilet. He doesn't personalize, generalize or project future doom from any single event. Explanatory style—the style we use to explain what happens to us—is a powerful index to personality.

Where I turn to Seligman more than McGehee is on the subject of earning a good feeling in order to be entitled to it. Pittman preaches the gospel of faith, of God's abundant love, which cannot be earned. It is a gift to be accepted. In contrast, Seligman presents this secular experiment to students and colleagues: "Suppose you could be hooked up to a hypothetical 'experience machine' that, for the rest of your life, would stimulate your brain and give you any positive feeling you desire." This includes love. Seligman continues, "Most of the people to whom I offer this imaginary choice refuse the machine. It is not just positive feelings we want, we want to be _entitled_ to our positive feelings."[7] I, for one, have more than just a desire to earn mine—I have a compulsion.

Our culture today advertises what Seligman calls "shortcuts to happiness," the idea of transformation through pills and scalpel, as referred to in the previous chapter. The shortcuts include not only drugs, but also "chocolate, loveless sex, shopping, masturbation, and television."[8] Trying to take shortcuts to joy and comfort leads to disastrous consequences, according to Seligman. "Legions of people... in the middle of great wealth are starving spiritually" because they fail to exercise personal strengths and virtues and thus don't feel entitled to good feelings. "Positive emotion alienated from the exercise of character leads to emptiness, to inauthenticity, to depression, and, as we age, to the gnawing realization that we are fidgeting until we die." Along the same line, the longest and most thorough psychological study of men across their entire lifetimes has been going on at Harvard since 1939. The strengths—"mature defenses," as Vaillant calls them—that hold up best and bring joy right into the eighth decade and beyond are altruism, the ability to postpone gratification, future-mindedness and humor.[9]

Seligman gives his students this weekend assignment: They are to engage in one pleasurable activity and one philanthropic activity, and write about both. Examples of the pleasurable activities the students pursued included "hanging out with friends or watching a movie or eating a hot fudge sundae." All of these "paled in comparison with the effects of the kind action." Examples of the latter included tutoring a nephew phoning for help with his third-grade arithmetic and helping an old woman shovel snow from her driveway. A business student reported that he had come to the University of Pennsylvania "to learn how to make a lot of money in order to be happy, but that he was floored to find that he liked helping other people more than spending his money shopping."[10]

Altruism as defined by Vaillant is "doing for others what they need, not what you want to do for them."[11] It's one of the characteristics of the men in his six-decade study who not only are still surviving, but are also thriving. Of the 76 inner-city men still living, 95 percent could still move heavy furniture, chop wood, walk two miles and climb two flights of stairs without tiring.[12] These hardy souls have a capacity not only to give love or service, but also to receive it graciously. As a Freudian psychiatrist, Valliant considers altruism to be a "mature" defense mechanism to use in the face of life's unavoidable losses and tragedies.[13] For Seligman, it is a way to find gratifying experiences and to discover one's strengths. He emphasizes that, for men especially, the ability to receive kindness is as important a part of signature strength as is giving it.[14]

Jean Shinoda Bolen, a Jungian-trained physician, knows that gratitude is a powerful feeling that comes to those who survive life-threatening illness or injury—an experience that cuts "close to the bone."[15] A natural response is one of wanting to "pay back" to God or life itself by serving others in some meaningful way. At the cancer center where I offer my services, many of the volunteers have had cancer and are there "paying back" with gratitude for having been spared. "Active kindness" is part of this behavior and the feeling behind it.[16]

What's the science in all this? Certainly, Seligman's measurements and methodologies in identifying signature strengths and their effects qualify as good science. The hardest endpoint measures, however, are found post-mortem. When our brains are autopsied and put under the microscope, they tell a story. Years ago, nuns belonging to the order of the American School Sisters of Notre Dame agreed to donate their brains to science upon their death. Included are 180 nuns who were born before 1917.

Of particular interest are those who develop Alzheimer's disease compared with the sisters who remain intellectually sound as they age. A distinguishing feature was found in the required autobiographies written many years before when the women were young and applied for admission into the order. Those who showed "strong emotional content" in what they wrote have survived best, according to research results.[17] The nuns with an optimistic outlook and positive emotions have survived longer and remained active. One unexpected finding is that a few of the nuns who remained active and upbeat to the very end of life showed classic signs of beta-amyloid plaques in brain autopsies. Like the women with cancer, they had Alzheimer's, but Alzheimer's did not have them. Others, who lived with less optimism and expressiveness, died earlier and had progressive signs of dementia.[18]

Additional long-term research projects, such as the MacArthur Studies of Successful Aging, show that good social emotional support and healthy interaction with others distinguishes healthy aging. In the MacArthur Studies, a cohort of 1,189 initially high-functioning older adults was followed for seven years.[19] The men and women who lived the longest and stayed active had kept a strong network of friends and an interest in learning new things.

That keeping the brain active will sustain health longer is the key finding in a recently published study in the *New England Journal of Medicine*.[20] The study has followed for 21 years a total of 469 older men and women and found that mental acuity was predicted by "use-it-or-lose-it" behaviors. An absorbing book or a challenging crossword puzzle are examples of means of keeping the mind active. In measuring the amount of dementia the men and women developed between sixty and seventy years of age, a significant difference was found between those who engaged regularly in mental activity and those who did not. Physical exercise did not appear to protect against dementia, with one exception. Frequent dancing, an activity that engages the mind as well as the body, did seem to confer protection.[21]

What these long-term, well controlled studies are telling us is that to enjoy mental, if not physical, health into old age, we will benefit by daily exercising our brain, practicing an optimistic outlook, maintaining a strong social support system, letting people inside our lives and responding to those who, in turn, open up their lives to us. Pittman scores better on this scientific tally than I do, with the possible exception of the amount of daily reading engaged in as mental exercise. My philosophy is that I am never too old to learn how to be "neurogenic"—that is, to keep my neurons growing. The rewarding experiences I have, whether at M. D. Anderson, in the Bolivian Andes or the Himalayas, or sitting with Pittman in the belly of the whale all contribute to arborizing my rhizomes and honoring my entelechy, which Aristole defined as *actualizing* one's essence as opposed to simply acknowledging its potential. I include entelechy to remind myself of something else the Greek philosopher was wise about. Most people, he suggested, are seeking more than just long, pleasant lives. They want an experience of flourishing, which neurobiologically calls for experiences and adventures that give us extra boosts of dopamine and endorphins and give the amygdala something to sing about. "Flourishing" is often felt by those who are so attached to something bigger outside themselves that they enter a state of flow.[22] Seligman found flow to be a characteristic state of those of his research subjects who exercise signature strengths in behalf of others.

The "call of service" is what Robert Coles, child psychiatrist and Pulitzer Prize-winning author, sees as "a witness to idealism."[23] I haven't experienced what I do for cancer patients in these terms, but I agree with what Coles's father said was the reason he helped people as a volunteer in nursing homes: "I like talking with the people I meet." He likes to hear their stories. I can actually feel a "state of flow" when I get caught up in the stories of people I meet at M. D. Anderson or at the hospice where I have volunteered. Does it help them to talk to a willing listener? The research evidence says it does, that stories and service go together.[24] Studies also show that people who, like me, give service find it is a way to lift their moods.[25] Research also shows that feelings of guilt may be relieved through service. I admit to both benefits and know that in volunteering I receive as much as or more than I give.

Service and other helping behaviors "light up" specific areas of the brain. What Damasio calls "the life of the spirit" includes recognition that humans have a responsibility to each other and to the natural world we live in. Brain correlates of experiences in which we show kindness and offer help have been identified by neurobiologists.[26] The return we receive for our "pay back" behavior—be it "pay back" to God or to life itself—is in the harmony and balance experienced in the brain and body. Exercising the discipline to pursue the life of the spirit becomes a source of joy, according to Damasio.[27] My Jungian teacher uses other words, but he is on the same path when he talks of the abundant life. Pittman's ways to transcend the self and experience the abundant life are complementary to the science of Aristotle, Spinoza, William James and Damasio. They are also are in accord with the psychological science of flow and signature strengths.

Like Seligman, Dr. McGehee inveighs against trying to use material "goodies" as a shortcut to happiness. Pittman tells his students that he has never seen "so much materialism and transformation of communication systems" side by side with a quest for spirituality.[28] Neither, he is convinced, will produce lasting feelings of gratification, much less happiness or rewards at the soul level.

So both of my teachers—McGehee and Seligman—agree that shortcuts won't cut it—"it" standing for a feeling of being real and connecting to something bigger than ego. In my small way, I am learning the same lesson from the Mabels and Arnies whose hand I may hold or foot I may rub or humor I may share. I leave feeling gratified and a little lighter and taller. My guess is that I am slowly tilting my temperamental set-point toward the brighter side.

CHAPTER 10

I'M HOME

This must be the way that human life worked....

If you cast your bread upon the waters and were

prepared to give it up for good, it would somehow

come back to you—albeit in another form.[1]

THE STORY

I'm sitting in the First Presbyterian Church in downtown San Antonio, not far from the historic chapel of the Alamo, attending a Saturday night formal wedding with my wife, Rita. In Houston, a short flight away, Pittman is preparing for the adult education class he is teaching at Christ Church Cathedral on "Mysticism 101." He's looking over what thirty-five class members wrote about their own "mystical" experiences. I've never had one. My scientific friends would say that this is understandable because such experiences are "not real;" they are "imaginary."

The prelude to the wedding service has just ended with the final notes of Bach's "Jesu, Joy of Man's Desiring." Now the house party is being seated to the accompaniment of the "Allegro Maestoso" movement of Handel's *Water Music*. I enjoy Baroque music, and my shadow must also, because it is staying quiet, along with my voices of depression. Rita and I whisper about times we have heard Bach and Handel at weddings.

Back in Houston, among the sketches and narratives that Pittman is reading, one in particular catches his attention. It's from a mother writing about her beautiful young daughter's "hopeless depression" and the "terrible hole" she and her family feel stuck in despite their repeated prayers. After a sleepless night, the mother takes a familiar shortcut the next morning to her work in a suburb. It's a country lane she uses often. She likes it because it is peaceful and gives her time to think. She reflects on the fact that although it's a quiet country road, she has never seen or heard any birds along the way, particularly on a cold winter day.

Suddenly that changes. A beautiful red bird flies in front of her slowly moving car, as if guiding it. The bird lands in the grass at the side of the road. The mother stops to watch it. It becomes a "spiritual experience," she writes. Something deep inside tells her the bird is there bringing her a message that there is hope for her daughter. "It took years, but the hope stayed in my heart," she said, proving to her that her "spiritual experience" was real and her faith well grounded.

A man in Pittman's class, who describes his experience as "semi-mystical," tells of sitting in his office and suddenly having "this intense sensation" that a girl "who was my first really 'big love' while in law school, is in serious trouble and needs help desperately." The next day he receives a call telling him that the woman was in a private plane crash and died shortly thereafter. The time coincided with his intense experience the day before. How to explain it? Mystery is to be experienced, not explained, Pittman tells his students.

Back at the wedding, they're now into the seating of the families. The deep, moving chords of Pachelbel's "Canon in D" are sounding in my ears. I am taken back immediately to the spring day Rita and I witnessed the outdoor graduation of our daughter Liz from a boarding school called Purnell in the green, rolling countryside of New Jersey. It was a golden moment watching the young women in white gloves and broad-brimmed straw hats as they marched in to the chords of Pachelbel. As that memory fades I look up from my reverie, and I hear a voice coming right out of the "Canon in D" being played by the ensemble in the church balcony. "I'm home, Dad," it says, and then repeats, "I'm home, Dad." Immediately, the voice becomes an image of our Tibetan puppy, Bodhi, wagging her black and white plume of a tail. It strikes me as a vision realer than real. And I know instantly that I am having my first mystical experience—complete with color—after a lifetime of mostly mundane, sometimes painful, episodes of strictly this-world reality. As I sit savoring the experience, I actually think I can feel my limbic loops lighting up with a numinosity that goes right into my amygdala, which really does "tingle." I don't mean to overstate, but the voice and vision don't fade even when the processional begins several minutes later with the resounding notes of Clarke's "Trumpet Voluntary" from the balcony.

My experience is so real, but inexplicable, that I say nothing even to Rita about it. I sense that it will never be repeated and that, as time passes, I will lose the strong feeling that it's "realer than real." I'll conclude then that it's simply God displaying the sense of humor Pittman has described. The joke here is on me, being presented with a voice saying, "I'm home, Dad," and then an image of a dog. *If that's how it plays out,* I'm thinking, *then there's no reason to say anything about it and raise questions about my going off the deep end even more. I'll save the experience to see what my therapist the priest says about it. He's the grand master of mystery.*

Meanwhile, back in Houston, the master is using the experiences of Mysticism 101 class members to confirm his conviction that many "ordinary" people have "extraordinary" things happen to them. However, most don't talk about them for the same reason I'm not inclined to. One in his class tells of seeing Jesus. I have been at the bedside of hospice patients who tell of seeing God as they die. I have never questioned such reports because what's "real" to any of us is what is experienced in our own brains. Other people are not walking in our shoes, much less being privy to what's inside our heads. I am aware of some of the theories on what the process of dying does to the brain, including hallucinations that may be produced. Yet I'm not inclined to believe that oxygen deprivation is the primal cause of seeing Jesus.

As the wedding ceremony proceeds, I continue to feel a lingering excitement from my own hallucination and mystical experience. It has presented me with a sequel of sorts to the story Pittman gave me at our very first session, now years ago. He said that by sacrificing a piece of my body, some sixteen inches of colon, in New York, I moved Liz from her stuck place in purgatory to a better realm. It's a story, a myth, involving an otherworldly evolution, which I am willing to accept. The sacrifice of my sigmoid also played a part in my own evolving. I have slowly come to recognize I was off-course and deviating badly from what my "acorn" nature was calling me to be. By nature I am an introvert who performed as a mother-pleasing extravert questing for fame and fortune. I finally had a painful wake-up call from my bursting belly. That's my story of evolving entelechy—Aristotle's word for the innate driving force behind becoming what one is meant to be. 𝓍

It's now the morning after hearing "I'm home, Dad" and seeing Liz as Bodhi. I smile as I reflect on my fantasy. Maybe Liz's upward progress after the sacrifice I made for her in New York got off track a little, and she ended up in the animal kingdom of the next realm. From there, she's coming home as Bodhi. This fits with the karmic theory that all of us keep recycling through this and other realms until we get our karmic points right and evolve on to become angels on earth as well as in heaven. It's a story that I now place alongside other myths to "explain" who we are and where we're headed. I don't disparage myths. I agree with Pittman that we're all living one archetypal story or another. He's convinced that his archetype is "wounded healer" and thinks mine is, too.

Rita and I are in another old San Antonio church, St. Mark's Episcopal, for the 9 A.M. service. We hear Bach again in the melody for the hymn "Christ Is Risen." I start feeling another mystical experience coming on, but it recedes. Then the preacher gives his sermon on "doubting Thomas," and for the first time I hear Thomas being cast as a good guy. In this version Thomas simply wants more than just to hear about the resurrection. He wants some deeper sensory experience of it, to feel the nail holes in Jesus' hands and the wound in Christ's side. Because I have been called a doubting Thomas and known not to believe many things, I feel better hearing a new interpretation of the story.

At the communion rail, following the sermon, I look up at the altar and feel a stream of endorphins going up and down my spine. Then I hear, "I'm home again, Dad," and see Bodhi. God's truth, that's the experience I have all over again. The telltale endorphin trilling is part of it.

Because my M.E. (mystical experience) continues to be realer than real to me, and not a one-time fantasy, I tell Rita. She doesn't laugh. She's happy for me as she sees me crying over a dead daughter who is back home as a puppy. Then Rita begins to have her own experiences with Bodhi. She discovers in this young dog some of the reckless behavior of Liz. We have a bridge in our house some fourteen feet above the dining and living room floor, and it connects our bedroom to Rita's meditation area on the second floor. There isn't any ceiling in this part of the house, just the inside of the vaulting roof lines. Over the next few months, Bodhi falls three times from this bridge onto the hard tile floor below. She's treated by the vet, limps for a while, then recovers completely, only to run too fast around the swimming pool and fall in. No one is outside except Tashi, her Tibetan brother, who doesn't know how to swim, either. Rita is inside the house meditating, and she hears these thrashing and splashing sounds outside. She runs down, sees Bodhi desperately gasping for air and trying to paddle her little legs to the one and only set of steps out of the pool. Rita saves her. So how many lives does this dog have? Another mystery.

I'm telling all this to Pittman the following Monday, my new day for sitting in the analytic container. I don't ask him if he believes it. It's my experience, and my temporal lobes and amygdala that feel the effect. It is also my story. In turn, he doesn't ask me if I believe his mystical experience of going out and doing a vision quest in the woods all alone, which he did. It's so powerful an experience he gives a sermon on it, without identifying himself as the mystic to whom it happened.

What Pittman did was to go into some woods and reenact an ancient Indian rite for becoming a warrior. The ritual consists of drawing a circle on the ground and making it into a clock. The initiate is to sit in the middle of the circle and observe and record for twenty-four hours what occurs around the clock. My therapist did this, not to reclaim the star basketball warrior in himself, but simply to sit, see and test whether what happens outside the circle changes who he is inside. In that night and day period, Pittman sees a large bird flying overhead; he watches a small fawn, a black snake, a streak of lightning, and a mother duck and her ducklings. Then he notices approaching rainclouds. A rainstorm—a deluge—occurs that leaves him cold, wet and hungry. As he watches the sun rise, he is visited by a "wise" owl and a feeling that he has experienced a condensed version of life itself.

"It is now the end of my twenty-four-hour lifetime," his journal states. "As I reread the accounts of my stationary journey, I realize that I have recorded ordinary events of animals, weather, lightning, and trees. Moses had his burning bush, St. Paul his blinding flash, and everyone his Christ. Perhaps now, I understand that what was great about them was not what happened to them, but that they were able to see the extraordinary in the ordinary."

Is Pittman any different because of his experience? He's the same in mind and body, but he notices he does have a change in lenses through which he sees the world, and the ordinary in it does strike him differently. Ordinary things, ordinary events, and ordinary people do look extraordinary to him. And, he realizes, they *are* extraordinary, and have been all along. All it took was a day and night in the woods to cleanse my teacher's doors of perception so that, as his favorite "wild-eyed" English engraver and poet, William Blake, said, he felt he could now see the world in a grain of sand.[2]

I remark to him, probably to reassure myself, "We're not crazy; we're just maverick guys having extraordinary things happen to us once in a while." We are like the men and women in Pittman's Mysticism 101. We're not different from a lot of other people in this country. Fifty-three percent of the adult population has said on Gallup polls that they have had mystical experiences.[3] But they don't talk about them. Some of them are even scientists who do talk, such as Richard Feynman, the Nobel physicist who didn't care what people said about him.[4] He knew what he had experienced. And so do I know. Pittman does, too. I resort to my scatological default and tell Pittman, "I don't give a shit what people think. It's my temporal lobe and limbic system that light up, not theirs."

Jung once remarked that "mystical experience is experience of archetypes."[5] He added that such experience is always numinous, full of the energy of archetypes. "Mystics are people who have a particularly vivid experience of the processes of the collective unconscious."

My mystical experience is akin to the "transfusions of transcendence" I receive periodically in the Colorado Rockies. I say "transfusions" because several times a year Rita has to take the Tibetans and me for our "fix" in the high country. "High" means anything from 8500 feet to 14,000. Our redwood house with solar paneling in the roof is at 8500. The peaks we try to "bag" are 14,000. Regardless of the time of year, the dogs find plenty of snowy inclines to slide and roll down. I feel the endorphins just watching them. My response to the Rockies comes unbidden from outside my awareness and, for me, involves something deep and archetypal.

On a trip to the mountains I have a flashback to ten years before. Liz is with me in the woods on our land. She's here on authorized leave from a drug recovery center in Manhattan where she is struggling to overcome addictions to heroin and cocaine. A young woman counselor about her age has accompanied her on the visit here. In the forest, there is only Liz walking with me on a tree version of a vision quest. I'm after a Douglas fir seedling I want to transplant near our house in order to watch it grow. I have been cautioned against this horticultural adventure. Douglas firs are particular about where they want their roots. They know they make beautiful Christmas trees in much demand by city slickers and countryfolk alike every December. They conjure up Norman Rockwell images of hearth and home and loving mothers. So I have to be very loving in the energy I carry with me on my quest for my seedling.

I finally find the one I want. It's about a foot high, and Liz watches me without a word in what I call the sound of sacred silence, which I can feel in my bones. I drop to my knees, an appropriate position for both digging up the baby tree and honoring the sacred silence. I feel the cold of rich soil as I carefully dig around tender roots and go deep enough to spare the taproot of my seedling. Liz has been watching closely and indicating that she, too, is absorbed in the birthing I hope to bring about. It is technically not a birth, but a transplanting, but for the baby tree and me it is a new beginning. I hope it is for Liz, too.

Liz starts getting cold standing still in the deep woods with giant Ponderosa and Lodgepole pines on every side. I tell her I picked this particular seedling because it is a survivor among these towering giants, which compete for the nourishment of sunlight and soil. There aren't many others like this little girl tree. I give her the feminine gender because I am becoming aware that the hardiest humans on this earth are female. I'm hoping that our younger daughter is no exception.

Liz decides to go back to the house, following our bootprints through the forest and, if necessary, using smoke from the chimney as a guide. I carefully extract my baby fir from her home and take her tenderly to the new one I have prepared for her. It's not a favorable time of year for transplanting, particularly a tree specimen that doesn't take to being moved. Nonetheless, I put in her new home and hole just the right mix of fertilizer the experts at the local hardware store have given me. Then I carefully fill the hole with good loose dirt for her "dendrites" to grow in and make healthy rhizome connections underground with the life that vibrates there.

I pat dirt around her tiny trunk and taproot—her "axon" I call it—and say a prayer over her, borrowing lines from Psalm twenty-three, which I identify with surviving. The new home I picked for this little tree is special. It is where Rita, the dogs and I can catch a glimpse of her as we drive up the last steep incline on the long dirt driveway to our house. However, the real reason I picked this spot is that I can stand in the small third-floor bathroom, where I perform my rituals of ablution, and watch her grow. The reasons I think she will grow are two: My heart has sent her powerful waves of loving energy, and her new home is directly adjacent to our large underground septic meadow.

These doings took place in the fall, a time of endings. However, I've learned enough Jungian from my teacher to know that endings are beginnings. The leaves and flowers of Indian summer were gone, and in their place were seeds everywhere. I have a fauna and flora mountain almanac that tells me to marvel at nature's proficiency in seed dispersal by wind, water, mammals and birds.[6] Even my little girl tree was perhaps dropping tiny, invisible seeds, from which, many years later, I imagined, would grow big Douglas firs. That's the destiny I wanted for my tiny Christmas tree.

And so it comes to pass. Ten years later, my tree has grown to be eighteen feet high. Liz is gone, but Bodhi is here, and her inexhaustible energy inspirits me. Periodically, in the chapel in Houston where we had a memorial service for Liz, I go to the communion rail to sip the wine, look up at the stained-glass windows above the altar and hear, "I'm home, Dad," all over again, and I feel the endorphin trills up and down my spine. I usually don't tell Rita, although the bonds between us deepen with each day, strengthening from shared sorrows. The voices of my depression have receded. My ego is now subordinate to my soul, reversing the position it held for a very long time.

Pittman and I are still sitting in the belly of the whale, but our perichoretic dance is much more graceful now that I have a better feel for the rhythm and the beat and have stopped thinking about the steps. On his part, Pittman still talks about the piano lessons his mother paid for him to take. It wasn't long before his teacher was telling Mrs. McGehee that her son should respond to a different calling, and he has. He has a different kind of music in his bones, and I know it well because it is making me whole. As a result I am able once again to hear the music of Mozart and the mountains and the singing of the trees, my Douglas fir in particular.

Back at 8500 feet, I'm smiling as I look at my evergreen tree while performing Pittman's rituals of ablution in the little third-floor bathroom of Chateau Les Justices. I smile because I suddenly realize that at last I'm embracing my shadow and loving the unloveable in me. My shit is my fir's fertilizer. And thanks to nature's alchemy, this means my dross is her gold and maybe the sacred really can be found in the profane. So, Liz, wherever you are in cosmic evolution, you have my blessings, and may God make His face to shine upon you. If I have contributed to transforming you, please know that you did the same for me.

THE SCIENCE

Certain environments facilitate the occurrence of cytoarchitectural changes in the brains of depressives.[1] An analytic container that provides a relationship of synchrony is one.

Pittman's "resonant" frequencies match mine, meaning that the beta and alpha frequencies that characterize his brain functioning and introverted personality are in sync with my own. Nature, which Pittman extols for transcending ego, is another trophic environment that is healing and promotes soundness in mind, body and soul.

"Sound" is a word derived from the German, meaning "whole" or "health." It is an energy that is especially noticeable in nature, where sound is often subliminal, but powerfully affecting. If we tap into the imperceptible music of mountains, forests and meadows, we become aware of a rhythm.[2] There is a tempo that entrains us and balances our breathing, heartbeat and brain waves.[3] The tenth cranial nerve transmits sound—its rhythm, tempo and pitch—from the brain to the vagus nerve, which has been found to regulate cardiac output and foster social engagement as well as to consolidate memory.[4] Sound produces powerful effects on the autonomic nervous system and can not only calm us, but also—through vagal effects and oxytocin, a bonding neurotransmitter—draw us closer to others.[5]

Nature, then, provides us with positive psychoacoustics, which Andrew Weil, a pioneer in integrative medicine, has shown to be healing.[6] The effects are subtle, archetypal and unconscious. David Cumes, a physician who has studied such effects, notes that a wilderness experience into "the archetype of sacred space" is "mystical and numinous."[7] But, he adds, it is also "difficult to reach." The countless days that Rita, our dogs and I have spent in the Indian Peaks Wilderness confirm to us that the space is sacred; we are there as visitors to honor the land and its forests, wildflowers, streams and mountains.

The "sound of silence" is also part of the trophic, nurturing environment of the mountains. Thomas Merton, a Trappist monk who championed contemplative prayer and silence, says, "When I am liberated by silence, when I am no longer involved in the measurement of life, but in the living of it, I can discover a form of prayer in which there is effectively no distraction. My whole life becomes a prayer. My whole silence is full of prayer.... Let me seek, then, the gift of silence, and poverty, and solitude, where everything I touch is turned into prayer; where the sky is my prayer, the birds are my prayer, the wind in the trees is my prayer, for God is all in all."[8]

As for the environment that a therapeutic relationship or analytic container should provide, it is like nature in its variable "weather" conditions, ranging from stormy to sunny. Bonded as my coauthor and I have become in the choppy waters and deep currents of the long sea journey upon which we embarked some five years before, our visions of mystery remain different. Pittman sees mystery as "unknowable" by definition and faults science for considering it a puzzle yet to be solved. I don't understand mystery but, now that I have experienced it, I recognize some of the markers by which science is starting to explore it empirically. Where my therapist and I remain firmly together is in mutual appreciation of the "miraculous" in the mundane, the extraordinary in the ordinary and the transcendent in the quotidian. All of which brings us back to recognition of the profane in the sacred or, in keeping with my theme, of finding gold underneath all the manure. Where we may differ is on methodology. I agree with Dr. Kandel's view of reductionism, which seeks to distill the essence out of experience and let its soul sing.[9] Pittman disavows the reductionistic and seeks truth in more mystical ways.

Synchronicity started us on this soulful voyage with my experience at Mount Sinai in the shadow of the valley of death in New York. And now we return to synchronicities. Mystical experience uses synchronicity as a marker, a cairn by which we know we are on the right path to understanding as much of the process as we can. Along the way we use science to provide us with more markers. Two such markers are acausality and nonlocality. Jung and his pen-pal patient, Nobel physicist Wolfgang Pauli, were pioneers in describing the "unexplainable" and extraordinary happenings ordinary people experience.

As we discussed at the start of this journey, what some leading-edge science is now suggesting to us on the subject of "mystery" and the "unexplainable" is that [1] acausality is a natural phenomenon, meaning that there can be such resonance or "empathy" between particles or people that what happens to one is "felt" by the other, even when far apart; [2] synchronicities do occur, demonstrating that meaningful, unpredictable events involving people and things are more than "funny coincidences"—they have something to tell us; and [3] nonlocality—action at a distance across space and time—is a principle of nature, including the human kind. Let us also add what neuroscience is discovering about "anomalous" experiences, such as people becoming "one," with much bigger realities. Through fMRI, we can now identify where in the medial prefrontal cortex we register our felt experience of "oneness" with another, animate or inanimate.

So what's the common denominator here in all this? A four-letter word for what makes the world go round: Love.[10] If this sounds more sentimental than scientific, then look at the empirical evidence. Starting with biofeedback, considered "heretical" in the 1960s, studies prove that ordinary individuals can control heart rate, muscle tension and skin temperature if given constant feedback by electronic instruments involving sight or sound. How do they do it? A common answer is that the subjects start to "feel one" with the instrument or with the monitor or the instructor. Yes, people can and do fall in love with machines as well as humans and pets, and we have profound, "silent," effects on all three.

At the Princeton Engineering Anomalies Research laboratory, ordinary people mentally exert "a statistically significant effect" on the performance of machines and "physical systems, whether mechanical, electromagnetic, quantum mechanical or nuclear."[11] Volunteer experimenters at the PEAR program are called operators and, without special instruction or training, they try to influence a machine that generates large sets of zeros and ones, showing no trend toward either zero or one. Another group of volunteers, known as "participants," are asked to visualize and extract details of a specific scene far away. In the case of the random number generators, the operators demonstrated the ability to significantly influence the behavior of the machine. In the other experiment, participants could accurately describe places they had never been to or seen.[12] One author contends that the findings provide "at least preliminary evidence of the possibility of some type of vital fifth force, such as the L energy," being responsible for the anomalous experiences of operators and participants.[13] To Pearsall, the "L" energy is "life energy," which, if proven, would join gravity, electromagnetic energy, and strong and weak nuclear forces as the physical forces moving matter, often without our awareness. I suggest that "L" also stands for love, whose power science is acknowledging more and more.

As we have seen, Jungian psychology has long held that the unconscious is a major player in what we do, think and feel. This means that much occurs without our willing or understanding it. When Malcolm Gillis stepped down after serving as president of Rice University for eleven years, he remarked about his attachment to outdoor ventures, "It's like church. It's in the wild we never see anybody…. I'm not introspective. I don't know why I feel this way. All that I know is I like it a lot and feel closer to nature and to God."[14] Dr. Gillis, introspective or not, is among many whose unconscious leads them to feel attached to something larger than themselves.

In recent years personality and social scientists have elaborated on "the illusion of conscious will"[15] and being "strangers to ourselves,"[16] the titles of two recent books on the subject from Harvard and the University of Virginia psychology departments. The books provide more confirmatory evidence on the fascinating unconscious feature of human nature, which has largely been the province of psychoanalysts.

Close to the time that these phenomena began achieving significant recognition, a centennial observance was being planned of Freud's much studied, but incomplete, *Project for a Scientific Psychology*. Freud's brilliant insights predicted the existence of brain cell synapses, but he died before he could establish psychoanalysis as a science. The goal of his unfinished project was "to furnish a psychology that shall be a natural science: that is, to represent psychical processes as quantitatively determinant states of specifiable material particles, thus making those processes perspicuous and free from contradiction."[17]

One hundred years later, in 1995, the New York Academy of Sciences organized a conference at which contemporary neuroscientists presented papers on what is now known about brain, mind and behavior and their relationship to Freud's incomplete project. In organizing the conference, Robert M. Bilder, a noted clinical neuropsychologist, observed that there seems to be a compulsion to observe anniversaries, which often "prompt odd behavior among their celebrants" and, in this case, "peculiar coincidences."[18] The first coincidence, Bilder reported, was discovering that the date set for the conference, November 4, was the same as the publication date of Freud's famous *Interpretation of Dreams* (November 4, 1900). Then Bilder "received an electronic mail transmission with a time-date stamp of 12:01 A.M., 100 years after the exact date on which Freud experienced his famous 'dream of Irma's injection.'" The email was from "an expert on the topic (of this particular dream)" but no mention was made of "the coincidence." Bilder asks, "Is it possible that in the world of dreams there is continuity not apparent to the waking?" Pittman answers with a resounding "yes." And he adds that those "coincidences" were none other than what Jung called synchronicities.

Another way of explaining what is involved in such anomalies is "resonance." The theory here is that not only physical systems and their environments, but the whole universe can be seen as operating on "sympathetic resonance," involving "synergistically interactive vibrations" and harmonic oscillation, which ordinary people can tap into, giving a feeling of being one with the universe. My friend Larry Dossey, a wise integrator of all these fields as well as a noted author and clinician, used to head an organization in Dallas called "Isthmus," devoted to bridging matter and spirit. Among Nobelists and other scientists invited to give presentations was biologist Lyall Watson, who perceived early on that a kind of resonance seems to pervade nature.[19] Not only can this universal resonance produce the "coincidences" in organizing weighty scientific conferences, it can be involved in interesting cases of a more mundane variety. Watson describes how a wide range of objects and organisms—from stones to cars to dogs and cats—may "resonate" with human creatures by taking on our "emotional fingerprints." All of this has helped me clear up a longstanding mystery of my own.

Only in hindsight across more than thirty years do I now understand why Rita talks to the cars she has had as though they share emotional imprints or fingerprints. I remember returning with her from an out-of-town conference before we were married and listening to her carry on a conversation with her Fiat, saying how she had missed it, what a fine vehicle it was, and how much faith she had in its starting right up despite a weak battery. And it always started. I also understood for the first time what is really meant by an engine "purring." It's simply showing love for its owner.

The neuroscientific take on this loving behavior has to do with experiments that show we not only "identify" with people or things we become closely attached to, but our very self-image or body sensations can be projected on to them. V. S. Ramachandran, M.D., Ph.D., director of the Center for Brain and Cognition at the University of California, San Diego, and adjunct professor at the Salk Institute for Biological Studies, has experimentally demonstrated this common experience: a "feeling that my car is part of me, so much so that I become infuriated if someone makes a small dent on it."[20] The brain's visual areas dispatch messages to the limbic, emotional brain, leading to a fired-up amygdala demanding that the hypothalamus turn on the norepinephrine. The professor holds that it's wrong to assume that "your 'self' is anchored to a single body that remains stable and permanent...." His experiments, he contends, "suggest the exact opposite—that your body image, despite all its appearance of durability, is an entirely transitory internal construct.... a shell... for passing on your genes to offspring."[21] Ramachandran suggests that when we love and deeply care for someone, not only may we become part of that person, but our souls—not merely our bodies—"have become intertwined."

"Intertwining" is a phenomenon also found in the experiences of heart transplant recipients. Pearsall[22] recorded reports of seventy-three such patients, including the experience of a young Hispanic who began using the word "copacetic" after his transplant—a word that his mother said is not found in Spanish and had never before been uttered by her son. This had been a favorite word of his donor, David, a young physician who had died in a car crash which his wife, Glenda, had survived. The "copacetic" recipient of David's heart changed from a vegetarian to a meat eater and from a lover of heavy metal music to a fan of rock-and-roll of the fifties. David's loves became his loves. And in recurrent dreams, the young man reported seeing "bright lights coming straight for him"—a description, according to Glenda, of the car crash that had killed her husband and injured her.

Harvard psychologist Jerome Kagan, in his book on *Galen's Prophecy,* suggests that Galen may have been right in suggesting that human personality corresponds to the four fundamental substances of fire, air, earth and water.[23] The healthy person is said to be characterized by "a balance of warm and cool, dry and moist energies." Kagan studies the power of temperament and its influence on "our living, working and loving throughout our life." He suggests, in the words of Pearsall, "that understanding more about temperament... can lead us to be more forgiving of the energy we sense coming from those around us."[24] Others have come to similar conclusions, using different terminology. Weil speaks of the "resident" frequencies that we carry in our brains and bodies and unconsciously project to others.[25] Most scientists are slow to accept these phenomena as "real," because there is no agreed-upon way to explain such energy transfer or cellular memories. The experiences of heart donors as well as recipients provide some empirical evidence for the phenomena Pearsall reports.

As for "nonlocal connections" between people and things, dreams reflect transactions in the real world that seem mysterious. A seventy-year-old artist authored a report in the peer-reviewed journal *Alternative Therapies in Health & Medicine*,[26] in which she reviewed the role of love in synchronicities, acausality and dreams. Her own experience with these phenomena involved her dogs Mah Dawg and Yo Dawg and a fellow artist and neighbor, Bill Shumway. "Without telling me," she wrote, "Bill had taken a picture of the dogs running full tilt on the gravel bar of the river where I live." He did it for the purpose of creating a painting of her animal companions. Later, inexplicably, Mah Dawg fell sick from what the local veterinarian believed was an epileptic seizure. "I was distraught at this news... and went to Bill's gallery" to tell him. "Although I rarely weep, I was sobbing against his chest as I told him I thought Mah would die.... He saw I was fearful and said, 'Peg, go back to the vet's. Mah will be all right.'"

As soon as Peg left the gallery, Bill rushed to his easel. Peg went directly to the vet. "I picked Mah up. She was woozy but fine and has remained so." Bill later confirmed that at almost exactly the time Mah collapsed, he had painted the dog out of his painting because he was dissatisfied with his rendering of her. Upon hearing the news of the dog's sudden illness, he quickly painted her back into the picture, and Mah recovered. Then Bill himself fell ill with a debilitating angina and was being assessed for emergency cardiac surgery. Unaware of her neighbor's condition, Peg had a dream of a male wolf and an arctic landscape. Meanwhile "Bill was choosing between life and death." Peg then heard of his critical condition, and was afraid he would die. That night, though, she dreamed of a white wolf bitch, holed up in a den "licking and playfully mauling three black male pups. Their romping delighted me. I awoke smiling, the fear gone. Bill was healing." And, in fact, he was, and soon recovered.[27]

Love as a power that heals a dog through a painting and a man through a dream is one thing. But visualizing the return of a dead daughter in the lively body and soul of a puppy is something else. Such hallucinating, involving my amygdala, hippocampus and the neocortex of the temporal lobe, is not uncommon in dreams. Epileptic seizures and other temporal lobe disorders also may produce hallucinations. However, I have no history of grand mal or focal temporal lobe seizures. My auditory hallucination of Liz, followed almost instantaneously by a clear image of our Tibetan dog Bodhi, was neither dream-like nor disorienting. My only sensation was that it was all "realer than real."

Transcendent experiences of being one with God are often reported by people during intense temporal lobe activation. Neurologists have long been aware that temporal lobe seizures can be accompanied by such feelings. There are other patients who never suffer epileptic seizures but who have a "temporal lobe personality." They have "heightened emotions and see cosmic significance in trivial events."[28] They may have a trait called hypergraphia, which motivates them to write hundreds of pages "filled with mystical symbols and notations." Some other patients have "focal," as opposed to grand mal, seizures. When these occur in the limbic system, the individuals may have "deeply moving spiritual experiences, including a feeling of divine presence and the sense that they are in direct communication with God.... Suddenly it all makes sense," many report.[29] Ramachandran finds it "ironic," given the great emphasis we place on the rational parts of the brain, that "Truth" should "derive from limbic structures concerned with emotions."[30]

Ramachandran and the rest of us without known brain lesions get "only occasional glimpses of a deeper truth." For him, these occur when he is "listening to some especially moving passage of music" or when he looks at Jupiter's moon through a telescope.[31] Pittman experienced some of these glimpses on his vision quest, which he credits for giving him eyes to see "the truth" all around him, the transcendent in the immanent. For me, mountains, music and my fir tree serve to stir the inlets of my soul. In particular, Pachelbel's "Canon in D" and Blue Lake, the high mountain lake where we scattered Liz's ashes, produce a glimpse of deeper truth. I like Karen Armstrong's description of transcendence as "a going beyond the self,"[32] which is what I feel when I'm caught up in the beauty of mountains, music and towering trees. It's not an ethereal flight into the heavenly, but a letting go of the self long enough for the music and mystery of this life to penetrate my soul.

Armstrong was eventually diagnosed with focal epilepsy, centered in the temporal lobe, and had occasional blackouts and fugue states. Although she experienced God in fugue states, her sense of transcendence and "ekstasis" came from such experiences as hearing T.S. Eliot's third poem of *Ash-Wednesday* or Tennyson's poetry.

If consciousness is "the great poem of matter," in the words of poet/naturalist Diane Ackerman,[33] then transcendence is the music that accompanies the poetry. As noted in chapter 6, the rostromedial prefrontal cortex is a region of the brain, near the center of the forehead, that is activated by poetry and music. It sparks our short-term and long-term memory and connects us to emotions that we feel when lifted out of ourselves.

Neuroscience is not the only discipline helping us to understand "the thin places" where we connect with mystery and something bigger than the ego. Quantum physics has also provided evidence of the realness of "extraordinary" experiences. The EPR phenomenon in that field tells us that there is a preexisting linkage, an entanglement, which continues to exist between subatomic particles once they are together.[34] When they are separated, and a change occurs in one, it occurs in the other across time and space. "When this nonlocal bond occurs between people, we call it 'love,'" Dr. Dossey believes.[35] This is not to suggest that "people and electrons experience love and empathy to the same degree." However, we can infer that across evolutionary time, such a primordial bonding slowly grew in complexity and infused all of nature, especially humans, until it became the experience we enjoy as love. Jung said that "the meeting of two personalities is like the contact of two chemical substances; if there is any reaction, both are transformed."[36]

Empathy, sympathy and a connectiveness that transforms are part of the design of this powerful "daimon" called love, which respects neither time nor space. "Sympatheia," from the Greek, means "feeling together." When we speak of the sympathetic nervous system, we are referring to how all its connections, reaching right into our cardiac brain as well as the limbic loops and neocortex upstairs, respond "sympathetically" to each other, with action in one part reverberating throughout the system. Babies feel resonance in the limbic synchrony they have with their mothers; lost dogs use it as a radar to find home, even at great distances. Researchers on this subject have collected dozens of accounts of "miraculous" returns. Bobbie, a collie, is an example. He was traveling with his owners from Ohio to a new home in Oregon, a place Bobbie had never been. On a stop in Indiana, Bobbie got lost. A diligent search failed to find him. The family gave up and resumed its journey west. Months later, Bobbie appeared at the family home in Oregon, still wearing his name tag and bearing unmistakable marks and scars.[37]

So if I have such resonance with a Tibetan pup named Bodhi, who in turn resonates with me in bonds of love for a dead daughter, then I'm willing to press the science here to explain the "mystery" of Liz's return in a new form. I tell all this to my shipmate the priest, and he gives me a blessing out of his little bottle of holy oil. He doesn't consider me crazy—maybe not even so sick anymore. He has carried on about the subject of love for as many years as he has been both priest and Jungian analyst. On occasion, he brings me down out of the clouds, or wherever Liz's realm is, and reminds me of how hard love is.

"Love is laborious and inefficient," he says, and at first I think I'm listening to a time management expert or factory foreman. But Pittman makes his point by asking what other human emotion is powerful enough to keep an ex-jock and his size 13D shoes in a room day after day, week after week, listening to the travails of the infirm in body, mind and soul. Pittman can love even people he doesn't like, meaning that he can give them an experience of synchrony, resonance and empathy. The reason I know he can do this is that he has persuaded me that one key to both healing and transcendence is the ability to love the unloveable, which not only means loving people we don't like, but, most of all, loving what is unloveable in ourselves.

It takes time, as I know too well. So does beauty, Pittman the poet adds. The tree in his yard through which he experiences God takes time to go through cycle after cycle of seasons, of birth and death, beginnings and endings. But it is a beauty to behold. So is my Douglas fir, still growing in Colorado, still dropping her seeds as winter comes. And as heavy snows bend her limbs, she is still evergreen and stately. She bears the legacy of kinship to the tallest reliably measured tree ever—a 413-foot Douglas fir in the Lynn Valley of British Columbia.[38] With such ancestry, I feel convinced that underground, my tree's "rhizome," her axon and dendrites will continue to arborize, as I pray mine do—along with Bodhi's and those of the spirit she embodies. With Pittman's help, I strive to keep resculpting my synapses so that my amygdala and soul sing. With such harmony Pittman and I should be able to congratulate each other on a truly striking cytoarchitectural feat.

Pittman and Blair

Liz and Blair

EPILOGUE

Jung described four stages to the analytical process: confession, elucidation, education and transformation.[1] About the fourth stage he writes, "Between doctor and patient, therefore, there are imponderable factors which bring about mutual transformation."[2] Jung was clear in his belief that a successful analysis was transforming for both the analysand and the analyst.

My transformation came about in innumerable, imponderable ways. As Blair reports, I continually admonished him to "trust the process." This was, in addition, a self-admonition. There is a grind to a long-term analytic relationship. That is why everything that comes into the relationship is "grist for the mill." It is particularly laborious when one is as sick as Blair was. The illness of depression drains the soul (anima). The result is lack of animation. Week after week we sat. Many times we said little and waited. We trusted the process. Because of my relationship with Blair Justice, my personal and professional life deepened as I beheld the empirical evidence that whatever psychoanalysis or psychotherapy is, it does have efficacy. Further, the experience of sitting with a colleague who has the ability to reflect on the subjective and objective processes at the same time has allowed me to learn some neurobiology and neuroscience from a truly competent professional in the field of healing.

Finally, I must thank Blair for integrating my thought and work into this collaborative effort. He read volumes of my sermons, papers and poems and listened to hours and hours of my taped lectures in order to incorporate my work into the book.

We do not know what heals. That remains a mystery. We know some of the things that set healing into motion. This book bears witness to many of those healing acts. It is the story of two ordinary men who developed a mutually transforming relationship in the course of the extraordinary task of healing and making whole.

I suspect that it is still difficult for even healthy men to express love for one another. My diploma thesis was entitled "Love in the Analytical Container: The Place of Eros, Logos and Agape in Psychoanalysis." I have grown to love Blair Justice. Not in any sentimental, trivial way, but with the kind of love that gets the ego out of the way and allows soul to connect with soul. Blair and I, scientist/writer and priest/analyst, have simply become soul mates.

J. Pittman McGehee
Houston, Texas

AFTERWORD

At 6:45 P.M. on Monday, February 23, 2004, Rita Justice answers the phone from a New York caller who says, "This is Brittany Justice's adoptive mother."

Elizabeth, our daughter, told us the last time we saw her alive that she had given birth to a baby girl and left her at St. Luke's-Roosevelt Hospital—the hospital where Liz later died—to be placed for adoption. "She was pretty, just like me," Liz said, "and I named her Brittany." Rita dutifully passed on to the nuns at the adoption agency our vital data with a note asking that, if Brittany's adoptive parents or Brittany herself ever wanted to connect with us, they just call us.

That night the Justices and Sedas, the adoptive parents, all get on the phone and become, as Gregory Seda says, "one family." We receive by overnight mail the next day a beautiful photo album showing Brittany from age seven weeks and a heroin baby to her present age of thirteen and an honor student admitted to the School for the Future, a selective public high school in New York. The resemblance to Liz is striking: fair skin, brown eyes, light hair, sweet smile.

Rita and I then fly to New York at Eastertime to become one family face to face, the Justices and Sedas, grandparents and parents of Brittany. Rita and I go to services at the Cathedral of St. John the Divine, where we often prayed when Liz was dying. Now we give thanks for a rebirth.

This book starts with a synchronicity, whose meaning Pittman McGehee explains to Blair. Now, Dr. McGehee, psychoanalyst and priest, says that the transforming energy—nonlocal, no doubt—that the two of us stirred up working together over the last five years has caused the first synchroncity to give birth to a second. This is the way a mystic explains it. Shaking his head, the patient/scientist suggests, "Couldn't it just be amazing grace?"

EPILOGUE II

On September 11, 2004, Blair Justice had his own inner terrorist attack. An angiogram detected significant arteriosclerosis and on that date he had quadruple bypass surgery. During the procedure, he suffered a stroke. The bypass surgery was a success, but the stroke left him with a condition known as aphasia. In simple terms, aphasia is inability or difficulty in finding words to express thoughts, or in finding the names of objects or persons. In Blair's case, it has affected his reading, writing, memory and speaking. What a devastating condition, especially for a man of words.

I visited him in the Intensive Care Unit and later in his hospital room. When he was released, I took communion to him at his home—a silent Eucharist in which, in my role as priest, I made both the commands and the responses. There was, even in those early days of recovery, a connection. Whatever we mean by soul, we brothers in that mystery knew we were still in the process. I had often admonished Blair to "trust the process." I now had to admonish myself to practice what I had preached.

As soon as he was able, Blair returned to his weekly analytic sessions in my office, that sacred space where we had spent so many years, nurturing him, treating his depressive illness and empowering his process of individuation. In the weeks of his absence, I had kept his standing appointment available for his return.

In the ensuing months, in small increments, his ability to speak and write did return. In the early weeks after the stroke, we would sit in silence, session after session, communicating at the nonverbal level, staying connected and waiting. Due to a strong will, a loyal and supportive wife, and excellent physical and speech therapy at the Texas Medical Center, two years hence, with the two greatest healers, mother nature and father time, he is near full recovery.

I would not sentimentalize any therapeutic or analytic process, especially the one we have reflected upon in these pages. Because the pain, terror, loss, depression and disability were great, I must admit the two years of Dr. Justice's recovery from his stroke were at times arduous. I never dreaded his coming, but I did anticipate his session each week, for I knew of its intensity. It was intense because of my deep empathy for him and because of the difficulty of holding the tension when we two wordsmiths couldn't use words to communicate. But we did hold on. We did persevere.

Blair is better. And because of my relationship with him, I am, too. It is my desire and hope that Blair Justice and I will continue our soulful relationship and go into the sunset together.

J. Pittman McGehee
Houston, Texas

NOTES

NOTES TO THE PREFACE

Because this book has science in it as well as soul, the Notes are meant to give more information on the new scientific treatment of soul as well as love and related subjects, both scientific and Jungian.

1. In the Bible there are two Lazaruses. One is the good friend whom Jesus revives after he is buried for three days in a tomb. The other is the diseased beggar rejected by the rich man in the parable of John 11. In this book, Lazarus is meant to represent all those suffering from disease and the stigma of disability, particularly clinical depression. Many consider that a major mood disorder that leaves a person feeling dead in every respect except the physical is a phenomenal experience, meaning that it is wholly subjective. However, the neuroimaging scans now used by neuroscientists are beginning to bestow some objectivity on phenomenal experience by peering into the fascinating cosmos of mind and brain. See more on this in chapter 1, where depression is described as "a trip to the land of nothingness."

2. Kessler, et al., 2003, p. 3096.

3. Eric Kandel, a Nobel-prize winning neuroscientist, and Joseph LeDoux, a leading researcher on synapses, led the conference.

4. Jung and Pauli, 1955. Jung was the acclaimed follower of Freud who split with his mentor and founded his own school of analysis and depth psychology, also called analytical psychology. As for Pauli, he was an eminent scientist, a winner of the Nobel Prize in physics, who was both a long-term patient and a colleague of Jung.

5. Siegel, 1999. Relationships that change us do so by providing us with an experience that generates new neurons and rewires connections (Gage, 2003; van Praag, et al., 2002).

6. Nerds are not geeks. See Lyndon, 2000. Also Bennis & Thomas, 2002. As to Blair's messiness, which is reflected in nests of papers and journals wherever he spends time, see Saxena, 2004, on PET scans of compulsive hoarders.

7. Surveys on physicians' wearing ties show that patients prefer this formality to the open collar. See Brandt, 2003.

8. Pittman's authority on this is Teilhard de Chardin, 1976.

9. Pursuit of many vocations may be characteristic of a person who never found himself, which might be the case here if self is equated with soul, as it is in Jungian terms.

10. See Rosen, 1993, for successful "egocide." See also Stevens, 1993.

11. Between depressions, I become overactive, mildly manic and driven by ideas and activities.

NOTES TO THE INTRODUCTION: THE STORY

1. Freud in Kandel, 1999, p. 505. Eric Kandel won a Nobel Prize for his work demonstrating that brain cells are altered by experience. For original quotation, see Freud, 1914/1957.

2. Kandel & Mack, 2003. Kandel's map of the brain's functional architecture includes elucidation of the powerful principles that cortical structure is malleable and that our very genes are responsive to social and environmental influences. This means that "insofar as psychotherapy works, it does so by creating an environment that permits modification of the brain" (p. 282) through explicit and implicit learning and memory. As to "cryoarchitectural," this refers to cell structure, and "biogenic amines" to neurochemicals important in depression—norepinephrine, dopamine and serotonin. See also Kraemer, 1992.

3. We (McGehee and Justice) spoke about our "wounds" at the "Open Questions on the Mystery of Healing" forum, University of Texas M. D. Anderson Cancer Center, March 6-7, 1999. My wounds were both physical (cancer) and psychological (our daughter Liz's descent into drugs and slow suicide). Similarly, Pittman spoke of wounds both physical (his experience of being nearly burned to death as a child) and psychological (his mother's untreated depression and his father's life of "quiet desperation"). James Hollis (1994), also a Jungian analyst, writes knowingly of such wounds in his fine little book, *Under Saturn's Shadow: The Wounding and Healing of Men.*

4. McGehee, 1996, p. 77.

5. Solomon, 2001.

6. The dendrites in the brain are like tree branches that touch dendritic branches of other cells, exchanging electrochemical messages. The "bushier" our neuronal trees are, the more connections we have and ways to deliver messages to different parts of the brain.

7. Jung & Pauli, 1955.

8. "Mystery" is more than a word to my partner. It is a felt experience in all that he intuits as "unknowable" about this world and the next. It is a word I have tried to avoid, since in science it is seen as an easy way for people to stop searching for answers. As to "mystic," I have learned from my wife, who has known Pittman as long as I have, that there are skilled healers who operate out of the unconscious to arrive at truth in ways that seem a mystery to me.

9. Barrett & Berman, 2001. Their studies suggest that patients whose psychotherapists reveal some of their own lives do better than those whose therapists do not self-disclose. Sullivan's interpersonal therapy focused on the patient's relationships with family, friends, coworkers, etc. It is now reported as coming into common use again, according to the *Harvard Mental Health Letter*, August 2004. Regardless of how a therapeutic alliance is achieved between doctor and patient, neuronal effects depend on the relationship providing an experience in which new learning about self occurs.

10. Freud as quoted in Goode, 2002, p. F5. In letters responding to an article by Goode, readers agreed that even in traditional psychoanalysis, therapist self-disclosure is efficacious.

11. Frattaroli, as quoted in Grossman, 2003, p. 74.

12. Jaffe, 1979/1983.

13. In a review of a book by Atul Gawande (2002), Gonzalez-Crussi, 2002, comments on how "a peculiar physics is going out of style" in the doctor-patient relationship. Historically, the prevailing metaphor placed the physician above the patient with intercommunicating vessels imagined as connecting the two. From the doctor fluid magically flowed down, healing the patient.

14. Miller, 2002, p. 4.

15. Brandt, 2003.

16. Watkins, 1990.

17. McGehee, *Re-Membering,* 2001c.

18. Quoted in McGehee, 2003b.

19. LeDoux, 1996; Lewis, Amini & Lannon, 2001. LeDoux's studies have convinced him that "much of what the brain does during an emotion occurs outside of conscious awareness" (p.267). This finding is in keeping with the clinical psychiatric experience of Lewis, Amini and Lannon, the source of the epigraph for the Science section. See also Pearsall, 1999, for what the heart may be communicating without our knowing it.

20. Solms & Turnbull, 2002; Siegel, 1999.

21. Lynch, 2000.

22. Thoreau, 1854/1983, p. 50.

23. Jung, 1954/1970a, p. 43, par. 87.

24. Damasio, 2003a.

25. Waldman, et al., 1978.

26. Kandel, 2002. This Nobel laureate and neuroscientist visits Houston especially to go to the Rothko Chapel to bathe in the bands of color of the artist's works.

27. Wilson, 1998, p. 264; Bolen, 1996.

28. Pinker, 2002.

29. Quartz & Sejnowski, 2002; Stevens, 1993. The book by the neuroscientists Quartz and Sejnowski has the subtitle, *What the New Brain Science Reveals about How We Become Who We Are.* Their findings jibe with the current evidence that the brain is changed by what we encounter in our culture and personal experience. See also Ridley, 2003.

30. Chodorow, 1997, p. 1.

31. Achterberg & Lawlis, 1978/1984; Simonton & Simonton, 1975.

32. Jung, as quoted by McGehee.

33. McGehee, 1996, p. 17.

34. Day & Semrad, 1978, pp. 199-241. The therapist, these authors emphasize, "must love the patient, expect him to change" (op. cit., p. 227).

35. Lewis, et al., op. cit., p. 207.

NOTES TO THE INTRODUCTION: THE SCIENCE

1. Lewis, et al., 2001, p. viii.
2. Newberg, d'Aquili, & Rause, 2001; Joseph, 2000. The limbic system, our "emotional brain," including the amygdala, is active in positive feelings, such as love and joy, as well as negative ones, such as fear and anger. Oxytocin, a bonding neurohormone, is involved in positive activation. See also LeDoux, 1996.
3. Kandel, 2002. Contemporary philosophers, as well as Jungians, would probably agree that there is "a place within our brains for a nonphysical being called mind or soul" which represents "the pattern of memories, habits, dispositions that constitute personality" (see review by M. Shermer, 2002, p. 76). Since Larry Dossey's 1989 book *Recovering the Soul: A Scientific and Spiritual Search*, a number of scientists and physicians have invoked the soul in the titles of their books. These range from Amen's *Healing the Hardware of the Soul* (2002) to Crick's *The Astonishing Hypothesis: The Scientific Search for the Soul* (1995), in which the author dismisses the soul as unnecessary for science to search for because it doesn't exist. In defining soul, Dossey, op. cit., p. 43, defers to Jung, who considered it to be "the radiant Godhead itself" and regarded consciousness as "the invisible, intangible manifestation of the soul." Jung saw the soul as unbounded and eternal. Rosen, 1989, p. 22, a psychiatrist and Jungian analyst, defines the soul as "that enlightening spirit or life-giving force which gives rise to those stabilizing, integrating powers that make a being whole and a person fully human.... The soul is the seat of... one's feelings and love (Eros)—in contrast to mind and intellect, which are the seat of thinking and reason (Logos)." Despite signs of the soul's recognition by science and Jungians, James Hollis, a Jungian author and lecturer, feels that "the soul has left modern psychology and psychiatry, and it must be retrieved and rekindled before individual and collective healing can occur" (see Rosen's foreword to Hollis, 2000, p. xiii).
4. Kandel, 2002.
5. In more technical terminology, we view the soul as a "nonlocal" essence that transcends time and space. This essence may be manifested through the brain, as when our amygdala "tingles," using Kandel's word, but it is not to be equated with the brain or any part of it. As Dossey, 1989, notes, "an electric signal might manifest through a television set but is not the same thing as the receiver itself" (p. 254). In *Reinventing Medicine*, 1999, Dossey adds that "the tendency of the ego" is "to deny a nonlocal, transpersonal dimension of the self" (p. 35). Some of the great names in science—Schrödinger, Einstein, Eddington, Planck—viewed reality as more than just physical matter bound by time and space and consciousness as more than an emergent property of brain cells. This view differs from that of Francis Crick, the DNA co-discoverer and Nobelist, who proposes that "a person's mental activities are entirely due to the behavior of nerve cells, glial cells and the atoms, ions and molecules that make them up and influence them" (Crick, 1995, p. 271). There is no soul to be found and no need to evoke it, according to Crick. We are "nothing but a pack of neurons" (p. 3).

6. LeDoux, 2003, p. 302.

7. Damasio, 2003a, p. 284.

8. Joseph, 2000.

9. Glenmullen, 2001.

10. Lewis, op. cit.

11. Frattaroli, 2002.

12. When we learn from interpersonal experience in such a way that understanding and a new perspective emerge, a cascade of effects occurs within the layers of the brain, reshaping cell synapses and receptors, generating proteins, changing genetic transcriptions, rewiring our story synthesizer in the cortical brain and rewriting our script of who and what we are. As Cozolino, 2002, p. 23, notes, there is good evidence that symptomatic and neural change "coincide with change in glucose metabolism... concentrations of neurotransmitters, and blood flow" to the brain. See Siegel, 1999; and Vaughan, 1997. See also van Praag, et al., 2002.

13. Merikle, 1992; Cumes, 1999, notes that "non-directed attention" occurs in wilderness experiences and benefits well-being more than directed awareness does.

14. LeDoux, 2002. Dossey, 1999, is convinced that the best medical diagnosticians "often employ nonlocal ways of knowing without being aware of it" (p. 168).

15. The self is "synaptic," as LeDoux, 2002, declares in the title of his book on the subject. To the extent that genes and experience constitute the self, the very focal point of their expression is the synapse. Synapses also provide the "way the psychological, social, moral, aesthetic or spiritual self is realized" (p. 3) in our brains and bodies, he states. Freud himself foresaw proof that such phenomena as synapses not only existed, but were important to psychological and physical science. His 1895 paper on the subject went unpublished for many years and was only resurrected when Sir Charles Sherrington, a Nobel laureate in neurophysiology, applied the name "synapses" to what Freud had thought were "contact barriers" connecting neurons.

16. Quartz & Sejnowski, 2002.

17. Ramachandran & Blakeslee, 1998. The word "limbic," which means "border" or "fringe," was used for this system because it is a fringe region of tissue surrounding deeper, more medial parts of the brain, including the hypothalamus and the thalamus. In turn, the limbic region lies underneath the neocortical mantle and has multiple connections to higher centers of the brain. It is extensively involved in emotional and social experiences and in what Jung called "psychic instincts" or archetypes.

18. Siegel, op. cit.; Vaughan, op. cit.; Ramachandran & Blakeslee, op.cit.

19. Lewis, op. cit. "Limbic resonance" seems to involve mechanisms that are psychophysiological, psychophysical and psychosocial/behavioral. Some researchers describe this kind of communication as depending on the sharing of "subtle energies" (Greene & Shellenger, 1996).

20. Solms & Turnbull, 2002, p. 279.

21. Vaughan, op. cit.

22. Stevens, 1993.

NOTES TO CHAPTER 1: THE SCIENCE

1. Peat, 1987, p. 11.
2. Jung & Pauli, 1955, p. 6. Einstein called Wolfgang Pauli his "spiritual heir." Pauli's "demand for precision and clarity earned him the title of 'the conscience of physics,'" according to the contemporary physicist Henry P. Stapp of Berkeley (Stapp, 1993/2003, p. 175). In any event, Pauli struck sympathetic chords in Jung when the physicist concurred that within nature itself synchronicities occur "beyond the bounds of explanation in terms of pure chance." Such happenings, the two of them decided, reflect "representations of archetypes in meaningful coincidences that defy causal explanation" (Stapp, op. cit., p. 180).
3. Polkinghorne, 1996, p. 196. Persisting entanglement among atoms has more recently been demonstrated in "teleporting"—the transfer of physical characteristics from one atom to another, in yet another demonstration of "quantum leaps." See Chang, 2004.
4. Jung, 1967b, p. xxiv. Marie-Louise von Franz, one of Jung's closest collaborators, notes that scientific minds, far separated geographically, can have intuitive flashes producing similar creative hypotheses on the same subject. She cites the synchronicity that linked Charles Darwin and A. R. Wallace. While Darwin was working on his origin-of-species project, he received a manuscript from a young biologist, Wallace, whom Darwin had never met. The manuscript "was a shorter but otherwise parallel exposition of Darwin's theory" (von Franz, 1964, p. 306). At the time Wallace was in the Molucca Islands in the Malay Archippelego. "He knew of Darwin as a naturalist but had not the slightest idea of the kind of theoretical work on which Darwin was at the time engaged" (ibid.). Von Franz hypothesizes that the archetype activated by such synchronicity produces, in effect, an "act of creation in time."
5. Wilmer, 1987/1993, p.169.
6. Wilson, 1982, p. 84.
7. Peat, op. cit., p. 6.
8. Ibid., pp. 5-6.
9. Sharp, 1991, p.133.
10. Wheeler, 1995; Hagelin, 1987.
11. Dossey, 1999, p. 166.
12. Peat, op. cit., p. 11.
13. McGehee, 2003a.
14. Bolen, 1996.
15. Justice, 2000.
16. Jung & Pauli, op. cit., pp. 31-33
17. Rosen, 1993, p. 224.
18. Ibid.
19. Peat, op. cit., p. 7.
20. Ibid.

21. See Bolen, 1996; and Hollis, 1993, 1994.

22. Justice, 2000. For a good understanding of how the "feeling brain" acts as both sensor and sentinel of our inner states, see Antonio Damasio, *Looking for Spinoza: Joy, Sorrow and the Feeling Brain,* 2003a.

23. Bolen, op. cit.; and Hollis, op. cit.

NOTES TO CHAPTER 2: THE STORY

1. Weil, 2002, p. 4. A "vine of despair that wraps around you" and going to "the country of nothingness" are expressions of experiences accessible only to the person who feels that way. But materialistic scientists as well as poets and Jungians, who already use such metaphors, recognize the reality of conscious "phenotypes"—that's each of us— who have our own way of feeling and experiencing. See Edelman, 2004, p. 146.

2. See Casey, 2001. For a book by a psychologist who not only wrote of her own illness, but reviewed depression historically in the "artistic temperament," see Jamison, 1994. Jamison tracked the genealogies of a long list of famous poets, writers, painters and composers, many of whom suffered from bipolar illness.

3. Hall, 2001, p. 163, husband of poet Jane Kenyon, quoting lines by his depressed wife.

4. Hollis, 1994. Styron, 1990, speaks of "the situation of the walking wounded." In "virtually any other serious sickness," outside of major depression, "a patient who felt similar devastation would be lying flat in bed.... His invalidism would be necessary, unquestioned and honorably attained. However, the sufferer from depression has no such option and therefore finds himself, like a walking casualty of war, thrust into the most intolerable social and family situations. There he must, despite the anguish devouring his brain, present a face approximating the one that is associated with ordinary events and companionship. He must try to utter small talk, and be responsive to questions, and knowingly nod and frown and, God help him, even smile" (pp. 62-63). The ranks of the wounded men that Hollis talks about and the walking wounded that Styron refers to have their counterparts in the millions of depressed women. The English novelist and critic Virginia Woolf said it involves "our looking-glass shame"— seeing oneself as plain or unattractive. See Breathnach, 1998, p. 82. Depression is more common in women than men, greater stress being one possible reason.

5. Wolpert, 1999; and Jamison, 1996, are good examples.

6. Weil, op. cit.

7. Manning, 2001, p. 266.

8. See Wolpert, 1999, p. 3. Wolpert, in his pain, echoes Styron, 1990, who said (p. 7), "Depression is a disorder of mood, so mysteriously painful and elusive in the way it be-comes known to the self—to the mediating intellect—as to verge close to being beyond description." What needs to be added is that lesser depressive disorders—not major clinical depression—can serve adaptive functions (Schmale, 1973). "Conservation-

withdrawal" is an appropriate stress response to overextending or failure to grieve when a loss occurs. See "Is Grief a Disease? Challenge for Medical Research," by George Engel, 1961, Schmale's longtime colleague in biopsychosocial research and clinical practice. Also see Gut, 1989, who studied what she called "productive" as well as "unproductive" depression. Even the manic phase of bipolar depression can produce much energy and creativity, as Dr. Suzanne Fiala acknowledges. In her mild manic periods, she says, "I just feel exquisitely, superbly good…. I am considered a 'high-functioning manic-depressive': my highs make me sharper, give me energy and an edge" (Fiala, 2004, p. 2925). My own experience with mild manic periods between my depressions has also been creative. I am flooded with ideas and projects. In such periods I have held down two jobs at the same time and have had "highs" from work, sex and writing. The crash afterwards is full of dread and shame.

9. Styron, 1990, p. 83. The struggle involves the "Sisyphean torment" of knowing that it is a disease from which recovery is often followed by recurrence (p. 75-76). Styron says that "we must still struggle to survive, and so we do—by the skin of our teeth" (p. 24).

10. Ibid. The noted humorist Art Buchwald, speaking of his own depression, said, "Everything was black, the trees were black, the road was black. You can't believe how the colors change unless you have it" (Buchwald, 1998 DRADA video).

11. Solomon, 2001.

12. Ibid., p. 53. Solomon also wrote a long piece in 1998 for the *New Yorker* on depression and his history with the disease, in which he described how he lay "frozen in bed" as he ran through his mind the steps and movements it would take to get to the bathroom for a shower. The sense that comes in depression is that not only does one's body stop moving, except by great effort, but that time itself is stuck in place. Karen Armstrong, 2004, p. 136, author and religion scholar, says "each second seemed a millennium."

13. Wolpert, 1999, p. vii. He is not alone in confessing how deadening clinical depression is, worse even than grief over the death of a loved one. Dick Cavett, the talk show host and writer who suffers from depression, had a psychiatrist who compared depression to the terrible grief the doctor himself experienced over the death of one of his parents. Cavett answered that grief is better; that at least it is a deep feeling. Depression is an "awful drone of nullity." Cavett's test for depression was simple: "You know you're depressed when you see a pill on your dresser that would cure you, and yet you don't have the motivation to get out of bed and take it" (Cavett, 1993 DRADA video). See DePaulo & Horvitz, 2002, pp. 10-11, 13.

14. Horder as quoted in Wolpert, 1999, p. 60.

15. See Jaffe, 1969/1983. Also Rosen, 1993, p. 4.

16. Rosen, 1993.

17. Center, et al., 2003, p. 3161.

18. Stevens, 1993, p. 104.

19. Wolpert, op. cit., p. 3.
20. See Justice, 1998, pp. 129-139, regarding Hall's locked-in syndrome.
21. Solomon, op. cit. Even the "father" of American psychology, William James, struggled for years with recurring bouts of depression. See Jamison, 1994.
22. Luther, 1982, p. 316.
23. Jung, 1958/1969, 1967a; Hillman, 1975.

NOTES TO CHAPTER 2: THE SCIENCE

1. Kessler, et al., 2003, p. 3095. Seligman, 2002, says, "Depression is now ten times as prevalent as it was in 1960, and it strikes at a much younger age.... This is a paradox, since every objective indicator of well-being—purchasing power, amount of education, availability of music and nutrition—has been going north, while every indicator of subjective well-being has been going south" (pp. 117-118). Easterbrook, 2004 (Part B) says the same thing: Despite increased longevity, rising incomes, decline in crime and other positive indicators, "the percentage of Americans who describe themselves as 'happy' has not increased since the early 1950s, while incidence of depression keeps rising—and was doing so long before the morning of Sept. 11, 2001."
2. Kessler, et al., 2003, p. 3097.
3. Brunk, 2003.
4. Goff, 2002, p. 2.
5. Skaer, et al., 2000, p. 1576. The cost includes 213 million prescriptions in 2003 for antidepressants alone.
6. Insell & Charney, 2003; Hensel, 2002; Marano, 2003, p. 59. Miller, 2004, reports that depression is the main cause of disability in women in the U.S. In the general population, it is second only to heart disease as a cause of lost healthy years of life. See *Harvard Mental Health Letter*, January 2004, p. 6.
7. Goff, op. cit.
8. Berkman, et al., 2003; Kessler, et al., op. cit. Regarding the comorbidity problem, "If you're diabetic, it's more difficult to control your diabetes. Depression also may increase the risk of Alzheimer's and stroke," according to Dr. Dennis Charney, head of NIMH's research program for depression (see Hales & Hales, 2004, p. 4). On the question of suicide, Solomon, 2004, p. A25, notes that "four percent to 10 percent of people who suffer from major depression commit suicide. Untreated depression is lethal," but, as Solomon adds, the Food and Drug Administration has announced changes requiring that labeling of some ten antidepressants reflect the warning that the medication may increase suicidal feelings in the first weeks of treatment. Thus, as the *New York Times* op-ed subhead for Solomon's piece on "A Bitter Pill," 2004, put it, "In trying to prevent suicide, we may actually abet it." At the same time, "Many people with severe depression go untreated, and have barren, miserable lives because of it." Psychopharmacology, of course, is just one form of treatment. Our book is

about changing brain chemistry and neurotransmission through relationship and new learning. As to the tradeoffs encountered in the frequent use of antidepressants, another one is that serotonin-enhancing medications can dampen libido and diminish romantic feelings toward longtime, loving partners. The antidepressants apparently disrupt neural circuits in brain modules interconnecting with limbic system nuclei and having to do with motivation and reward. The caudate nucleus, in particular, seems affected. Also see Fisher, 2004 and O'Connor, 2004.

9. "The reward system may be more vulnerable, response to stress more intense or the formation of addictive habits quicker in some people, especially those suffering from depression, anxiety or schizophrenia, and those with antisocial or borderline personality" (*Harvard Mental Health Letter*, 2004, July, p.2).

10. Wolpert, 1999, viii. Depression is particularly underdiagnosed in men. Rather than cry or talk about it, as most depressed women do, depressed men are more likely to express anger, frustration, feelings of futility and physical problems, such as gastro-intestinal complaints. Men are less likely to talk about their symptoms, whatever they may be. Stigma is a factor in men's refusal to show or disclose their true feelings, even to their physicians. A 2004 poll found that 52 percent of men believe depression carries a stigma (*Parade*/Research!America Health Poll—see Hales & Hales, 2004). "Real men" don't get depressed, and if they do, their legacy tells them to tough it out. See Swartz and Margolis, 2003, p. 15. James Hollis, in his book *Understanding Saturn's Shadow: The Wounding and Healing of Men,* maintains that fear underlies shame in men. Our fears, he says, have to do with fear of "not measuring up" (1994, p. 24) and fear of ridicule if we disclose how we feel. The anger over having to hold in both fear and shame is often turned inward and manifests as part of our depression. However, what has been called "perhaps the cruelest type of depression" is suffered by women, who experience postpartum depression. They hear such remarks as, "How can you possibly be sad? This is the happiest time of your life." See Bender, 2004, p. 31.

11. Goode, 2003, p. F5; Center, et al., 2003. To her credit, Dr. Suzanne J. Fiala, a Seattle physician, has, in her own words, come out of "the closet" and publicly acknowledged in *JAMA* that "I have bipolar disorder: manic depression." See Fiala, 2004, p. 2924.

12. Solomon, 2001, p. 366. "Depression is not a weakness, but a highly treatable medical disease," says Dr. Richard Carmona, the U.S. Surgeon General. "Even strong men develop depression and should not be discouraged or intimidated from seeking help for fear they'll look weak" (see Hales & Hales, 2004, p. 4). Among the "strong men" is NFL former star Terry Bradshaw, featured on the June 20, 2004 cover of *Parade* magazine. Tough or not, 41 percent of men polled said that are less likely to seek treatment if depressed. Caving in to stress or becoming depressed may also involve genetics. Recently, researchers have found further evidence for the "diathesis-stress theory," which predicts that "individuals' sensitivity to stressful events depends on their genetic makeup." People with a short form of a gene called 5-HTT were more prone to depression after stressful life events (see Caspi, et al., 2003, p. 386). The 5-HTT gene helps regulate serotonin, a neurotransmitter deficient in depression. A

short allele (form) of the gene encodes expression of a protein that serves as a serotonin transporter responsible for the reuptake of the neurochemical into the presynaptic cell after it has been released into the synaptic cleft to signal the adjacent neuron. The 5-HTT gene has been found to "moderate the influence of stressful life events on depression" (ibid.). Individuals with a short form were more likely to exhibit more depressive symptoms. As to a predisposition, "negative affect" (NA) is now being considered by some researchers as part of one's temperament or "diathesis" (constitutional disposition).

13. Yudofsky, 2003.

14. Solomon, op. cit.

15. Lesch, 2004, pp. 174-184. He says, "Given the psychobiologic complexity of depressive disorders, it is not surprising that the identification of specific genetic factors is extremely difficult and continues to be among the last frontiers of gene hunting" (p. 182). Also see Siegel, 1999, p. 20.

16. Goff, 2002, p. 5.

17. Lewis, et al., 2001. The American Psychological Association has assembled a task force to address the controversy between scientists who demand empirical proof of the efficacy of psychotherapy and clinicians who insist that the relationship with the patient is a key factor with nuances that escape objective measurement (Carey, 2004). See note 19 for a related issue.

18. Olfson, et al., 2002, pp. 203-209. Between 1987 and 1997, the number of Americans treated for depression increased from 1.7 million to 6.3 million. The number of those taking antidepressants climbed from 37 percent to nearly 75 percent. In 2003 alone, the number of prescriptions for antidepressants and other drugs affecting the central nervous system climbed 17 percent. The percentage of patients receiving psychotherapy declined from 71 to 60.

19. Luhrmann, 2000. Some ten years earlier, a depressed William Styron was bemoaning "the schism between the believers in psychotherapy and the adherents of pharmacology" (1990, p. 11). It is an issue that psychiatrist Elio Frattaroli has written passionately about in *Healing the Soul in the Age of the Brain: Why Medication Isn't Enough.* Empirical evidence now convincingly tells us that recovery from depression is not an either-or undertaking. It is not either believing in talk therapy or a commitment to psychopharmacology. Neuroscience, particularly social neuroscience, is showing that the chemistry in the brain is changed by learning, by relationship and by experience. Talk, in the right relationship resulting in a felt experience of learning, can change synapses as well as antidepressants can. The neuronal resculpting is likely to be longer-lasting as a result of changing what we know about ourselves and why we are here. This should be good news, particularly for the estimated 1.5 million depressed people who do not benefit from antidepressants.

20. Solomon, op. cit., p. 31.

21. Ibid., pp. 31-32. Alongside the depressive effects of modernity are the risk factors of age, culture, gender, marital status, substance abuse and poor physical health. For

instance, a higher rate of depressive symptoms in females is one of the most robust epidemiological findings (Angst, 1997). Marital status is another consideration. Divorced or separated individuals have higher rates of depression (Bland, 1997). For major depression, the highest prevalence rates are found in persons eighteen to forty-five years old, particularly women. Rates of mild-to-moderate depression increase with age up to sixty-five years, after which there is a decline (Horwath & Weissman, 1995).

22. Seligman, 2002, p. 118. The nucleus accumbens, a cluster of nerve cells beneath the cerebral hemispheres, plays a principal part in the brain's reward system. It has been called the brain's "pleasure center" (Higgins, 2004) and is activated by the neurotransmitter dopamine (Ikemoto & Panksepp, 1999). When a person performs an action that satisfies a need, dopamine is released into this region of the limbic system. In nature, as in much of human life, reward usually comes with effort and after delay. "Shortcuts" are attempts to get an immediate reward with minimal personal effort. Their effect is temporary, and the aftermath is negative, requiring more and more "shortcuts"or heavier and heavier "doses" to produce a reward. Some recent research indicates that hitting behavior and other cruelty may also activate the nucleus accumbens and become addictive (Higgins, 2004).

23. Solomon, op. cit.

24. Kandel, 1998; LeDoux, 2002.

25. Frattaroli, 2002; Solms & Turnbull, 2002.

26. Lewis, et al., 2001; Amen, 1998.

27. Amen, op. cit.

28. Davidson, 1998, pp. 16-17. Contrary to popular belief, "right brained" people are not the happy, visionary types while "left brainers" are cognitive and rational. "The right hemisphere seems to be more sensitive to negative emotion, while high activity in the left hemisphere is associated with happiness" (Carter, R., 1998, p. 101). Clinical depression is associated with a smaller left prefrontal cortex (Gold, 1998).

29. Siegel, 1999, p. 142. Clusters of cells in the amygdala and orbitofrontal cortex serve as "social responders" and participate in the creation of meaning—all part of the neurobiology of interpersonal experience. The orbitofrontal cortex is just behind the eyes and in a strategic position at the top of the limbic system to influence the association cortex responsible for thought and consciousness.

30. Ibid., p. 272. A sense of meaning is considered a biological imperative, serving the well-being of both psyche and soma.

31. Vaughan, 1997; Siegel, 1999.

NOTES TO CHAPTER 3: THE STORY

1. Wolpert, 1999, p. 82. Biologist Wolpert follows his own words with those of the French poet Antonin Artaud, who said, with excusable hyperbole: "No one has ever

written, painted, sculpted, modeled, built or invented except literally to get out of hell." Sadness, even the "malignant" kind of depression, has helped some artists, poets, writers and scientists to do their best work. However, people in general must also have something else working for them. In *Consilience*, E. O. Wilson, the eminent Harvard biologist, says (1998, p. 264,) that people "must have a sense of larger purpose" to keep from yielding to despair. He insists that we need one god or another to believe in, and the god cannot be science.

NOTES TO CHAPTER 3: THE SCIENCE

1. Lewis, et al., 2001, p. 64. See also Siegel, 1999, on attunement and resonance.
2. Kandel, 1999; Kandel, 2001.
3. Siegel, 1999, pp. 272-273. Success in psychotherapy often depends on the degree to which "there is a direct resonance between the primary emotional, psychobiological state of the patient and that of the therapist." This nonverbal communication between the two is "mediated by the right hemisphere of one person and that of the therapist" (p. 298).
4. Pearsall, 1999; Childre, et al., 1999.
5. McCraty, et al., 2001.
6. Krucoff, et al., 2001; Levin, 2001; Benor, 2001.
7. Levin, 2001; Dossey, 1999; Dossey, 2000. See also the pioneering "action-at-a-distance" work of Jahn & Dunne, 1997.
8. Solms & Turnbull, 2002.
9. Pert, 1997; Dossey, 2003a. Perhaps paradoxically, the "tapping into" universal consciousness is best done unconsciously. Intuition operates largely out of the unconscious and requires right-hemisphere-to-right hemisphere communication with another person. We process and store much "knowing" in our unconscious. Myers, 2002, p. 29, says, "Our minds process vast amounts of information outside of consciousness, beyond language. Inside our ever-active brain, many streams of activity flow in parallel, function automatically, are remembered implicitly, and only occasionally surface as conscious words."
10. As discussed in Schroeder, 2001, p. 153. Sir James Jeans, 1938, British mathematician, astronomer and physicist contended that "there is wide measure of agreement.... that the stream of knowledge is heading towards a non-mechanical reality; the universe begins to look more like a great thought than a great machine."
11. Schroeder, op. cit.
12. Consciousness is more than the neurological state of being awake. It is also awareness of both the world we live in and the world that lives in us. Much of the world living in us is unconscious and involves our archetypal heritage. Exploring and valuing this deeper inner world leads to a better understanding of who we are and what we are called to do in the outer world. See Hopcke, 1999; Solms & Turbull, op. cit.

13. Feynman, 1998.
14. Schulz, 1998, p. 120. The posterior cingulate gyrus, a structure involved in decision-making and problem-solving as well as the processing of emotional stimuli, also shows decreased activity in the brains of compulsive savers or hoarders (see Preface note 6).
15. McCraty, et al., 1998.
16. Armour & Ardell, 2004; and Armour, 2003.
17. Levenson, 1972/1983/2005, p. 70.
18. LeDoux, 2002, p. 262.
19. Siegel, op. cit.; LeDoux, op. cit.
20. Benor, op. cit.
21. Dossey, 2003a.
22. As quoted in Malinin, 1979. Carrel won the Nobel Prize in medicine or physiology in 1912 for his seminal research on vascular suturing, perfusion and transplantation of blood vessels and organs. He is the only known medical scientist Nobelist to describe himself as a mystic. In 1902 he had traveled to Lourdes with sick patients on a holy pilgrimage. He witnessed the "miracle" healing of a woman who was unconscious and near death. His 1935 book, *Man the Unknown*, sold 900,000 copies in nineteen countries. The *British Medical Journal* gave it an unfavorable review and said that "Dr. Carrel, the man of science, shelters under the same hat as Dr. Carrel the mystic."
23. Real, 1997, p. 22. A senior faculty member of the Family Institute of Cambridge, Real also correctly notes, "Hidden depression drives several of the problems we think of as typically male: physical illness, alcohol and drug abuse, domestic violence, failures in intimacy, self-sabotage in careers."
24. For generations, males have been taught early on not to be a "crybaby," which means, regardless of age, to "be a man" and "don't be a wimp." So hubris, shame and shadow become natural carriers for such scripting.

NOTES TO CHAPTER 4: THE STORY

1. See Bennis & Thomas, 2002.
2. McGehee, 1998a.
3. Lewicki & Czyzewski, 1992; Merikle, 1992; Merikle & Reingold, 1998; LeDoux, 1996.
4. McGehee, op. cit.
5. Becker, 1973.
6. Mikulincer, et al., 2003.
7. Becker, op.cit.
8. Dossey, 1999, p. 205.
9. Newberg, D'Aquili, & Rause, 2001. "There is not one of us who has not laid awake at night… and wondered what it is all about," says *The Martian Chronicles* author Ray Bradbury, as quoted in Carreau, 2004a. Not just science fiction, but now also serious science,

is concerned with questions of "Where do we come from?," "What are we?," and "Where are we going?"—issues having to do with origin, identity and destiny. Theoretical physics, especially the rising field of string theory, is now proposing that the universe existed before the Big Bang, before the beginning of time. (See Veneziano, 2004.) From another perspective, the "ultimate questions" in physics have to do with science's quest for a Theory of Everything. Physics is still wrestling with reconciling Einstein's general theory of relativity with quantum mechanics. The first is a theory of gravity and the second has to do with the behavior of all physical objects, including the subatomic. See Newton, 2004; and Greene, 2004.

10. Dossey, 2000, p. 12.
11. McGehee, op. cit.
12. Blake & Ostriker, 1977, p. 181, "The Marriage of Heaven and Hell," plate 4.
13. McGehee, 1992.
14. Dossey, 2003a, p. 299.
15. Ibid.
16. Justice, 1998, p. 241.
17. McGehee, 1999c. Physicist Chet Raymo, 1998, says, "The Hebrew and Christian scriptures tell us that God created the first man and woman out of the slime of the Earth, breathed life into them, and pronounced them good. The myth is consistent with our current understanding of the nature of life. According to the best scientific theories, we are literally animated slime. Now we must relearn to think ourselves 'good'" (p. 197). Dust, slime or shit, letting our goodness prevail in life is a perennial challenge.
18. Delbruck, 1985.
19. Dossey, 2003a, pp. 300-301.
20. As quoted by Dossey, op. cit.
21. Russell, 2003, p. 121.
22. Ibid., pp. 121-122.
23. Freeman, 2000.
24. Gomes, 1996, p. 214: "There is in Celtic mythology the notion of 'thin places' in the universe, where the visible and the invisible world come into their closest proximity." Raymo, 2004, writes of the Celtic emphasis on the immanent.
25. Schroeder, 2001, p. 171.

NOTES TO CHAPTER 4: THE SCIENCE

1. In 2005, "four decades after the 'God is Dead' controversy," 94 percent of Americans believed in the existence of God, (http://www.saviorquest.com/news2/pollgod.htm, accessed 9/5/08).
2. Puchalski, 2001.
3. Schroeder, 2001, p. 184.

4. Ibid., p. 182.

5. Schwartz (with Simon), 2002.

6. Ibid., p. xxiii.

7. Remen, 2001.

8. Ibid.

9. Chargaff, 1987, p. 199.

10. Raymo, 1998, pp. 47-48. Cosmologists tell us that not only is the universe infinite, it is also multiple—meaning that we and all the unknown dwellers in the cosmos are living in one or another "multiverse" levels, from I through IV. All this is no longer science fiction or metaphysics. "The frontiers of physics have gradually expanded to incorporate ever more abstract (and once metaphysical) concepts such as round Earth, invisible electromagnetic fields, time slowdown at high speeds, quantum superpositions, curved space and black holes. Over the past several years the concept of a multiverse has joined the list." And under consideration is even the idea that each of us, somewhere in these parallel universes, has an alter ego, identical to us in every respect (Tegmark, 2004, p. 41).

11. Raymo, op. cit., p.48.

12. Remen, op. cit.

13. Cardena, Lynn & Krippner (Eds.), 2000.

14. Blake & Ostriker, 1977, p. 506. "To see the world in a grain of sand" is the opening line of Blake's poem "Auguries of Innocence," first published in 1863, thirty-six years after Blake's death.

15. Jeans, 1981, p. 204.

16. Schrödinger, 1969, p. 145.

17. More "hardheaded" scientists still wrestle with "the problem of consciousness." But many would agree that it involves being "conscious of being conscious" and having some sense of self (Edelman, 2004, p. 161). Francis Crick, who turned to brain studies after co-discovering the structure of DNA, and Christof Koch provided in their framework of consciousness a self that can plan and act, using the frontal cortex, in response to a sensing carried on in the back of the brain—in the occipital, parietal and temporal lobes. See Crick & Koch, 2003; also Moore, 2003.

18. McGehee, 2001c. Pittman also argues that while he defines mystery as "the unknowable," science says it is "a problem waiting to be solved." The truth is that many believe there will always be mystery and as they try to understand some of its manifestation, they do so with humility, wonder and awe. See Davies, 1983 and 1992; Chargaff, 1987; and Feynman, 1998.

19. Amen, 2002.

20. Vaughan, 1997.

21. David Bohm quoted in Weber, 1990, pp. 101 and 151.

22. Johnson, 2002, pp. D1, D2.

23. Reynolds, c. 2003. I am indebted to the Very Reverend Joe Reynolds for lighting up a part of my brain with a little humor, which his predecessor, McGehee, considers a

spiritual exercise. Joking, humor and laughter can produce dopamine from our nucleus accumbens brain area in the limbic system. When a woman's orbital prefrontal cortex was accidentally touched in surgery, she suddenly laughed, so this area may also be involved. The limbic system is involved not only in laughing, but also in smiling, which one can even see on the faces of animals, particularly dogs. See Johnson, 2004; and Ackerman, 2004a.

24. *The Book of Common Prayer*, 1972, p.469.

NOTES TO CHAPTER 5: THE STORY

1. Solomon, 2001, p. 15.

NOTES TO CHAPTER 5: THE SCIENCE

1. In his book *The Two-Million-Year-Old Self*, Anthony Stevens,1993, provides a comprehensive insight into the archetypes and reveals how the archetype of the "two-million-year-old Self" becomes manifest in our dreams and illnesses.

2. Erik H. Erikson is well recognized for his work on, and writings about, the stages of human development through the lifespan, the sources of identity and the interdependence of individual growth and historical/cultural change. His work has deeply influenced contemporary psychology. See Erikson, 1997.

3. The contents of the collective unconscious are known as archetypes. In his famous essay "Archetypes of the Collective Unconscious," Jung gave a number of examples of archetypes and transformation processes in which they appear (Jung, 1959/1969a). Jung said that an archetype is in itself irrepresentable but has affect which makes visualization of the archetypal images and ideas possible.

4. Jung described archetypes as preformed tendencies to create images and compared them to dry riverbeds to be filled with the water's of experience. See Wilmer, 1987/1993, pp. 56-57.

5. Stevens, op. cit., p. 20.

6. In his book *The God Gene: How Faith is Hardwired into our Genes*, Dr. Dean Hamer, 2004, reveals that the inclination towards religious faith may be related to certain genes. See also Newberg, et al., 2001, *Why God Won't Go Away*; and Collins, 2006.

7. Stevens, op. cit., p. 87, suggested that the laws whose operation is apparent throughout nature apply to the psyche as well. In other words, deficiencies in environmental (social) conditions will result in susceptibility to (mental) disease.

8. *Metanoia* is a Greek word for conversion, a capacity to "turn again," to change. (See Armstrong, 2004, p. 270.) *Paranoia* (derangement) is a mental disorder characterized by the presence of delusions, often of a persecutory character (*Websters's New World*

Stedman's Concise Medical Dictionary, 1987, New York: Webster's New World and William & Wilkins).

9. Stevens, op. cit., pp. 86-87.

10. Ibid., p. 25.

11. The work that I did with the city of Houston is the basis for *Violence in the City* (Justice, 1996).

12. Stevens, op. cit.

13. See d'Aquili & Newberg, 1999; Kandel, 2006; Solms & Turnbull, 2002; and Restak, 2003.

NOTES TO CHAPTER 6: THE STORY

1. Stern, 2001, p. 1047. Leading the list of processes in the head that are "shrouded in mystery" is the unconscious. Scientists, Jung noted, tend to take one of two positions on the unconscious: "There is no unconscious" (Jung, 1964, p. 23), or "the unconscious is nonsense" (p. 102). The evidence today in neuroscience and various branches of psychology, is that "we are more than what we are aware of" (LeDoux, 2002, p. 27), "consciousness is a much smaller part of our mental life than we are conscious of" (Jaynes, 1976, p. 23), and conscious will is largely an "illusion" (Wegner, 2002). Wilson, 2002, cites research on "lack of awareness of one's own feelings" (p. 11) as well his own studies on the "adaptive unconscious" (p. 17).

2. McGehee, March 24, 1991. Whether God speaks to us in our dreams, as various faiths attest, or whether we prefer to think He does, the words conveyed may bear an important message. In the Talmud, the collection of ancient Rabbinic writings, it is said that "a dream not interpreted is like a letter to the self unread" (McDonald, 2003, p. 5). Even without this admonition, Pittman was not about to ignore the message of his dream.

3. Thoreau, 1854/1983, p. 50. Thoreau recorded in his *Walden* essay "Economy," that he had realized while living in the woods that "what is called resignation is confirmed desperation." This is the heavy feeling that economic depression is known to engender in people.

4. Mr. J. B. McGehee had memories of his own father trying to make ends meet. Now, as a father himself, he was struggling with his own failed dreams as his younger son looked on. Pittman grew up wanting to give to his father and mother what they dreamed of having, but never got—a theme Jung called living the unlived lives of one's parents. Pittman sees his dream as freeing him of such responsibility.

5. Joan of Arc is quoted as saying, "I hear voices telling me what to do. They come from God." She was told that "they come from your imagination." Joan replied: "Of course, that is how messages of God come to us." The words in Pittman's dream could have come from several sources, including God. What matters, he decides, is that he claims them as true.

6. Sanford, 1968/1989.

7. Jung, 1964, p. 102.

8. Dr. McGehee can cite Jung himself on not letting the church stand between an individual and God: "We are so captivated by and entangled in our subjective consciousness that we have forgotten the age-old fact that God speaks chiefly through dreams and visions.... the Christian puts his Church and his Bible between himself and his unconscious; and the rational intellectual does not yet know that his consciousness is not his total psyche" (Jung, op. cit.).

9. McGehee, May 2004, "Burn the Barn" presentation at the "Mythical Journeys" conference in Atlanta.

10. Raymo, 1998, pp. 256-257.

11. Buber, 1958/1987, p. 34. Buber's *I-Thou* applies to the relationship to our true self as well as to others. The story is told that when Buber died and went to heaven, God didn't ask him, "Why weren't you more like Moses?" but "Why weren't you more like Buber?"

12. Raymo, op. cit., p. 257. Jungian analyst Jean Shinoda Bolen says that "I-Thou is about love and intimacy and trust between two souls" or between a person and a divine presence (see Bolen's *Close to the Bone: Life-Threatening Illness and the Search for Meaning*, p. 115). Raymo shows us that such bonding is not confined to humans, but extends to relationships between humans and other animals.

13. Ibid. As we have seen, there are moments of clarity and insight that come to artists, poets and scientists, producing illumination and an "intense feeling of euphoria lasting two or three days." See Herrmann, 2004, p. 49.

14. Raymo, op. cit., p. 262; and Teilhard De Chardin, 1959. Raymo comments that Teilhard de Chardin is "too mystical to appeal to scientists and too worldly to satisfy traditional theologians.... Yet many of Teilhard's intuitions strike me as on the mark" (Raymo, op. cit., p. 264). Cosmologist Fred Hoyle, according to physicist Paul Davies, has "a teleological God (somewhat like that of Aristotle or Teilhard de Chardin) directing the world toward a final state in the infinite future" (Herrmann, 2004, p. 49).

15. Gomes, 1996.

16. O Riordian, 1996.

17. My locomotive-busting tornado dream would be classified by Wilmer (1987/1993, p. 218) as a Type 5, "The Explosive Dream."

NOTES TO CHAPTER 6: THE SCIENCE

1. Diamond, 1962.

2. Hobson & McCarley, 1977.

3. Frattaroli, 2002.

4. Freud, 1900/1952/1980, p. 7. Jung felt that he himself had fought a lifelong battle, to prove the validity of both the collective unconscious and the idea that "dreams and

their symbols are not stupid and meaningless. On the contrary, dreams provide the most interesting information for those who take the trouble to understand their symbols" (Jung, 1964, p. 102).

5. Solms & Turnbull, 2002.

6. Ibid., p. 212.

7. Authorities such as Solms have suggested that "neuroscientists are finding that their biological descriptions of the brain may fit together best when integrated by psychological theories Freud sketched a century ago" (Solms, 2004, p. 82). Hobson replies that "major aspects of Freud's thinking are probably erroneous." Dreams, he says, have nothing to do with release of repressed urges, but are due to chemical changes that accompany sleep. These "determine the quality and quantity of dream visions, emotions and thoughts" (Hobson, 2004, p. 89). And the debate continues.

8. Vaughan, 1997, pp. 10-13.

9. Ibid., p. 33.

10. Hobson, 2002, p. 150.

11. Ibid., p. 88.

12. Schulz, 1998, p. 33.

13. See Goldberg, 1983.

14. See Sheldrake, 2003, p. 268. Otto Loewi is reported to have awakened in the middle of the night in 1921 with the idea for an experiment. He quickly wrote himself a note and went back to sleep. The next morning he couldn't read what he had written. But the following night, he again woke up; this time he remembered what he had written the night before. He went directly to his laboratory and, from the experiment he conducted, he proved that one of the ways nerve impulses are transmited is chemically. In 1936 he was awarded a Nobel Prize. See also Bard & Bard, 2002.

15. Dossey, 1999, p. 1.

16. Ibid., p. 3.

17. Sheldrake, op. cit., p. 246.

18. Dunne, 1927/2001.

19. Cole, p. 2003, p. 146. According to Shermer, 2004, p. 32, "the law of large numbers" also "guarantees that one-in-a-million miracles happen 295 times a day in America."

20. The dreams I have of this kind seem to take place between conscious and unconscious states. The fact that my funny "Chopsticks" dream was pleasant and not high in visual content suggests that it occurred in non-REM sleep shortly after I fell asleep. (See Gazzaniga, 1988, on sleeping and dreaming.) Such straightforward dreams without much imagery seem to come more from cognitive than emotional brain centers. Fontana, 2003, classifies dreams according to "dream levels." Level 1 dreams have been described as preconscious, not as deep as those drawing on material from the personal unconscious (Level 2) or from the collective unconscious (Level 3), which Jung called "grand" dreams. The deeper we go in the brain, to the paleomammalian or repitilian layer, the oldest level, the more universal the dream themes seem to be. "Borderline"

dreams, involving regions between cognitive and emotional layers, may be considered liminal. My "automatic writing" dreams seem liminal, a mix of Level 1 and Level 2. They are cognitive in terms of giving me ideas or solutions that I get excited about. If Loewi's prizewinning dream could be considered "liminal," combining Level 1 and Level 2, such dreams may be a good thing.

21. McGehee, 1996. Pittman lectures on the powerful symbols in the biblical story of Jonah: storm, sea, bowels of a boat, belly of a great fish, and Jonah's coming to himself. Archetypal symbols are considered the bridge between the conscious and unconscious. They are charged with great energy and numinosity. If love and anger are both involved, activated brain circuits run through the amygdala to the insula, a part of the cortex that registers somatic sensations. When we are "thrown into" experiencing an archetype and integrate its message or revelation, a transcendent function is served, according to Jungian theory. It facilitates our becoming who we are and what we are meant to be. In the process, we tend to become "whole" and experience more fully the nature of our inner and outer worlds. The deeper we go into the unconscious, the more archetypal power we encounter. In my experiences of psychic storm, I come to terms with my own darkness of shit and shame, anger and guilt. In bringing them to light I have the opportunity to transform them into something good. Bolen, 1996, notes that in major depression and serious illness—"close to the bone" experiences—we are presented with both danger and opportunity, as indicated by the Chinese pictograph for crisis. She sees "illness as a descent of the soul into the underworld" (p. 9). It is in that deep level of the soul and unconscious that the rich resources for healing are to be found.

22. Sacks, 1973/1990, 1991; Bolen, 1996; Remen, 2001.

23. Diamond, 1962.

24. Ibid., p. 19.

25. Sacks, 1991.

26. Ibid., p. 369.

27. Joseph, 2000, p. 78.

28. Sacks, 1991. Somatic memory lies in the deep layers of the limbic system and the amygdala. Certain archetypal symbols and sound can reach into that space and temporarily restore wholeness and "awakenings" to damaged brains and bodies. See also Oliver Sacks's book, *Awakenings*, 1973/1990, and the award-winning movie by that name. Music that touches the soul has the power to lift us out of our disability by activating deeper brain centers that are still whole.

29. Ibid.

30. Joseph, op.cit.

31. As quoted by Sacks, 1991, p. 369.

32. Dr. Rita Charon's "narrative medicine" is designed to give medical students, residents and physicians a deeper understanding of how a patient experiences his or her illness and the meaning it has to the patient. The doctors and students write the patient's

story, as they have heard it, and then check back with the patient to see if they captured what was important. In a "parallel" chart, the doctors and students write their own reactions to the patient and glean new insights into themselves as well as a better understanding of the sick people they treat (Charon, 2004).

33. Bolen, op. cit., pp. 115 and 113.
34. Solms & Turnbull, op. cit., p. 91.
35. McGehee, 2001c, April 18.
36. Solms & Turnbull, op. cit.
37. Damasio, 1999, as summarized in Eakin, 2003.
38. Ibid.
39. Damasio, 2003a, p. 139.
40. Ibid.
41. Frattaroli, op. cit., p. 8.
42. Ibid., p. 6.
43. Harlow, 1868, p. 327. Gage was a construction foreman laying down railroad tracks in the 1840s. He was using a tamping rod to press down a charge of dynamite in a rock formation. The charge suddenly exploded and shot the rod through Gage's frontal lobe and out the top of his skull. Physically Gage made a rapid recovery, but he was a changed man in personality. Those who knew him said he was "no longer Gage."
44. Goldberg, 1983, p. 77.
45. Ramachandran & Blakeslee, 1998, p. 195.
46. See Samuels, Shorter, & Plaut, 1986/1987, p. 153.
47. Edinger, 2002, p. 15.
48. Stevens, 1993.
49. Damasio, 2003a.
50. Hillman, 1991, p. 243. Trying to ignore the garbage is like pretending shit doesn't stink. To become a whole person requires consciousness of the darkest corners of the unconscious so as to use the compressed power of the shadow in the service of life.
51. McGehee, 2001b, April 7.
52. Solms & Turnbull, op. cit.
53. Edinger, op. cit.

NOTES TO CHAPTER 7: THE STORY

1. Cozolino, 2002; and Ketter, et al., 2003.
2. Jung wrote that "within the soul from its primordial beginnings there has been a desire for light and an irrepressible urge to rise out of the primal darkness.... The longing for light is the longing for consciousness" (1961/1989, p. 269).
3. Jung, 1971/1976, pp. 426-427, par. 709.
4. Cohen, 2004.
5. Cohen, 2001.

NOTES TO CHAPTER 7: THE SCIENCE

1. Ketter, et al., 2003, pp. 938-939, suggested that negative versus neutral words provoke a higher brain activity in certain areas. This has been documented in the studies using functional magnetic resonance imaging (fMRI). See also Solm & Turnbull, 2002; Siegel, 1999; and Damasio, 1999.

2. LeDoux noted that "the brain states and bodily responses are the fundamental facts of an emotion, and the conscious feelings are the frills that have added icing to the emotional cake." In other words, emotions did not evolve as linguistically differentiated conscious feelings, but as brain states and bodily responses (1996, p. 302). See also Cozolino, 2002.

3. Spears, 1990.

4. Ibid., p. 1.

5. In his book *The Emotional Brain: The Mysterious Underpinnings of Emotional Life*, Joseph LeDoux states that "the amygdala is, in essence, involved in the appraisal of emotional meaning. It is where trigger stimuli do their triggering." The amygdala plays a special role in taking care of fear responses in all species that have an amygdala (LeDoux, 1996, p. 169).

6. Ibid., pp. 200-204.

7. Justice, 2000, pp. 77-78.

8. Wilmer, 1987/1993, pp. 96-106.

9. Netting, 2000.

10. Curtis & Biran, 2001; and Curtis, et al., 2004.

11. Haidt, 2003, pp. 857-860.

12. Haidt, 2001; Seligman, 2002, p. 8.

13. Haidt, op. cit.

14. Damasio, 2003.

15. Gershon, 1998. See also Armour, 2003; and Armour & Ardell, 2004.

16. Gershon, op. cit., p. xiii.

17. Pert, as quoted in *Brain/Mind Bulletin,* 1986, January 20.

18. Hawking, 2001.

19. Ibid., pp. 82-86, 196.

20. In their book *Anger Kills*, Redford and Virginia Williams have summarized the results of their several-decades-long scientific research on the role of stress on various diseases, with special reference to the effects of the hostility complex that involves anger, cynicism (a mistrusting attitude regarding the motives of people in general) and aggression (the behavior to which many hostile people are driven by the anger). These characteristics of the hostility complex relate to bodily changes that place many people at higher risk of developing severe, life-threatening illnesses, such as heart attack, stroke or cancer (Williams & Williams, 1997, pp. 35-92).

21. Kiecolt-Glaser, et al., 2003.

22. Siegel, 1999. See also Porges, 1998.

23. Siegel, op. cit.; and Schore, 1994.
24. Darwin, 1872/1965, introduced the general class of innate or inherited emotions (such as rage, fear, disgust, joy, shame, anguish, and surprise); that is, emotions that have not been learned by the individual. To support this theory, Darwin indicated the similarity of expressions both within and between species, and noted that these expressions are present in persons who were born blind and thus lacked the opportunity to learn them.
25. Miller, 1998.
26. Damasio, 2003, p. 156; and Haidt, 2003.
27. Haidt, op. cit.
28. Ibid.
29. Ogden, 1990, p. 108.
30. It has been estimated that, in the United States, there are about 42,000 to 65,000 ostomies each year (involving any opening from the abdomen for the removal of feces or urine). Source: http://tinyurl.com/q9cnm4 (accessed 10/20/07). See also Routh, 2003.
31. Barrie, 1997.
32. Hawkins, 2002, p. 76.
33. Ibid.
34. Ibid., pp. 263-264.
35. Prager, 2003, p. 2333.
36. Harlow, 1868, p. 327. See also chapter 6, science note # 43.
37. Pearce, 2002. See also Mascolo, et al., 2003.
38. Cohen, 2002b.
39. Cohen, 2002c.
40. D'Aquili & Newberg, 1999.
41. Hendrick & Hendrick, 2005, pp. 205-211.
42. A documentary movie entitled *Two Towns of Jasper* was produced by the ABC News program "Nightline," DVD released in 2006. See also the movie *Jasper, Texas,* directed by Jeff Byrd and Jeffrey W. Byrd, released in 2004.

NOTES TO CHAPTER 8: THE STORY

1. Carmony & Elliot, 1980.
2. Ibid., p. 165.
3. Ibid.
4. Tillich, 1952/2000.
5. See LeDoux, 2003; and d'Aquili & Newberg, 1999.
6. Artress, 1996, p. 29.
7. McGehee, 1996.
8. Jung said that "we should not try to 'get rid' of a neurosis, but rather to experience what it means, what it has to teach, what its purpose is. We should even learn to be thankful

for it, otherwise we pass it by and miss the opportunity of getting to know ourselves as we really are. A neurosis is truly removed only when it has removed the false attitudes of the ego. We do not cure it—it cures us" (1964/1070, p. 170, par. 361).

9. Pinkola Estes, 1995.

NOTES TO CHAPTER 8: THE SCIENCE

1. Jung, 1966, pp. 81-83, par. 127.
2. MacLennan, 2002.
3. Schwartz & Begley, 2002, p. 321.
4. MacLennan, op. cit, p. 308.
5. Jung, 1959/1969b, pp. 79-80, paragraph 155. See also MacLennon, op. cit.
6. West, 2000, p. 34.
7. Dr. Andrew von Eshenbach's lecture at the M. D. Anderson Cancer Center, January 17, 2003 (Trainee Speakers Series), Houston, Texas.
8. Artress, op. cit, pp. 63-64. In *The Washington Cathedral: This Bible in Stone*, Robert Kendig, 1995, provides a complete history of the cathedral as well as a full description of its large and impressive windows, including the great west rose window (p. 121).
9. Artress, op. cit.
10. Berger, 2003.
11. Elliot, 2003.
12. Rothman & Rothman, 2003.
13. Nuland, 2004.
14. Schwartz & Begley, op. cit., p. 250.
15. Ibid., p. 72.
16. Damasio, 2003, p. 36.
17. Ibid., p. 269.
18. McGehee, 1999c.
19. Capra, 2000, p. 11.
20. McGehee, 2002.

NOTES TO CHAPTER 9: THE STORY

1. Vaillant, 2002.
2. See Karen Armstrong's story in *The Spiral Staircase* (2004) on her own unrelenting depression.
3. Fordyce, 1988, p. 282.
4. Rosen, 1994.
5. Larry Dossey, 1997, has long extolled the value of pet animals. "Pets provide us the opportunity to unite unconditionally with another living being. They teach us to

love. Love, in a general sense, involves a relaxing of personal boundaries and a willingness to 'become one' with someone else. And to flourish, love requires surrendering our rigid sense of individuality that creates distance and separateness.... Pets bring us back to the realization of our unity with other living things. They help us remember who we are" (p. 15). Fine, 2000, provides a comprehensive theoretical overview and examples of practical implementations of this type of therapy.

6. Justice, 1998, pp. xi-xii.
7. Ibid. See interviews with breast cancer patients.
8. McGehee, 2004.

NOTES TO CHAPTER 9: THE SCIENCE

1. Seligman, 2002.
2. Midlarsky, 1991.
3. Vaillant, 2002, p. 25.
4. Ibid., pp. 62-64.
5. Damasio, 2003b, p. 227.
6. Seligman, 1975.
7. Seligman, 2002, p. 8.
8. Ibid.
9. As described in Seligman, 2002, p. 10.
10. Seligmman, 2002, p. 9.
11. Vaillant, op. cit., p. 71.
12. Selligman, 2002, p. 10, neatly summarizes Vaillant's results.
13. Vaillant, op. cit., pp. 60-64.
14. Seligman, 2002, pp. 134-161.
15. Bolen, 1996.
16. Zukav, 2000.
17. Danner, Snowdon, & Friesen, 2001.
18. Snowdon, 2001.
19. Seeman, et al., 2001.
20. Verghese, et al., 2003.
21. Ibid.
22. Csikszentmihalyi, 1997.
23. In his book *The Call of Service: A Witness to Idealism*, Dr. Robert Coles (1993) examines the idealistic motives of people who engage in volunteer work. One of the main messages of this book is that those who give are as much receivers and learners as they are givers.
24. Ibid., p. xiii.
25. Ibid.
26. Damasio, 2003a, p. 284.

27. Dr Antonio Damasio (ibid., p. 283) writes that the practice of the life of the spirit means doing something to alleviate human suffering. He also suggests that science can be combined with the best of humanistic tradition to permit a new approach that will lead to human flourishing (Damasio, 2003a, p. 283).
28. McGehee, 1996.

NOTES TO CHAPTER 10: THE STORY

1. Armstrong, 2004, p. 142.
2. Blake & Ostriker, 1977, p. 506 ("Auguries of Innocence").
3. Cardena, Lynn, & Krippner, 2000, p. 407.
4. Feynman, 1988.
5. Jung, 1950/1980, p. 98, par. 218.
6. Cushman & Jones, 1993.

NOTES TO CHAPTER 10: THE SCIENCE

1. A therapeutic relationship or experience in which self learning occurs can change the very structure (architecture) of a cell (cyto) of the brain. When neurons and their synapses change, neurotransmitters (serotonin, norepinephrine, dopamine, and acetylcholine) are usually affected. This has been demonstrated by advances in neuroimaging techniques. This means that the power of the "nonmaterial" (relationships, experience, and talk) can visibly affect the material—brain cells and body.
2. Weil, 1997.
3. Ibid.
4. Ibid.
5. According to polyvagal theory, the phylogenetic development of the mammalian vagus is paralleled by specialized communications between hypothalamus and the medullary source nuclei of the visceral vagus, which facilitates the enduring pair-bonds. For a detailed description of this mechanism, see Porges, 1998.
6. Psychoacoustics is a new scientific field that studies the effects of sound on consciousness. In the recording of *Sound Body, Sound Mind: Music for Healing*, Dr. Andrew Weil (1997) used a special technology (the beat set at a frequency to influence brain waves), which allow the listener to enter states of consciousness different from a normal waking state. Such deep relaxation is by itself healing. According to Dr. Weil, this music may be used to encourage any kind of healing—physical, mental, emotional and spiritual.
7. Cumes, 1998, p. 114.
8. Merton, 1999, pp. 91-92.
9. Kandel, 2002.

10. Walsh, 1996.
11. Dossey, 1996, pp. 8-15.
12. Pearsall, 1998, p. 45.
13. Ibid., p. 44.
14. Dr. S. Malcolm Gillis is a distinguished professor of economics, who has dedicated his career to teaching and applying economic analysis to important issues in public policy in nearly twenty countries. From 1993 to 2004, Dr. Gillis served as the sixth president of Rice University in Houston, Texas.
15. Wegner, 2002.
16. Wilson, 2002.
17. Freud, 1985/1996, p. 295.
18. Bilder, 1998, p. ix.
19. Watson, 1992.
20. Ramachandran & Blakeslee, 1998, p. 60.
21. Ibid, pp. 61-62.
22. Pearsall, op. cit., pp. 75-77.
23. Kagan, 1997.
24. Pearsall, op. cit., p. 133.
25. Weil, op. cit.
26. Mayo, 1998.
27. Ibid., p. 98.
28. Ramachandran & Blakeslee, op. cit., p. 180.
29. Ibid., p. 179.
30. Ibid.
31. Ibid.
32. Armstrong, 2004, p. 177.
33. Ackerman, 2004, p. 19.
34. Polkinghorne, 1989, p. 93, explains the Einstein–Podolski–Rosen Paradox (EPR), which refers to the consequence of quantum theory: "once two systems interact with each other, then a measurement on one system can produce an instantaneous change in the state of the other system, even if they are by then widely separated from each other." See also Polkinghorne, 1996.
35. Dossey, 1996, p. 13.
36. Jung, 1933, p. 49.
37. Stelljes, 2005.
38. Pakenham, 2003; and Fanselow & Miller, 2001.

NOTES TO THE EPILOGUE

1. Jung, 1954/1966, p. 55, par. 122.
2. Ibid., p. 72, par. 164.

BIBLIOGRAPHY

Achterberg, J., & Lawlis, G. F., 1978/1984. *Imagery and Disease: A Diagnostic Tool for Behavioral Medicine*. Champaign, IL: Institute for Personality and Ability Testing.

Ackerman, D., 2004a. *An Alchemy of Mind: The Marvel and Mystery of the Brain*. New York: Scribner's.

Ackerman, D., 2004b. We are our words. *Parade*, May 30. pp. 8, 10.

Adler, G., 1966. *Studies in Analytical Psychology*. New York: G. P. Putnam's Sons.

Allen, J., 2000. Biology and transactional analysis II: A status report on neurodevelopment. *Transactional Analysis Journal*, 30, 4, 260.

Amen, D. G., 1998. *Change Your Brain, Change Your Life: The Breakthrough Program for Conquering Anxiety, Depression, Obsessiveness, Anger, and Impulsiveness*. New York: Three Rivers Press.

Amen, D. G., 2002. *Healing the Hardware of the Soul: How Making the Brain-Soul Connection Can Optimize Your Life, Love, and Spiritual Growth*. New York: Free Press.

Armour, J. A., 2003. *Neurocardiology: Anatomical and Functional Principles*. Boulder Creek, CA: HeartMath.

Amour, J. A., & Ardell, J. L. (Eds.), 2004. *Basic and Clinical Neurocardiology*. London: Oxford University Press.

Angst, J., 1997. Presentation: The course of affective disorders, part II: Epidemiology of major depression in women. Psychiatric Association conference, May 17-22.

Armstrong, K., 2004. *The Spiral Staircase: My Climb Out Of Darkness*. New York: Alfred A. Knopf.

Artress, L., 1996. *Walking a Sacred Path: Rediscovering the Labyrinth as a Spiritual Tool*. New York: Riverhead Trade.

Bair, D., 2003. *Jung: A Biography*. Boston: Little, Brown.

Bard, A. S., & Bard, M. G., 2002. *The Complete Idiot's Guide to Understanding the Brain*. Indianapolis, IN: Alpha Books.

Barrett, M., & Berman, J., 2001. Is psychotherapy more effective when therapists disclose information about themselves? *Journal of Consulting and Clinical Psychology*, 69, 4, 597-603.

Barrie, B., 1997. *Don't Die Of Embarrassment: Life After Colostomy*. New York: Simon & Schuster.

Bateson, A. C., 2001. *Composing a Life*. New York: Grove/Atlantic.

Batson, C. D., Ahmad, N., Lishner, D. A., & Tsang, J., 2002. Empathy and Altruism. In C. R. Snyder & S. J. Lopez (Eds.), *Handbook of Positive Psychology,* pp. 485-198. Oxford: Oxford University Press.

Becker, E., 1973. *The Denial of Death*. New York: Free Press.

Belitz, C. & Lundstrom, M., 1998. *The Power of Flow: Practical Ways to Transform Your Life with Meaningful Coincidence*. New York: Three Rivers Press.

Bell, C., 2000. *Comprehending Coincidence: Synchronicity and Personal Transformation*. West Chester, PA: Chrysalis Books.

Bender, E., 2004. Childbirth, aging boost women's depression risk. *Psychiatric News*, June 18, p. 31.

Bennis, W. G., & Thomas, R. J., 2002. *Geeks & Geezers*. Boston: Harvard Business School Press.

Benson, H., & Stark, M., 1997. How large is faith? In J. M. Templeton (Ed.), *How Large is God? The Voices of Scientists and Theologians,* pp. 95-112. Philadelphia, PA: Templeton Foundation Press.

Benor, D. J., 2001. *Spiritual Healing: Scientific Validation of a Healing Revolution*. Southfield, MI: Vision Publications.

Berger, L., 2003. Books on health: Transformation by Pill or Scalpel. In the *Science Times* of the *New York Times*, May 20, p. D7.

Berkman, L., et al., 2003. Effects of treating depression and low perceived social support on clinical events after myocardial infarction. *JAMA, 289* (23), 3106-3116.

Bernbaum, E., 1990. *Sacred Mountains of the World*. San Francisco: Sierra Club Books.

Bernstein, J., 1982. *Science Observed: Essays Out of My Mind*. New York: Basic Books.

Bilder, R. M., 1998. Preface in R. M. Bilder & F. LeFever (Eds.), *Neuroscience of the Mind on the Centennial of Freud's "Project for a Scientific Psychology."* Annals of the New York Academy of Sciences, 843, ix-xii.

Bilder, R. M., & LeFever, F. (Eds.), 1998. *Neuroscience of the Mind on the Centennial of Freud's "Project for a Scientific Psychology."* Annals of the New York Academy of Sciences, 843.

Blake, W., 1863. *Poems*. Edited by Dante Gabriel Rossetti. (Including "Auguries of Innocence").

Blake, W., 1977. *William Blake: The Complete Poems*. Edited by A. Ostriker. London: Penguin Books.

Bland, R., 1997. Epidemiology of affective disorders: A review. *Canadian Journal of Psychiatry, 42,* 367-377.

Bly, R., 1991. The long bag we drag behind us. In C. Zweig & J. Abrams (Eds.), *Meeting the Shadow: The Hidden Power of the Dark Side of Human Nature,* pp. 6-12. New York: Tarcher/Putnam.

Bohm, D., 1980. *Wholeness and the Implicate Order*. London: Routledge & Kegan Paul.

Bolen, J. S., 1996. *Close to the Bone: Life-Threatening Illness and the Search for Meaning*. New York: Scribner.

Book of Common Prayer of the Episcopal Church, 1972. New York: Seabury Press.

Breathnach, S. B., 1998. *Something More: Excavating Your Authentic Self*. New York: Warner Books.

Brain/Mind Bulletin. Pursuit of peptides opens doors. January 20, 1986, p. 2.

Brandt, L. J., 2003. On the value of an old dress code in the new millennium. *Archives of Internal Medicine, 163,* 1277-1281.

Breger, L., 1967. Function of dreams. *Journal of Abnormal Psychology Monograph, 72* (5), 1-28.

Brody, A., Saxena, S., Stoessel, P., et al., 2001. Regional brain metabolic changes in patients with major depression treated with either paroxetine or interpersonal therapy. *Archives of General Psychiatry*, *58*, 631-640.

Brunk, D., 2003. Depression may hit over one-third of adolescents (Study of more than 3,000 teens). *Pediatric News*, February, p. 23.

Buber, M., 1958/1987. *I and Thou*. Translated by R.G. Smith. New York: Collier Books.

Buchwald, A., 1998. DRADA video in which Buchwald describes his depression. (DRADA is the Depression and Related Affective Disorders Association),

Buechner, F., 1973. *Wishful Thinking: A Theological ABC*. New York: HarperCollins.

Caile, L., 2000. *A Life at Treeline*. Nederland, CO: Perigo Press.

Capra, F., 2000. *The Tao of Physics: An Exploration of the Parallels between Modern Physics and Eastern Mysticism* (25th Anniversary Edition). Boston: Shambhala Publications.

Cardena, E., Lynn, S. J., & Krippner, S. C. (Eds.), 2000. *Varieties of Anomalous Experience: Examining the Scientific Evidence*. Washington, DC: American Psychological Association.

Carmony, D., & Elliott, J., 1980. *New Harmony, Indiana: Robert Owen's Seedbed for Utopia*, Reprinted 1999 from the *Indiana Magazine of History*, LXXVI, September 1980, pp. 161-261.

Carreau, M., 2004a. Looking for a reason to explore new worlds. *Houston Chronicle*, April 16, p. 4A.

Carreau, M., 2004b. Mysterious "dark energy" still expanding universe. *Houston Chronicle*, May 18, p. 4A.

Carey, B., 2004. For psychotherapy's claims, skeptics demand proof. *Science Times* of the *New York Times*, August 10, pp. D1, D4.

Carter, C. S., 1998. Neuroendocrine perspectives on social attachment and love. *Psychoneuroendocrinology*, *23* (8), 779-818.

Carter, R., 1998. *Mapping the Mind*. Berkeley, CA: University of California Press.

Casey, N. (Ed.), 2001. *Unholy Ghost: Writers on Depression*. New York: Morrow/Harper Collins.

Caspi, A., Sugden, K., Moffitt, T., et al., 2003. Influence of life stress on depression: Moderation by a polymorphism in the 5-HTT gene. *Science*, *301*, 386-389.

Cavett, D., 1993. DRADA video in which Cavett describes his experience with depression. (DRADA is the Depression and Related Affective Disorders Association).

Center, C., Davis, M., Detre, T., et al., 2003. Confronting depression in physicians. A consensus statement. *JAMA*, *289* (23), June 18, 3161-3166.

Chaker, A. M., 2003. Do you need a pill to stop shopping?—For antidepressant makers, shopaholics are a new market. *Wall Street Journal*, January 2 (page unknown).

Chalmers, D., 1995. The Puzzle of Conscious Experience, *Scientific American*, *273* (6), December, 82-3.

Chang, K., 2004. Scientists teleport not Kirk, but an atom. *New York Times*, June 17, p. A21.

Charon, R., 2004. Narrative and medicine. *New England Journal of Medicine*, *350* (9), 862-864.

Chargaff, E., 1987. Engineering a molecular nightmare. *Nature, 327,* 199-200.

Childre, D. L., & Martin, H. (with Beech, D.), 1999. *The HeartMath Solution.* San Francisco: HarperCollins.

Chodorow, J., 1997. Introduction to C.G. Jung, *Jung on Active Imagination.* Princeton, NJ: Princeton University Press, p. 1.

Clark, M. (Ed.), 1991. *Prosocial Behavior.* Newbury Park, CA: Sage.

Cohen, R. M., 2001. Cases: Trouble with "The Bag" is in the head. *Science Times* of the *New York Times,* February 27 (http://tinyurl.com/cgvftc).

Cohen, R. M., 2002a. Confronting cancer: Cases: When cancer pain is more than pain. *Science Times* of the *New York Times,* April 9 (http://tinyurl.com/d54csl).

Cohen, R. M., 2002b. Cases: My body, my prison, my dreams. *Science Times* of the *New York Times,* May 28, D5.

Cohen, R. M., 2002c. Cases: Diseases that stay out of sight. *Science Times* of the *New York Times,* December 10, D5.

Cohen, R. M., 2004. *Blindsided: Lifting a Life Above Illness: A Reluctant Memoir.* New York: HarperCollins.

Cole, K. C., 2003. *Mind Over Matter: Conversations with the Cosmos.* New York: Harcourt.

Coles, R., 1993. *The Call of Service: A Witness to Idealism.* New York: Houghton Mifflin.

Collins, F. S., 2006. *The Language of God: A Scientist Presents Evidence for Belief.* New York: Free Press.

Conlan, R. (Ed.), 1999. *States of Mind: New Discoveries about How Our Brains Make Us Who We Are.* New York: Wiley.

Corsi, P. (Ed.), 1991. *The Enchanted Loom: Chapters in the History of Neuroscience.* Oxford: Oxford University Press.

Cozolino, L., 2002. *The Neuroscience of Psychotherapy: Building and Rebuilding the Human Brain.* New York: W. W. Norton.

Creek, W., 1999. *Now Here's a Man Who Knows His Shit.* Ontario, OR: Possum Press.

Crick, F., 1995. *The Astonishing Hypothesis: The Scientific Search for the Soul.* New York: Touchstone.

Crick, F., & Koch, C., 2003. A framework for consciousness. *Nature Neuroscience, 6* (2), 119-126.

Csikszentmihalyi, M., 1990. *Flow: The Psychology of Optimal Experience.* New York: Harper-Collins.

Csikszentmihalyi, M., 1993. *The Evolving Self: A Psychology for the Third Millennium.* New York: HarperCollins.

Csikszentmihalyi, M., 1996. *Creativity: Flow and the Psychology of Discovery and Invention.* New York: HarperCollins.

Csikszentmihalyi, M., 1997. *Finding Flow: The Psychology of Engagement with Everyday Life.* New York: Basic Books.

Cumes, D., 1998. *Inner Passages, Outer Journeys: Wilderness, Healing, and the Discovery of Self.* Saint Paul, MN: Llewellyn Publications.

Cumes, D., 1999. *The Spirit of Healing: Venture into the Wilderness to Rediscover the Healing Force*. Saint Paul, MN: Llewellyn.

Curtis, V., Aunger, R., & Rabie, T., 2004. Evidence that disgust evolved to protect from risk of disease. *Proceedings of the Royal Society of Biological Sciences, 271*, Supplement 4, S131-S133.

Curtis, V., & Biran, A., 2001. Dirt, disgust, and disease: Is hygiene in our genes? *Perspectives in Biology and Medicine, 44*, 1, 17-31.

Cushman, R., & Jones, S. (with Knopf, J.), 1993. *Boulder County Nature Almanac*. Boulder, CO: Pruett.

Damasio, A., 1999. *The Feeling of What Happens: Body and Emotion in the Making of Consciousness*. New York: Harcourt Brace.

Damasio, A., 2003a. *Looking for Spinoza: Joy, Sorrow, and the Feeling Brain*. New York: Harcourt.

Damasio, A., 2003b. Feelings of emotions and the self. In J. LeDoux, J. Debiec, & H. Moss (Eds.), *The Self: From Soul to Brain*. Annals of the New York Academy of Sciences, 1001, 253-261.

Damasio, A., 2003c. Mental Self: The person within. *Nature, 423*, 227.

Danner, D. D., Snowdon, D. A., & Friesen, W. V., 2001. Positive emotions in early life and longetivity: Findings from the nun study. *Journal of Personality and Social Psychology, 80*, 5, 804-813.

D'Aquili, E. G., & Newberg, A. B., 1999. *The Mystical Mind: Probing the Biology of Religious Experience*. Minneapolis, MN: Fortress Press.

Darwin, C., 1872/1965. *The Expression of the Emotions in Man and Animals*. Chicago: Chicago University Press.

Davidson, R. J., 1998. Understanding positive and negative emotion. *Discovering Our Selves: The Science of Emotion*, pp. 16-17. Executive summary of conference sponsored by the Library of Congress, National Institute of Mental Health and National Institutes of Health, Washington, D.C.

Davidson, R. J., 2000. Affective style, psychopathology and resilience: Brain mechanisms and plasticity. *American Psychologist, 55*, 1196-1214.

Davidson, R. J., Kabat-Zinn, J., Schumacher, J., et al., 2003. Alteration in brain and immune function produced by mindfulness meditation. *Psychosomatic Medicine, 65*, 564-570.

Davidson, R. J., Scherer, K. R., & Goldsmith, H. H. (Eds.), 2003. *Handbook of Affective Sciences*. Oxford: Oxford University Press.

Davies, P., 1983. *God & the New Physics*. New York: Simon & Schuster.

Davies, P., 1992. *The Mind of God: The Scientific Basis for a Rational World*. New York: Simon & Schuster.

Dawkins, R., 2003. *A Devil's Chaplain: Reflections on Hope, Lies, Science, and Love*. New York: Houghton Mifflin.

Day, M., & Semrad, E., 1978. Schizophrenic reactions. In A. M. Nicholi, Jr. (Ed.), *The Harvard Guide to Modern Psychiatry*, pp. 199-241. Cambridge, MA: Harvard University Press.

Delbruck, M., 1985. *Mind from Matter: An Essay on Evolutionary Epistemology.* Oxford: Blackwell Publishing.

DePaulo, J., & Horvitz, L., 2002. *Understanding Depression: What We Know and What We Can Do about It.* New York: Wiley.

De Quincey, C., 2002. *Radical Nature: Rediscovering the Soul of Matter.* Montpellier, VT: Invisible Cities Press.

De Quincey, C., 2002. Stories matter, matter stories. *Ions: Noetic Sciences Review,* 60, June-August, pp. 9-23, 44-45.

Diamond, E., 1962. *The Science of Dreams.* Garden City, NY: Doubleday.

Dossey, L., 1989. *Recovering the Soul: A Scientific and Spiritual Search.* New York: Bantam Books.

Dossey, L., 1996. What's love got to do with it? *Alternative Therapies in Health and Medicine,* 2 (3), 8-15.

Dossey, L., 1997. The healing power of pets: A look at animal-assisted therapy. *Alternative Therapies in Health and Medicine,* 3 (4), 8-16.

Dossey, L., 1999. *Reinventing Medicine: Beyond Mind-Body to a New Era of Healing.* San Francisco: HarperSanFrancisco.

Dossey, L., 2000. Immortality. *Alternative Therapies in Health and Medicine,* 6 (3), 12-17, 108-115.

Dossey, L., 2003a. *Healing Beyond the Body: Medicine and the Infinite Reach of the Mind.* Boston: Shambhala.

Dossey, L., 2003b. Living Dangerously: Risk-taking and Health. *Alternative Therapies in Health and Medicine,* 9 (6), 10-14, 94-96.

Dowling, J., 1992. *Neurons and Networks: An Introduction to Neuroscience.* New York: Belknap Press.

Dunne, J. W., 1917/2001. *Experiment with Time.* New York: Hampton Roads Publishing.

Dyson, F., 1988. *Infinite in All Directions.* New York: Harper & Row.

Eakin, E., 2003. I feel, therefore I am. *New York Times,* April 19 (http://tinyurl.com/cv67sv).

Easterbrook, G., 2003. *The Progress Paradox: How Life Gets Better while People Feel Worse.* New York: Random House.

Easterbrook, G., 2004. Commentary: A paradox of progress: Stepped-up stress: Even as the modern world has dramatically improved our material lives, many of us are feeling increasingly worse. *Los Angeles Times,* February 23, Part B.

Eccles, J. C., 1991. *Evolution of the Brain: Creation of the Self.* London: Routledge.

Eccles, J. C., & Robinson, D. N., 1984. *The Wonder of Being Human: Our Brain and Our Mind.* New York: Free Press.

Edelman, G., 2004. *Wider Than the Sky: The Phenomenal Gift of Consciousness.* New Haven, CT: Yale University Press.

Edinger, E., 1972. *Ego and Archetype*. New York: Penguin.

Edinger, E., 1990. *Anatomy of the Psyche: Alchemical Symbolism in Psychotherapy*. LaSalle, IL: Open Court.

Edinger, E., 2002. *Science of the Soul: A Jungian Perspective*. Toronto: Inner City Books.

Edinger, E., 2004. *The Sacred Psyche: A Psychological Approach to the Psalms*. Transcribed and edited by J. D. Blackmer. Toronto: Inner City Books.

Eiseley, L., 1946/1957. *The Immense Journey*. New York: Vintage Books.

Eliade, M., 1972. *The Sacred and the Profane: The Nature of Religion*. Translated by W. R. Trask. New York: Harcourt.

Elliot, C., 2003. *Better than Well: American Medicine Meets the American Dream*. New York: W. W. Norton.

Engel, G., 1961. Is grief a disease? Challenge for medical research. *Psychosomatic Medicine*, *23*, 18-22.

Erikson, E. H., 1997. *The Life Cycle Completed* (Extended Version). New York: W. W. Norton.

Evans, R., 1964. *Conversations with Carl Jung and Reactions from Ernest Jones*. Princeton, NJ: D. Van Nostrand.

Fanselow, J., & Miller, D., 2001. *Lonely Planet British Columbia*. Oakland, CA: Lonely Planet.

Feeney, M., 2000. At 95, U.S. poet has rhymes. *Houston Chronicle*, Sept. 4, p. 3D.

Feiner, A. H., 2000. *Interpersonal Psychoanalytic Perspectives on Relevance, Dismissal and Self-Definition*. New York: Jessica Kingsley.

Feynman, R. P., 1985. *"Surely You're Joking, Mr. Feynman!": Adventures of a Curious Character*. London: Vintage.

Feynman, R. P., 1988. *What Do You Care What Others Think: Further Adventures of a Curious Character*. New York: W. W. Norton.

Feynman, R. P., 1998. *The Meaning of It All: Thoughts of a Citizen Scientist*. Reading, MA: Perseus.

Fiala, S., 2004. Normal is a place I visit. *JAMA*, *291*, 2924-2926.

Fine, A. H. (Ed.), 2000. *Handbook of Animal-Assisted Therapy: Theoretical Foundations and Guidelines for Practice*. San Diego, CA: Academic Press.

Fisher, H., 2004. *Why We Love: The Nature and Chemistry of Romantic Love*. New York: Holt.

Fontana, D., 2003. *The Secret Language of Dreams*. San Francisco: Chronicle Books.

Fordyce, W. E., 1988. Pain and suffering: A reappraisal. *American Psychologist*, *43* (4), 276-283.

Fox, E., 1984. *A Feeling for the Organism: The Life and Work of Barbara McClintock*. New York: Holt.

Fox, J., 1997. *Poetic Medicine: The Healing Art of Poem-Making*. New York: Tarcher.

Frank, A., 1995. *The Wounded Storyteller: Body, Illness, and Ethics*. Chicago: University of Chicago Press.

Frankl, V., 1997. *Man's Search for Meaning* (Revised edition). New York: Pocket Books.

Frattaroli, E., 2002. *Healing the Soul in the Age of the Brain: Why Medication Isn't Enough*. New York: Penguin Group.

Freeman, W., 2000. *How Brains Make Up Their Minds*. New York: Columbia University Press.

Freud, S., 1914. On narcissism: An introduction. In *Complete Psychological Works*, standard ed., vol. 14. London: Hogarth Press, 1957, pp. 67-102.

Freud, S., 1900/1952/1980. *On Dreams*. Translated by J. Strachey. New York: W. W. Norton.

Freud, S., 1957. *A General Selection from the Works of Sigmund Freud*, John Rickman (Ed.). New York: Liveright.

Freud, S., 1966. *The Ego and Mechanisms of Defense*. New York: International Universities Press.

Freud, S., 1985/1996. Project for a Scientific Psychology. In J. Strachey (Ed.), *The Standard Edition of the Complete Psychological Works of Sigmund Freud*. Vol. 1, 229-397. London: Hogarth Press.

Gage, F. H., 2003. Brain, repair yourself. *Scientific American*, 289, 3, September, pp. 47-53.

Gardner, M., 1986. *The Sacred Beetle and Other Great Essays in Science*. New York: Meridian.

Gawande, A., 2002. *Complications: A Surgeon's Notes on an Imperfect Science*. New York: Holt.

Gazzaniga, M., 1988. *Mind Matters: How Mind and Brain Interact to Create Our Conscious Lives*. Boston: Houghton Mifflin.

Gershon, M. D., 1998. *The Second Brain: The Scientific Basis of Gut Instinct and a Groundbreaking New Understanding of Nervous Disorders of the Stomach and Intestine*. New York: HarperCollins.

Gioia, D., 2002. *Can Poetry Matter? Essays on Poetry and American Culture*. Saint Paul, MN: Graywolf Press.

Glenmullen, J., 2001. *Prozac Backlash: Overcoming the Dangers of Prozac, Zoloft, Paxil and Other Antidepressants with Safe, Effective Alternatives*. New York: Simon & Schuster.

Goff, V., 2002. Depression: A decade of progress, more to do. *National Health Policy Forum Issue Brief*, 786, Washington, D.C.

Gold, P., 1998. The high costs of stress. *Discovering Ourselves: The Science of Emotion*, pp. 30-31. Executive summary of conference sponsored by the Library of Congress, National Institute of Mental Health and National Institutes of Health, Washington, D.C.

Goldberg, P., 1983. *The Intuitive Edge*. Los Angeles: Tarcher.

Gomes, P., 1996. *The Good Book: Reading the Bible with Mind and Heart*. New York: William Morrow.

Gomes, P., 2002. *The Good Life: Truths That Last in Times of Need*. San Francisco: Harper.

Gonzalez-Crussi, F., 2002. Oops: Book review of *Complications: A Surgeon's Notes on an Imperfect Science* by Atul Gawande. *New York Times,* April 7 (http://tinyurl.com/devngz).

Goode, E., 2002. Therapists redraw line on self-disclosure. *New York Times*, January 1, p. F5.

Goode, E., 2003. Doctors' toughest diagnosis: Own mental health. *New York Times*, July 8, p. F5.

Gould, S., 1999. *Rock of Ages: Science and Religion in the Fullness of Life*. New York: Ballantine.

Green, J., & Shellenberger, R., 1993. The subtle energy of love. *Subtle Energies*, 4, 31-55.

Green, J., & Shellenberger, R., 1996. The healing energy of love. *Alternative Therapies in Health and Medicine*, 2, 46-56.

Greene, B., 2004. *The Fabric of the Cosmos: Space, Time and the Texture of Reality*. New York: Knopf.

Groopman, J., 2004a. *The Anatomy of Hope: How People Prevail in the Face of Illness*. New York: Random House.

Groopman, J., 2004b. The Biology of Hope. *Science & Spirit*, May-June, pp. 56-61.

Grossman, L., 2003. Can Freud Get His Job Back? *Time*, January 20, pp. 74-78.

Gut, E., 1989. *Productive and Unproductive Depression*. New York: Basic Books.

Hacking, I., 2004. Minding the brain: Review of *Looking for Spinoza: Joy, Sorrow and the Feeling Brain*. *New York Review of Books*, June 24, pp. 32-36.

Hagelin, J., 1987. Is consciousness the unified field? A field theorist's perspective. *Modern Science and Vedic Science*, 1, 28-87.

Haidt, J., 2001. The emotional dog and its rational tail: A social intuitionist approach to moral judgement. *Psychological Review*, 108, 814-834.

Haidt, J., 2003. The moral emotions. In R. J. Davidson, et al., (Eds.), *Handbook of Affective Sciences*, pp. 852-870. Oxford: Oxford University Press.

Hales, D., & Hales, R. E., 2004. Too tough to seek help? *Parade*, June 20, pp. 4-6.

Hall, D., 2001. Ghost in the House. In Nell Casey (Ed.), *Unholy Ghost: Writers on Depression*, pp. 162-172. New York: HarperCollins.

Hamer, D., 2004. *The God Gene: How Faith is Hardwired into Our Genes*. New York: Anchor Books.

Hansel, B., 2002. Executives get personal about mental health. *Houston Chronicle*, August 4, p. 1.

Hardcastle, V. (Ed.), 1999. *Where Biology Meets Psychology*. Cambridge, MA: MIT Press.

Harlow, J., 1868. Recovery from passage of an iron bar through the head. *Massachusetts Medical Society Publications*, 2, 327-347.

Harvard Mental Health Letter. Interpersonal psychotherapy. (M. C. Miller, Ed.) August, 2004, pp. 1-3.

Harvard Mental Health Letter. SAMe reconsidered. (M. C. Miller, Ed.) January, 2004, p. 6.

Harvard Mental Health Letter. The addicted brain. (M. C. Miller, Ed.) July, 2004, pp. 1-4.

Hatfield, H., Cacioppo, J., & Rapson, R., 1994. *Emotional Contagion*. Cambridge, MA: Cambridge University Press.

Hawking, S., 2001. *The Universe in a Nutshell*. New York: Bantam Books.

Hawkins, D. R., 2002. *Power vs. Force: The Hidden Determinants of Human Behavior*. Carlsbad, CA: Hay House.

Hendrick, G., & Hendrick, W., 2005. *Why Not Every Man? African Americans and Civil Disobedience in the Quest for the Dream*. Chicago: Ivan R. Dee Press.

Hensel, B., 2002. Executives speak of depression. *Houston Chronicle*, August 4, p. B1.

Herrmann, R. L., 2004. *Sir John Templeton: Supporting Scientific Research for Spiritual Discoveries* (Rev. Ed.). Philadelphia, PA: Templeton Foundation Press.

Higgins, E., 2004. Understanding the "joy" of aggression. *Current Psychiatry Online*, *3*, July, pp. 1-2.

Hillman, J., 1975. *Re-Visioning Psychology*. New York: HarperPerennial.

Hillman, J., 1991. The cure of the shadow. In C. Zweig & J. Abrams (Eds.), *Meeting the Shadow: The Hidden Power of the Dark Side of Human Nature,* pp. 242-243. New York: Tarcher/Putnam.

Hobson, J. A., & McCarley, R., 1977. The brain as a dream-state generator: An activation-synthesis hypothesis of the dream process. *American Journal of Psychiatry*, *134*, 1335-1348.

Hobson, J. A., 1988. *The Dreaming Brain: How the Brain Creates Both the Sense and the Nonsense of Dreams*. New York: Basic Books.

Hobson, J. A., 2002. *Dreaming: An Introduction to the Science of Sleep*. Oxford: Oxford University Press.

Hobson, J. A., 2004. Counterpoint: Freud Returns? Like a Bad Dream. *Scientific American*, May, p. 89.

Holden, C., 2001. "Behavioral" addictions: Do they exist? *Science*, *294*, 980-982.

Hollis, J., 1993. *The Middle Passage: From Misery to Meaning in Midlife*. Toronto: Inner City Books.

Hollis, J., 1994. *Under Saturn's Shadow: The Wounding and Healing of Men*. Toronto: Inner City Books.

Hollis, J., 2000. *The Archetypal Imagination*. College Station: Texas A&M University Press.

Hollis, J., 2003. *On This Journey We Call Our Life: Living the Questions*. Toronto: Inner City Books.

Holton, G., 1965. The false images of science. In L. B. Young (Ed.), *The Mystery of Matter,* pp. 637-648. London: Oxford University Press.

Hopcke, R., 1999. *A Guided Tour of the Collected Works of C. G. Jung*. Boston: Shambhala.

Horrigan, B., 1995. Dean Ornish, MD: Healing the heart, reversing the disease. *Alternative Therapies in Health and Medicine*, *1* (5), 84-92.

Horrigan, B., 1999. Jeff Levin, MPH, Ph.D.: The Power of Love. *Alternative Therapies in Health and Medicine*, 5(4), 79-86.

Horwath, E., & Weissman, M. M., 1995. Epidemiology of depression and anxiety disorders. In M. T. Tsung, M. Tohen, & G. E. P. Zahner (Eds.), *Textbook in Psychiatric Epidemiology,* pp. 317-344. New York: Wiley.

Howell, P., & Hall, J., 2002. *Locked Into Life*. Boise, ID: Tea Road Press.

Ikemoto, S., & Panksepp, J., 1999. The role of nucleus accumbens dopamine in motivated behavior: A unifying interpretation with special reference to reward-seeking. *Brain Research Review*, *31*, 6-41.

Inside Story: Understanding the Power of Feelings, 2002. Boulder Creek, CA: Institute of HeartMath.

Insel, T., & Charney, D., 2003. Research on major depression: Strategies and priorities. *JAMA*, *289* (23), 3167-3168.

Jacoby, M., 1994. *Shame and the Origins of Self-Esteem*. Translated by D. Witcher. London and New York: Routledge.

Jaffe, A. (Ed.), 1979/1983. *C. G. Jung: Word and Image*. Bollingen Series XCVII. Princeton, NJ: Princeton University Press.

Jahn, R. G., & Dunne, B. J., 1997. *Science of the Subjective* [Technical Notes.]. Princeton, NJ: Princeton University.

James, W., 1890. *Principles of Psychology*. New York: Holt.

James, W., 1902/1982. *The Varieties of Religious Experience*. New York: Penguin Books.

Jamison, K., 1994. *Touched With Fire: Manic-Depressive Illness and the Artistic Temperament*. New York: Free Press Paperback.

Jamison, K., 1996, *An Unquiet Mind*. New York: Vintage Books.

Janata, P., Birk, J., Van Horn, J., et al., 2002. The cortical topography of tonal structures underlying western music. *Science*, 298, 2167-2179.

Jaynes, J., 1976. *The Origin of Consciousness in the Breakdown of the Bicameral Mind*. Boston: Houghton Mifflin.

Jeans, J., 1938 (reprint of 1931 edition of 1930 book). *The Mysterious Universe*. New York: Macmillan.

Jeans, J., 1981. *Physics and Philosophy*. New York: Dover.

Johnson, G., 2002. Years of research yield nothing, and that's good news for scientists. *New York Times,* February 5, pp. D1-D2.

Johnson, R. A., 1986. *Inner Work: Using Dreams and Active Imagination for Personal Growth*. San Francisco: Harper & Row.

Johnson, R. A. (with Ruhl, J. M.), 1998. *Balancing Heaven and Earth*. San Francisco: Harper.

Johnson, S. M., 2004. *Mind Wide Open: Your Brain and the Neuroscience of Everday Life*. New York: Scribner.

Joseph, R., 1993. *The Naked Neuron: Evolution and the Languages of the Body and Brain*. New York: Plenum.

Joseph, R., 2000. *The Transmitter to God: The Limbic System, the Soul, and Spirituality*. San Jose: University of California Press.

Joseph, R. (Ed.), 2002. *NeuroTheology: Brain, Science, Spirituality, Religious Experience*. San Jose: University of California Press.

Jung, C. G., 1933. *Modern Man in Search of a Soul*. Translated by W. Bell and C. Baynes. New York: Harvest.

Jung, C. G., 1950/1980. The Tavistock lectures. In *Collected Works*, Vol. 18, pp. 5-182. Translated by R. F. C. Hull. Princeton, NJ: Princeton University Press. (Original work published in 1935.)

Jung, C. G., 1954/1966. Problems of modern psychotherapy. In *Collected Works*, Vol. 16, pp. 53-75. Translated by R. F. C. Hull. Princeton, NJ: Princeton University Press. (Original work published in 1935.)

Jung, C. G., 1954/1970a. Introduction to Wickes's "Analyse der Kinderseele." In *Collected Works*, Vol. 17, pp. 37-46. Translated by R. F. C. Hull. Princeton, NJ: Princeton University Press. (Original work published in 1931.)

Jung, C. G., 1954/1970b. Marriage as a psychological relationship. In *Collected Works*, Vol. 17, pp. 187-201. Translated by R. F. C. Hull. Princeton, NJ: Princeton University Press. (Original work published in 1931.)

Jung, C. G., 1958/1969. Psychotherapists of the clergy. In *Collected Works*, Vol. 11, pp. 327-347. Translated by R. F. C. Hull. Princeton, NJ: Princeton University Press. (Original work published in 1932.)

Jung, C. G., 1959/1969a. Archetypes of the collective unconscious. In *Collected Works,* Vol. 9, part I, pp. 3-41. Translated by R. F. C. Hull. Princeton, NJ: Princeton University Press. (Original work published in 1954.)

Jung, C. G., 1959/1969b. Psychological aspects of the Mother Archetype. In *Collected Works,* Vol. 9, part I, pp. 75-112. Translated by R. F. C. Hull. Princeton, NJ: Princeton University Press. (Original work published in 1954.)

Jung, C. G., 1959/1969c. Aion: Researches into the phenomenology of the Self. In *Collected Works,* Vol. 9, part II. Translated by R. F. C. Hull. Princeton, NJ: Princeton University Press. (Original work published in 1951.)

Jung, C. G., 1960/1969. Synchronicity: An acausal connecting principle. In *Collected Works*, Vol. 8, pp. 417-531. Translated by R. F. C. Hull. Princeton, NJ: Princeton University Press. (Original work published in 1952.)

Jung, C. G., 1961/1989. *Memories, Dreams, Reflections* (Revised Edition). Translated by R. and C. Winston; recorded and edited by A. Jaffe. New York: Vintage Books.

Jung, C. G., 1964. Approaching the unconscious. In C. G. Jung, et al., *Man and His Symbols,* pp. 18-103. Garden City, NY: Doubleday.

Jung, C. G., 1964/1970. The state of psychotherapy today. In *Collected Works,* Vol. 10, pp. 157-173. Translated by R. F. C. Hull. Princeton, NJ: Princeton University Press. (Original work published in 1934.)

Jung, C. G., 1966. On the relation of analytical psychology to poetry. In *Collected Works,* Vol. 15, pp. 65-83. Translated by R. F. C. Hull. Princeton, NJ: Princeton University Press. (Original work published in 1931.)

Jung, C. G., 1967a. The philosophical tree. In *Collected Works*, Vol. 13, pp. 251-349. Translated by R. F. C. Hull. Princeton, NJ: Princeton University Press. (Original work published in 1954.)

Jung, C. G., 1967b. Foreward to R. Wilhelm, *The I Ching,* pp. xxi-xxxix. Translated by Cary F. Baynes. Princeton, NJ: Princeton University Press.

Jung, C. G., 1971/1976. Psychological Types. In *Collected Works*, Vol. 6. A revision by R. F. C. Hull of the translation by H. G. Baynes. Princeton, NJ: Princeton University Press. (Original work published in 1921.)

Jung, C. G., & Pauli, W., 1955. *The Interpretation and Nature of the Psyche.* London: Routledge & Kagan.

Jung, C. G., von Franz, M.-L., Henderson, J., Jacoby, J., & Jaffe, A., 1964. *Man and His Symbols.* Garden City, NY: Doubleday.

Justice, B., 1996. *Violence in the City.* Fort Worth, TX: Texas Christian University Press.

Justice, B., 1998. *A Different Kind of Health: Finding Well-Being despite Illness*. Houston: Peak Press.

Justice, B., March 6, 1999a. Can Pain Co-Exist With Well-Being? Lecture at Conference on Open Questions about the Mystery of Healing, University of Texas M. D. Anderson Cancer Center, Houston.

Justice, B., 1999b. *Visits with Violet: How to Be Happy for 100 Years*. Houston: Peak Press.

Justice, B., 2000. *Who Gets Sick: How Beliefs, Moods and Thoughts Affect Your Health* (Revised Edition). Houston: Peak Press.

Kabat-Zinn, J., 1990. *Full Catastrophe Living: Using the Wisdom of Your Body and Mind to Face Stress*. New York: Dell.

Kagan, J., 1997. *Galen's Prophecy: Temperament and Human Nature*. Boulder, CO: Westview Press.

Kandel, E. R., 1998. A new intellectual framework for psychiatry. *American Journal of Psychiatry*, 155 (4), 457-469.

Kandel, E. R., 1999. Biology and the future of psychoanalysis: A new intellectual framework for psychiatry revisted. *American Journal of Psychiatry*, 156 (4), 505-534.

Kandel, E. R., 2001. The molecular biology of memory storage: A dialogue between genes and synapses. *Science*, 294, 1033-1038.

Kandel, E. R., September 28, 2002. Radical Reductionism in Science and Art: The Biology of Memory Storage and Minimalist Art. New York Academy of Sciences Conference on The Self: From Soul to Brain, Mount Sinai School of Medicine, New York.

Kandel, E. R., & Mack, S., 2003. A parallel between radical reductionism in science and in art. In J. LeDoux, J. Debiec, & H. Moss (Eds.), *The Self: From Soul to Brain*. Annals of the New York Academy of Sciences, 1001, 272-294.

Kandel, E. R., 2006. *In Search of Memory: The Emergence of a New Science of Mind*. New York: Norton.

Karen, R., 2001. *The Forgiving Self: The Road from Resentment to Connection*. New York: Doubleday.

Kast, V., 1991. *Joy, Inspiration, and Hope*. College Station: Texas A&M University Press.

Keller, J. C., 2004. Dawkins drops bombs on religion. *Science & Theology News*, January, p. 3.

Kendig, R. E., 1995. *The Washington National Cathedral: This Bible in the Stone*. McLean, VA: EPM Publications.

Kessler, R., Berglund, P., & Demler, O., 2003. The epidemiology of major depressive disorder: Results from the National Comorbidity Survey Replication (NCS-R). *JAMA*, 289 (23), 3095-3105.

Ketter, T. A., Wang, P. W., Lembke, A., & Sachs, N., 2003. Physiological and pharmacological induction of affect. In R. J. Davidson, et al. (Eds.), *Handbook of Affective Sciences*, pp. 930-962. New York: Oxford University Press.

Kiecolt-Glaser, J. K., Bane, C., Glaser, R., & Malarkey, W. B., 2003. Love, marriage, and divorce: Newlyweds' stress hormones foreshadow relationship changes. *Journal of Consulting and Clinical Psychology, 71*, 176-188.

Kisselgoff, A., 2005. Flowers rain on a conductor as he ends and begins roles. *New York Times*, May 29, pp. B1, B7.

Koenig, H., 1998. Spirituality and medical outcomes. Presentation at Spirituality & Healing in Medicine-IV & V conference, Houston, March 22.

Kraemer, G., 1992. A psychological theory of attachment. *Behavioral and Brain Sciences, 15*, 493-541.

Kramer, P., 1993. *Listening to Prozac: A Psychiatrist Explores Antidepressant Drugs and the Remaking of the Self*. New York: Viking.

Krucoff, M. W., Crater, S. W., Green, C. L., et al., 2001. Integrative noetic therapies as adjuncts to percutaneous intervention during unstable coronary syndromes: The monitoring & actualization of noetic training (MANTRA) feasibility pilot. *American Heart Journal, 142,* pp. 760-769.

Krucoff, M. W., 2002. The MANTRA Study Project. Presentation at conference on "The Psychology of Health, Immunity and Disease," Hilton Head, SC, Dec. 9-15.

Kunitz, S. J., 1979. *The Poems of Stanley Kunitz, 1928-1978*. Boston: Little, Brown.

Kunitz, S. J., 2000. *The Collected Poems*. New York: Norton.

Laney, M. O., 2002. *The Introvert Advantage: How to Thrive in an Extrovert World*. New York: Workman.

LeDoux, J., 1996. *The Emotional Brain: The Mysterious Underpinnings of Emotional Life*. New York: Touchstone.

LeDoux, J., 2002. *Synaptic Self: How Our Brains Become Who We Are*. New York: Viking Penguin.

LeDoux, J., 2003. The self: Clues from the brain. In J. LeDoux, J. Debiec & H. Moss (Eds.), *The Self: From Soul to Brain*. Annals of the New York Academy of Sciences, 1001, 298, 295-304.

LeDoux, J., Debiec, J., & Moss, H. (Eds.), 2003. *The Self: From Soul to Brain*. Annals of the New York Academy of Sciences, 1001. New York: NYAS.

Lennox, J., 2001. *Aristotle's Philosophy of Biology*. Cambridge, UK: Cambridge University Press.

Lesch, K., 2004. Gene-environment interaction and the genetics of depression. *Journal of Psychiatry and Neuroscience, 29*, 174-184.

LeShan, L., 1989/1994. *Cancer As a Turning Point: A Handbook for People with Cancer, Their Families, and Health Professionals* (Revised edition). New York: Plume.

LeShan, L., 1975. *How to Meditate: A Guide to Self-Discovery*. New York: Bantam Books.

Levenson, E. A., 1972/1983/2005. *The Fallacy of Understanding/The Ambiguity of Change*. Hillside, NJ: The Analytic Press.

Levenson, E. A., 2000. Foreward in A. H. Feiner, *Interpersonal Psychoanalytic Perspectives on Relevance, Dismissal and Self-Definition*. New York: Jessica Kingsley.

Levin, J. S., 2001. *God, Faith, and Health: Exploring the Spirituality-Healing Connection*. New York: Wiley.

Levine, P. A. (with Frederick, A.), 1997. *Waking the Tiger: Healing Trauma*. Berkeley, CA: North Atlantic Books.

Levine, S., 1987. *Healing Into Life and Death*. New York: Anchor Books.

Levine, S., 1997. *A Year to Live: How to Live This Year as If It Were Your Last*. New York: Bell Tower.

Lewicki, P., & Czyzewski, M., 1992. Nonconscious acquisition of information. *American Psychologist*, 47, 796-781.

Lewin, R., 1999. *Complexity: Life at the Edge of Chaos* (2nd Edition). Chicago: University of Chicago Press.

Lewis, T., Amini, F., & Lannon, R., 2001. *A General Theory of Love*. New York: Vintage.

Levy, B., Slade, M., Kunkel, S., & Kasl, S., 2002. Longevity increased by positive self-perceptions of aging. *Journal of Personality and Social Psychology*, 33, 261-270.

Luhrmann, T. M., 2000. *Of Two Minds: The Growing Disorder in American Psychiatry*. New York: Knopf. [Published in 2001 by Vintage with the title *Of Two Minds: An Anthropologist Looks at American Psychiatry.*]

Luks, A. (with Payne, P.), 1991. *The Healing Power of Doing Good: The Health and Spiritual Benefit of Helping Others*. New York: Fawcett.

Luther, M., 1982. *Day By Day We Magnify Thee: Daily Readings for the Church Year Selected from the Writings of Martin Luther, 1483-1546*. Philadelphia, PA: Fortress Press.

Lynch, J. J., 1977. *The Broken Heart: The Medical Consequences of Loneliness*. New York: Basic Books.

Lynch, J. J., 2000. *A Cry Unheard: New Insights into the Medical Consequences of Loneliness*. Baltimore, MD: Bancroft Press.

Lyndon, N., 2000. The inner nerd. *The (London) Times*, July 12, Times 2 Cover Story, pp. 3-5.

MacLennan, B., 2002. Evolutionary neurotheology and the varieties of religious experience (Extended Version). In R. Joseph (Ed.), *NeuroTheology: Brain, Science, Spirituality, Religious Experience*, pp. 305-314. San Jose: University of California Press.

Malinin, T. I., 1979. *Surgery and Life: The Extraordinary Career of Alexis Carrel*. New York: Harcourt Brace Jovanovich.

Manning, M., 2001. The Legacy. In Nell Casey (Ed.), *Unholy Ghost: Writers on Depression*, pp. 256-269. New York: HarperCollins.

Marano, H., 2003. The depressive suite. *Psychology Today*, May/June, pp. 59-66.

Martin, B., 1950. *Miracle at Carville*. Edited by E. Wells, Garden City, NY: Doubleday.

Mascolo, M. F., Fisher, K. W., & Li, J., 2003. Dynamic development of component systems of emotions: Pride, shame, and guilt in China and the United States. In R. J. Davidson, et al. (Eds.), *Handbook of Affective Sciences,* pp. 375-409. Oxford: Oxford University Press.

Matsuoka, Y., Yamawaki, S., Inagaki, M., Akechi, T., & Uchitomi, Y., 2003. A volumetric study of amygdala in cancer survivors with intrusive recollections. *Biological Psychiatry*, 54, 736-743.

Matthews, P.M., & McQuain, J., 2003. *The Bard on the Brain*. New York: The Dana Press.

Mayo, P. M., 1998. Dreams as nonlocal connections. *Alternative Therapies in Health & Medicine, 4,* (5), 97-98.

MacLennan, B., 2002. Evolutionary neurotheology and the varieties of religious experience. In R. Joseph (Ed.), *NeuroTheology: Brain, Science, Spirituality, Religious Experience,* pp. 305-314. San Jose: University of California Press.

McCraty, R., Atkinson, M., Tomasino, D., et al., 1998. The electricity of touch: Detection and measurement of cardiac energy exchange between people. In K. Pribram (Ed.), *Brain and Values: Is a Biological Science of Values Possible?* pp. 359-380. Mahwah, NJ: Erlbaum.

McCraty, R., Atkinson, M., & Tomasino, D., 2001. *Science of the Heart.* Boulder Creek, CA: Institute of HeartMath .

McCraty, R., & Childre, D., 2003. *The Appreciative Heart: The Psychophysiology of Positive Emotions and Optimal Functioning.* Boulder Creek, CA: Institute of HeartMath.

McDonald, A., 2003. Is there an amygdala and how far does it extend: An anatomical perspective. In P. Shinnick-Gallagher, A. Pitkanen, A. Shekhar, L. Cahill, (Eds.), *The Amygdala in Brain Function: Basic and Clinical Approaches.* Annals of the New York Academy of Sciences, 985, 1-21.

McGehee, J. P., Sept. 9, 1990. The Day My Father Died. Sermon, Christ Church Cathedral, Houston.

McGehee, J. P., March 24, 1991. Father Comes in a Dream. Sermon, Christ Church Cathedral, Houston.

McGehee, J. P., 1992. Homily. Christ Church Cathedral, Houston.

McGehee, J. P., 1996. *Love in the Analytic Container: The Place of Eros, Logos and Agape in Psychoanalysis.* In fulfillment of Jungian diploma, C. G. Jung Institute of Dallas.

McGehee, J. P., May 15, 1998a. The Power of Darkness. Lecture, C. G. Jung Center, San Antonio.

McGehee, J. P., 1998b. How Do Symbol and Story Heal the Spirit? Houston Seminar series.

McGehee, J. P., March 5, 1999a. Meaning and Healing: The Place of Suffering in the Making of Soul and in the Healing Arts. Keynote lecture at Conference on Open Questions about the Mystery of Healing. University of Texas M. D. Anderson Cancer Center, Houston.

McGehee, J. P., 1999b. Alcohol and the Thirst for Spirit. Lecture.

McGehee, J. P., 1999c. Love and Wholeness: The Place of Eros, Logos and Agape in Analytical Psychology. Lecture.

McGehee, J. P., 1999d. Axis Mundi, the Symbol of the Tree. Lecture.

McGehee, J. P., Sept. 15, 2000a. Personal Narratives for Refractions of the Spirit: The Power of the Personal Story. Lecture, University of Houston.

McGehee, J. P., September 2000b. Denial of Death: A Commentary on Ernest Becker's book. Lecture, Kincaid School, Houston.

McGehee, J. P., 2000c. Mysticism 101. A course at the Center for Theologicial Studies, Houston.

McGehee, J. P., January 27, 2001a. Fleshing Out the Soul: A Theology of the Body. Lecture at the Conference on Paths to Healing, Houston.

McGehee, J. P., April 7, 2001b. The Abundant Life: The Lois Peckham Lecture Series, Christ Church Cathedral, Houston.

McGehee, J. P., April 18, 2001c. Re-Membering: A Psychology of Story. Houston Seminar Series lecture.

McGehee, J. P., March 9, 2002. Mystical Paths to Wholeness. Houston Seminar Series lecture.

McGehee, J. P., 2003a. *The Collected Poems of Pittman McGehee*. Edited and printed by Mary Sieber and Micki Simms.

McGehee, J. P., 2003b. What Is Your Weltanschauung? The Women's Institute Fall Lecture, November 23.

McGehee, J. P., 2004. Burn the Barn. Mythics Journeys presentation, May 24.

Menninger, K. A., 1956. *Man against Himself*. New York: Harvest Books.

Menninger, K. A., 1959. *Love against Hate*. New York: Harvest Books.

Merikle, P. M., 1992. Perception without awareness: Critical issues. *American Psychologist*, 46 (6), 792-795.

Merikle, P. M., & Reingold, E. M., 1998. On demonstrating unconscious perception: Comment on Draine and Greenwald (1998). *Journal of Experimental Psychology*, *127*, 3, 203-310.

Merton, T., 1958/1999. *Thoughts in Solitude*. New York: Farrar, Straus, and Giroux.

Merton, T., 1969. *Contemplative Prayer*. New York: Herder and Herder.

Midlarsky, E., 1991. Helping as coping. In M. Clark (Ed.), *Prosocial Behavior,* pp. 238-264. Newbury Park, CA: Sage Publications.

Mikulincer, M., Florian, V., & Hirschberger, G., 2003. The existential function of close relationships: Introducing death into the science of love. *Personality and Social Psychology Review*, 7 (1), 20-40.

Miller, M. (Ed.), 2002. How much should psychotherapists tell about themselves? *Harvard Mental Health Letter*, October, pp. 3-6.

Miller, M. (Ed.), 2004. Women and depression: How biology and society make women more vulnerable to mood disorders. *Harvard Mental Health Letter*, May, pp. 1-4.

Miller, W. I., 1998. *The Anatomy of Disgust*. Cambridge, MA: Harvard University Press.

Moore, P., 2003. *Being Me: What It Means to be Human*. Chichester, UK: Wiley.

Moore, T., 1992. *Care of the Soul: A Guide for Cultivating Depth and Sacredness in Everyday Life*. New York: HarperPerennial.

Myers, D. G., 2002. *Intuition: Its Powers and Perils*. New Haven, CT: Yale University Press.

Neborski, R., 2003. Shame and guilt from a developmental neuroscience perspective: Implications for technique in intensive short-term dynamic psychotherapy. *Ad Hoc Bulletin of Short-Term Dynamic Psychotherapy*, 7, 1.

Netting, J., 2000. The "yuck" factor. *NatureNews,* 16 October (http://tinyurl.com/d4moz2).

Newberg, A., D'Aquili, E., & Rause, V., 2001. *Why God Won't Go Away: Brain Science and the Biology of Belief*. New York: Ballantine Books.

Newton, R. G., 2004. Weird Science: The author of the "The Elegant Universe" explains cutting-edge ideas in theoretical physics. *New York Times*, April 11, p. 12.

Nicholi, A. M., Jr. (Ed.), 1978. *The Harvard Guide to Modern Psychiatry*. Cambridge, MA: Harvard University Press.

Nuland, S. B., 2004. Getting in nature's way: A review of *The Pursuit of Perfection: The Promise and Perils of Medical Enhancement* by S. M. Rothman and D. J. Rothman. *New York Review of Books, 51* (2), February 12 (http://www.nybooks.com/articles/16899).

Nygren, A., 1953/1989. Agape and Eros. In A. Soble (Ed.), *Eros, Agape, and Philia: Readings in the Philosophy of Love*, pp. 85-95. Saint Paul, MN: Paragon House.

O'Connor, A., 2004. Has the romance gone? Was it the drug? *New York Times*, May 4, D8.

O Riordian, J. J., 1996. *The Music of What Happens: Celtic Spirituality: A View from the Inside*. Dublin: Columba Press.

Ogden, T. H., 1990. *The Matrix of the Mind: Object Relations and Psychoanalytic Dialogue*. New York: Jason Aronson.

Olfson, M., Marcus, S. C., Druss, B., et al., 2002. National trends in the outpatient treatment of depression. *JAMA, 287*, 203-209.

Ornish, D., 1995. Interview by Horrigan, B. (See Horrigan, 1995.)

Ornish, D., 1998. *Love and Survival: The Scientific Basis for the Healing Power of Intimacy*. New York: HarperCollins.

Ornstein, R., & Sobel, D., 1987/1999. *The Healing Brain: Breakthrough Discoveries about How the Brain Keeps Us Healthy*. Cambridge, MA: Malor Books.

Owen, R., & Clayes, G., 1991. *A New View of Society and Other Writings*. London: Penguin Classics.

Pakenham, T., 2002. *Remarkable Trees of the World*. New York: W. W. Norton.

Paul, E. F., Miller, F. D., & Paul, J. (Eds.), 1999. *Human Flourishing*. Cambridge: Cambridge University Press.

Pearce, J. C., 2002. *The Biology of Transcendence: A Blueprint of the Human Spirit*. Rochester, VT: Park Street Press.

Pearsall, P., 1998. *The Heart's Code: Tapping the Wisdom and Power of Our Heart Energy*. New York: Broadway Books.

Pearsall, P., 2001. *Miracle in Maui* (Updated edition). Maui, HI: Inner Ocean.

Peat, F. D., 1987. *Synchronicity: The Bridge between Matter and Mind*. New York: Bantam.

Pennebaker, J., 1997. *Opening Up: The Healing Power of Expressing Emotions*. New York: Guilford.

Persinger, M., 1987. *Neuropsychological Bases of God Beliefs*. New York: Praeger.

Pert, C. B., 1997. *Molecules of Emotion: Why You Feel the Way You Feel*. New York: Simon & Schuster.

Petit, T., & Ivy, G., *Neural Plasticity: A Lifespan Approach*. New York: Liss.

Pinker, S., 2002. *The Blank Slate: The Modern Denial of Human Nature*. New York: Viking Penguin.

Pinkola Estes, C., 1995. *Women Who Run with the Wolves: Myths and Stories of the Wild Woman Archetype*. New York: Ballantine Books.

Polkinghorne, J., 1989. *The Quantum World*. Princeton, NJ: Princeton University Press.

Polkinghorne, J., 1996. *The Faith of a Physicist: Reflections of a Bottom-Up Thinker*. Minneapolis, MN: Fortress Press.

Polkinghorne, J., 1998a. *Belief in God in an Age of Science* (The Dwight Harrington Terry Foundation Lectures on Religion in the Light of Science and Philosophy). New Haven, CT: Yale University Press.

Polkinghorne, J., 1998b. *Science and Theology: An Introduction*. London: SPCK/Fortress Press.

Porges, S., 1998. Love: An emergent property of the mammalian autonomic nervous system. *Psychoneuroendocrinology*, *23* (8), 837-861.

Powell, L., Shahabi, T., & Thoresen, C., 2003. Religion and spirituality: Linkages to physical health. *American Psychologist*, *58* (1), 36-52.

Prager, K. M., 2003. Alice's Husband. *JAMA, 289*, 2333.

Pribram, K. (Ed.), 1998. *Brain and Values: Is a Biological Science of Values Possible?* Mahwah, NJ: Erlbaum.

Puchalski, C., 2001. Reconnecting the science and art of medicine. *Academic Medicine*, *76* (12), 1224-1225.

Quartz, S. R., & Sejnowski, T. J., 2002. *Liars, Lovers, and Heroes: What the New Brain Science Reveals about How We Become Who We Are*. New York: William Morrow.

Ramachandran, V. S., & Blakeslee, S., 1998. *Phantoms in the Brain: Probing the Mysteries of the Human Mind*. New York: Quill William Morrow.

Ramachandran, V. S., 2004. *A Brief Tour of Human Consciousness: From Impostor Poodles to Purple Numbers*. New York: Pi Press.

Raymo, C., 1998. *Skeptics and True Believers: The Exhilarating Connection between Science and Religion*. New York: MJF Books.

Raymo, C., 2004. *Climbing Brandon: Science and Faith on Ireland's Holy Mountain*. New York: Walker.

Real, T., 1997. *I Don't Want to Talk About It: Overcoming the Secret Legacy of Male Depression*. New York: Simon & Schuster.

Remen, R., 1997. *Kitchen Table Wisdom*. New York: Riverhead Trade.

Remen, R., 2000. *My Grandfather's Blessings: Stories of Strength, Refuge and Belonging*. New York: Riverhead Books.

Remen, R., 2001. *The Will to Live and Other Mysteries*. Sounds True Cassettes.

Restak, R., 2003. *The New Brain: How the Modern Age is Rewiring Your Mind*. Emmaus, PA: Rodale.

Reynolds, J., c. 2003. Presention in an adult Sunday school class.

Richardson, W. M., & Slack, G. (Eds.), 2001. *Faith in Science: Scientists Search for Truth*. London: Routledge

Ridley, M., 2003. *Nature Via Nurture: Genes, Experience & What Makes Us Human*. New York: HarperCollins.

Rilke, R., 1992. *Duino Elegies*. Translated by D. Oswald. Einsiedeln, Switzerland: Daimon Verlag.

Robbins, M., 2004. Meditation apparently activates positive areas within the brain. *Discover*, January, p. 45.

Rosen, D., 1989. Modern medicine and the healing process. *Humane Medicine: A Journal of the Art and Science of Medicine,* 5, 18-23.

Rosen, D., 1993. *Transforming Depression: Healing the Soul through Creativity.* New York: Penguin.

Rothman, S. M., & Rothman, D. J., 2003. *The Pursuit of Perfection: The Promise and Perils of Medical Enhancement.* New York: Knopf.

Routh, D. K., 2003. Focus on clinical health psychology: Ostomy culture. *The Health Psychologist, 25,* 1, 8-10.

Rowe, J. W., & Kahn, R.L., 1998. *Successful Aging.* New York: Pantheon.

Rudd, P., 2001. Molecular Grace. In W. M. Richardson & G. Slack (Eds.), *Faith in Science: Scientists Search for Truth,* pp. 87-102. London: Routledge.

Rufus, A., 2003. *Party of One: The Loner's Manifesto.* New York: Marlowe.

Russell, P., 2003. *From Science to God: A Physicist's Journey into the Mystery of Consciousness.* Novato, CA: New World Library.

Sacks, O., 1973/1990. *Awakenings.* New York: HarperPerennial.

Sacks, O., 1991. Neurology and the Soul. In P. Corsi (Ed.), *The Enchanted Loom: Chapters in the History of Neuroscience,* pp. 366-370. Oxford: Oxford University Press.

Salovey, P., Mayer, J., & Rosenhan, D., 1991. In M. Clark (Ed.), *Prosocial Behavior,* pp. 215-237. Newbury Park, CA: Sage.

Samuels, A., Shorter, B., & Plaut, F., 1986/1987. *A Critical Dictionary of Jungian Analysis.* London: Routledge.

Sanford, J., 1968/1989. *Dreams: God's Forgotten Language.* San Francisco: HarperSanFrancisco.

Saxena, S., Brody, A. L., Maidment, K. M., et al., 2004. Cerebral glucose metabolism in obsessive-compulsive hoarding. *American Journal of Psychiatry, 161,* 1038-1048.

Scaer, R., 2001. *The Body Bears the Burden: Trauma, Dissociation, and Disease.* New York: Haworth Medical Press.

Schmale, A. H., 1973. The adaptive role of depression in health and disease. In J. P. Scott & E. C. Senay (Eds.), *Separation and Depression: Clinical & Research Aspects.* Washington, D. C.: American Association for the Advancement of Science.

Schore, A., 1994. *Affect Regulation and the Origin of the Self: The Neurobiology of Emotional Development.* Hillsdale, NJ: Erlbaum Associates.

Schrödinger, E., 1969. *What Is Life?* And *Mind and Matter.* London: Cambridge University Press.

Schroeder, G., 1997. *The Science of God: The Convergence of Scientific and Biblical Wisdom.* New York: Free Press.

Schroeder, G., 2001. *The Hidden Face of God: Science Reveals the Ultimate Truth.* New York: Simon & Schuster.

Schulz, M. L., 1998. *Awakening Intuition.* New York: Three Rivers Press.

Schwartz, G. E. (with Simon, W. L.), 2002. *The Afterlife Experiments: Breakthrough Scientific Evidence of Life after Death.* New York: Atria.

Schwartz, J. M., & Begley, S., 2002. *The Mind and the Brain: Neuroplasticity and the Power of Mental Force.* New York: ReganBooks/HarperCollins.

Scott, J. P., & Senay, E. C. (Eds), 1973. *Separation and Depression: Clinical & Research Aspects.* Washington, D. C.: American Association for the Advancement of Science.

Seeman, T. E., et al., 2001. Social relationships, social support, and patterns of cognitive aging in healthy, high-functioning older adults: MacArthur Studies of Successful Aging. *Health Psychology, 20,* 4, 243-255.

Seligman, M. E., 1975. *Helplessness: On Depression, Development, and Death.* San Francisco: Freeman.

Seligman, M. E., 1991. *Learned Optimism.* New York: Knopf.

Seligman, M. E., 2002. *Authentic Happiness: Using the New Positive Psychology to Revive Your Potential for Lasting Fulfillment.* New York: The Free Press.

Selye, H., 1946. The general adaptation syndrome and the diseases of adaptation. *Journal of Clinical Endocrinology,* 6 (2), 117-230.

Selye, H., 1976. *Stress in Health and Disease.* Boston: Butterworth.

Selye, H., 1976. *Stress of Life* (Revised edition). New York: McGraw-Hill.

Shamdasani, S., 2003. *Jung and the Making of Modern Psychology: The Dream of a Science.* Cambridge: Cambridge University Press.

Shapiro, F., 2001. *Eye Movement Desensitization and Reprocessing: Basic Principles, Protocols and Procedures* (2nd edition). New York: Guilford Press.

Shapiro, F. (Ed.), 2002. *EMDR as an Integrative Psychotherapy Approach: Experts of Diverse Orientations Explore the Paradigm Prism.* Washington, DC: American Psychological Association Books.

Sharp, D., 1991. *Jung Lexicon: A Primer of Terms and Concepts.* Toronto: Inner City Books.

Sheldrake, R., 2003. *The Sense of Being Stared At: And Other Aspects of the Extended Mind.* New York: Crown.

Shermer, M., 2002. The soul problem: Review of *The Problem of the Soul: Two Visions of Mind and How to Reconcile Them* by Owen Flanagan, Ph.D. *Psychology Today,* November-December, 76-80.

Shermer, M., 2004. Miracle on probability street. "Skeptic" column, *Scientific American,* August, p. 32.

Shinnick-Gallagher, P., Pitkanen, A., Shekhar, A., & Cahill, L. (Eds.), 2003. *The Amygdala in Brain Function.* Annals of the New York Academy of Sciences, 985. New York: NYAS.

Siegel, D. J., 1999. *The Developing Mind: Toward a Neurobiology of Interpersonal Experience.* New York: Guilford Press.

Simonton, O.C., & Simonton, S., 1975. Belief systems and the management of the emotional aspects of malignancy. *Journal of Transpersonal Psychology,* 7, 29-47.

Singer, J., 1994. *Boundaries of the Soul: The Practice of Jung's Psychology* (Revised and updated edition). New York: Anchor Books.

Skaer, T., Sclar, D., Robison, L. & Galin, R., 2000. Trends in the rate of depressive illness and use of antidepressant pharmacotherapy by ethnicity/race: An assessment of office based visits in the United States, 1992-1997. *Clinical Therapeutics, 22* (12), 1575-1589.

Snowdon, D., 2001. *Aging with Grace: What the Nun Study Teaches Us about Leading Longer, Healthier, and More Meaningful Lives.* New York: Bantam Books.

Snyder, C. R., & Lopez, S. J. (Eds.), 2002. *Handbook of Positive Psychology.* Oxford: Oxford University Press.

Soble, A. (Ed.), 1989. *Eros, Agape, and Philia: Readings in the Philosophy of Love.* Saint Paul, MN: Paragon House.

Solms, M., & Turnbull, O., 2002. *The Brain and the Inner World: An Introduction to the Neuroscience of Subjective Experience.* New York: Other Press.

Solms, M., 2004. Freud returns. *Scientific American,* May, pp. 82-88.

Solomon, A., 1998. Anatomy of Melancholy. *New Yorker,* January 12, p. 46.

Solomon, A., 2001. *The Noonday Demon: An Atlas of Depression.* New York: Scribner.

Solomon, A., 2004. A Bitter Pill. Op-ed essay. *New York Times,* March 29, p. A25.

Spears, R. A., 1990. *Forbidden American English: A Serious Compilation of Taboo American English.* Chicago: Passport Books.

Sperry, R. W., 1990. Forebrain commissurotomy and conscious awareness. In C. Trevarthen, (Ed.), *Brain Circuits and Functions of the Mind: Essays in Honor of Roger W. Sperry,* pp. 371-388. Cambridge: Cambridge University Press. (Reprinted with permission from *The Journal of Medicine and Philosophy,* 1977, 2).

Stapp, H. P., 1993/2003. *Mind, Matter, and Quantum Mechanics.* New York: Springer-Verlag.

Stein, J., 2003. Just Say Om. *Time,* August 4, pp. 48-56.

Stein, M., 1998. *Transformation: Emergence of the Self.* College Station: Texas A&M University Press.

Stein, S. (with Blochman, L.), 1963. *Alone No More: The Story of a Man Who Refused To Be One of the Living Dead.* Carville, LA: The Star.

Stelljes, Susan, 2005. *Wonder Dog, the Story of Silverton Bobbie.* Portland, OR: For the Love of Dog Books.

Stern, P., 2001. Sweet dreams are made of this. *Science, 294,* 1047.

Sternberg, R., 1986. A triangular theory of love. *Psychological Review, 93,* 119-135.

Sternberg, R., & Barnes, M. (Eds.), 1998. *The Psychology of Love.* New Haven, CT: Yale University Press.

Stevens, A., 1991. The shadow in history and literature. In C. Zweig & J. Abrams (Eds.), *Meeting the Shadow: The Dark Side of Human Nature,* pp. 27-29. New York: Tarcher/ Putnam.

Stevens, A., 1993. *The Two Million-Year-Old-Self.* College Station: Texas A&M University Press.

Stix, G., 2003. Ultimate self-improvement. *Scientific American, 289,* 3, September, pp. 44-45.

Styron, W., 1990. *Darkness Visible: A Memoir of Madness.* New York: Random House.

Swanson, L. W., 2003. *Brain Architecture: Understanding the Basic Plan.* Oxford: Oxford University Press.

Swartz, K. L., & Margolis, S., 2004. Depression and anxiety. *The Johns Hopkins White Paper.* Baltimore: Johns Hopkins Medicine.

Tabor, M. B. W., 1995. A poet takes the long view, 90 years long. *New York Times,* November 30, p. B1.

Tangney, J., & Dearing, R., 2002. *Shame and Guilt.* New York: Guilford.

Tegmark, M., 2003. Parallel universes: Not just a staple of science fiction, other universes are a direct implication of cosmological observations. *Scientific American,* May, pp. 41-51.

Teilhard De Chardin, P., 1959. *The Phenomenon of Man.* Translated by Bernard Wall, translation revised in 1965. New York: Harper & Row. (Original work published in 1955.)

Templeton, J. M. (Ed.), 1997. *How Large is God? The Voices of Scientists and Theologians.* Philadelphia, PA: Templeton Foundation Press.

Thoreau, H., 1854/1983. *Walden.* New York: Penguin Classics.

Tierney, J., 2004. Politics on the brain? Resorting to M.R.I.'s for partisan signals. *New York Times,* April 20, pp. A1, A17.

Tillich, P., 1952/2000. *The Courage to Be.* New Haven: Yale University Press.

Torrey, E. F., 1995. *Surviving Schizophrenia: A Manual for Families, Consumers and Providers.* New York: HarperPerennial.

Trevarthen, C. (Ed.), 1990. *Brain Circuits and Functions of the Mind: Essays in Honor of Roger W. Sperry.* Cambridge: Cambridge University Press.

Tsung, M. T., Tohen, M., & Zahner, G. E. P. (Eds.), 1995. *Textbook in Psychiatric Epidemiology.* New York: Wiley.

Turkington, C., 1999. *The Brain Encyclopedia.* New York: Checkmark Books.

Tyndall, J., 1897. *Fragments of Science.* New York: D. Appleton.

Unger, J. B., McAvay, G., Bruce, M. L., Berkman, L., & Seeman, T., 1999. Variation in the impact of social network characteristics on physical functioning in elderly persons: MacArthur Studies of Successful Aging. *The Journals of Gerontology Series B: Psychological Sciences & Social Sciences, 54,* S245-S251.

Vaillant, G. E., 1977/1995. *Adaptation to Life.* Cambridge, MA: Harvard University Press.

Vaillant, G. E., 2002. *Aging Well: Surprising Guideposts to a Happier Life from the Landmark Harvard Study of Adult Development.* Boston: Little, Brown.

Van Praag, H., Schinder, A., Christie, R., Toni, N., Palmer, T., & Gage, F., 2002. Functional neurogenesis in the adult hippocampus. *Nature, 415,* 1030-1034.

Vaughan, S., 1997. *The Talking Cure: The Science behind Psychotherapy.* New York: Putnam.

Vedantam, S., 2002. Negative view? It may be brain "knob." *Washington Post,* February 12.

Veneziano, G., 2004. The myth of the beginning of time: String theory suggests that the Big Bang was not the origin of the universe but simply the outcome of a pre-existing state. *Scientific American,* May, pp. 54-65.

Verghese, J., Lipton, R. B., Katz, M., et al., 2003. Leisure activities and the risk of dementia in the elderly. *New England Journal of Medicine, 348,* 2508-2516.

Von Eschenbach, A., 2002. Spirituality and Medicine. Invited distinguished lecture, University of Texas Medical School, Houston, November 6, 2002.

Von Franz, M.-L., 1964. Science and the unconscious. In Jung, et al., *Man and His Symbols*, pp. 304-310. Garden City, NY: Doubleday.

Wade, N. (Ed.), 1998. *The Science Times Book of the Brain*. New York: The Lyons Press.

Waldman, D., Rothko, M., & Malamud, B. (Designer), 1978. *Mark Rothko: A Retrospective*. New York: Harry Abrams.

Walsh, A., 1996. *The Science of Love: Understanding Love and Its Effects on Mind and Body*. Buffalo, NY: Prometheus Books.

Watkins, C., 1990. The effects of counselor self-disclosure: A research review. *The Counseling Psychologist*, 18, 477-500.

Watson, L., 1986. *Gifts of Unknown Things*. New York: Simon and Schuster.

Watson, L., 1992. *The Nature of Things: The Secret Life of Inanimate Objects*. Rochester, VT: Destiny Books.

Weber, R., 1990. *Dialogue with Scientists and Sages: The Search for Unity*. London: Arkana.

Wegner, D.M., 2002. *The Illusion of Conscious Will*. Cambridge, MA: MIT Press.

Wehr, G., 2003. *Jung and Steiner: The Birth of a New Psychology*. Translated by M. Jaeckel. Great Barrington, MA: Anthroposophic Press.

Weil, A., 1997. *Sound Body, Sound Mind: Music for Healing* (audio/disc). New York: Upaya.

Weil, A., 2002. Coping with depression: An integrative approach. *Self Healing*, November, p. 4

Weil, A., 2003. Introduction. *Healer: Transforming the Inner and Outer Wounds*. Vol. 2, Archetypes of the Collective Unconscious. New York: Tarcher/Putnam.

Weiner, J., 2004. This is your brain on drugs. *New York Times Book Review*, May 9, section 7 p. 15.

West, M. G., 2000. *Exploring the Labyrinth: A Guide for Healing and Spiritual Growth*. New York: Broadway Books.

WGBH, 2001. *Methuselah Tree*. NOVA television. Boston.

Wheeler, J. A., and Mehra, J. (Eds.), 1973. *The Physicist's Concept of Nature*. Boston: D. Reidel.

Wheeler, J., 1995. *At Home in the Universe*. New York: Springer-Verlag.

Whitmont, E., 1993. *The Alchemy of Healing Psyche and Soma*. Berkeley, CA: Homeopathic Educational Services; North Atlantic Books.

Wilhelm, R., 1967. *The I Ching*. Translated by Cary F Baynes. Princeton, NJ: Princeton University Press.

Williams, J. K., 1964. *The Wisdom of Your Unconscious Mind*. Englewood Cliffs, NJ: Prentice-Hall.

Williams, J., 2004. Mind-body proof: For Einstein, it was all relative. *Science & Theology News*, May, p. 12.

Williams, R., & Williams, V., 1997. *Anger Kills: Seventeen Strategies for Controlling the Hostility That Can Harm Your Health*. New York: HarperPaperbacks.

Wilmer, H. A., 1987/1993. *Practical Jung: Nuts and Bolts of Jungian Psychotherapy.* Wilmette, IL: Chiron Publications.

Wilson, E. O., 1998. *Consilience: The Unity of Knowledge.* New York: Knopf.

Wilson, R. A., 1982. Mere Coincidence? *Science Digest*, 90 (1), January, pp. 80-85, 95.

Wilson, R. A., 1999. The individual in biology and psychology. In V. Hardcastle (Ed.), *Where Biology Meets Psychology,* pp. 357-374. Cambridge, MA: MIT Press.

Wilson, T. D., 2002. *Strangers to Ourselves: Discovering the Adaptive Unconscious.* Cambridge, MA: Harvard University Press.

Winson, J., 1986. *Brain and Psyche.* New York: Vantage Books.

Wolman, R., 2001. *Thinking With Your Soul.* New York: Harmony Books.

Wolpert, L., 1999. *Malignant Sadness: The Anatomy of Depression.* New York: The Free Press.

Woods, J., 2004. Study asks whether chemicals and communion are the same. *Science & Theology News*, May, p. 7.

Woolf, V., 1928/1993. *Orlando: A Biography.* New York: Harvest Books.

Yardley, J., 2004. Beauty contestant fights for right of self-improvement. *New York Times*, June 17, p. A4.

Yoon, C.K., 2004. Taller trees? The limit is plumbing. *New York Times*, April 27, p. D1.

Young, L. B. (Ed.), 1965. *The Mystery of Matter.* London: Oxford University Press.

Young-Eisendrath, P., & Hall, J. (Eds.), 1987. *The Book of the Self: Person, Pretext, and Process.* New York: New York University Press.

Young-Eisendrath, P., & Hall, J., 1991. *Jung's Self Psychology: A Constructivist Perspective.* New York: Guilford.

Yudofsky, S., 2003. Stigma and Psychotic Illness. Presentation at the 10th annual "Health Care and the Arts" series, University of Texas Health Science Center, Houston, March 25.

Zald, D., Mattson, D., & Prado, J., 2002. Brain activity in ventromedial prefrontal cortex correlations with individual differences in negative affect. *Proceedings of the National Academy of Sciences*, 99 (4), 2450-2454.

Zeman, A., 2002. *Consciousness: A User's Guide.* New Haven: Yale University Press.

Zukav, G., 2000. *Soul Stories.* New York: Simon & Schuster.

Zweig, C., & Abrams, J. (Eds.), 1991. *Meeting the Shadow: The Hidden Power of the Dark Side of Human Nature.* New York: Tarcher/Putnam.

INDEX

Made in the USA